Economic Myths:

Making Sense of Canadian Policy Issues

THIRD EDITION

Patrick Luciani

Toronto

Canadian Cataloguing in Publication Data

Luciani, Patrick
    Economic myths: making sense of Canadian policy issues

3rd ed.

ISBN 0-201-61436-7

Canada – Economic policy – 1991-.2. Canada – Economic conditions – 1991-.   I. Title.

HC115.L824 2001   338.971   C00-932203-5

ISBN 0-201-61436-7

Vice President, Editorial Director: Michael Young
Executive Acquisitions Editor: Dave Ward
Marketing Manager: Steve Iacovelli
Developmental Editor: Suzanne Schaan
Production Editor: Jennifer Therriault
Copy Editor: Gail Marsden
Production Coordinator: Patricia Ciardullo
Page Layout: Joan M. Wilson
Art Director: Mary Opper
Cover Design: Anthony Leung
Cover Image: Eyewire

1 2 3 4 5 05 04 03 02 01

Printed and bound in Canada

Table of Contents

Preface.. vi

Introduction 1

PART I MYTHS ABOUT THE MARKET AND PRICE CONTROLS 9

Chapter 1 Rent Controls and Housing................................10
Rent controls are needed during a housing shortage.

Chapter 2 Pay Equity and the Law 18
Pay equity should be backed by law.

Chapter 3 Preserving the Family Farm 26
The family farm should be preserved as a way of life.

Chapter 4 Minimum Wages and the Working Poor 36
Higher minimum wages are a good way to help the working poor.

Chapter 5 Education and Wages 44
A university education is losing its value.

Chapter 6 Banking and Business.. 52
Canadian banks make too much profit.

PART II MYTHS ABOUT TRADE AND COMPETITION 61

Chapter 7 The North American Free Trade Agreement 62
NAFTA was a bad deal for Canada.

Chapter 8 The Status of Canadian Manufacturing........................ 70
Canadian manufacturing is disappearing.

Chapter 9 Valuing the Dollar.. 77

We need a lower dollar in order to be competitive.

Chapter 10 Buying Canadian.. 85

Buy Canadian means more jobs.

Chapter 11 Immigrant Employment................................... 94

Immigrants steal jobs from Canadians.

PART III MYTHS ABOUT THE ROLE OF GOVERNMENT... 103

Chapter 12 Government Spending and Future Security.. 104

The government can't afford an aging population.

Chapter 13 Examining the GST... 112

The GST is a bad tax.

Chapter 14 Taxes and the Quality of Life 120

Higher taxes mean less work (and vice versa).

Chapter 15 National Debt and the Future 129

The national debt will bankrupt the country.

PART IV MYTHS ABOUT GROWTH AND THE ENVIRONMENT... 139

Chapter 16 Environmental Protection and the Law 140

We have a right to a clean environment regardless of cost.

Chapter 17 Nonrenewable Resources..............................149

We are running out of nonrenewable resources.

Chapter 18 The Cost of Recycling 156

Recycling always makes good business sense.

Chapter 19 Zero-Growth and the Environment 165

No-growth policies will save the environment.

PART V OTHER ECONOMIC MYTHS 173

Chapter 20 Small Business 174

Small businesses drive the economy.

Chapter 21 Government Statistics 182

Government statistics never lie.

Chapter 22 Economic Policies 192

Wise economic policies can always control business cycles.

Chapter 23 High Unemployment 201

We can't do much about high unemployment.

Chapter 24 Quebec and Sovereignty 211

The cost of separation will be manageable for Quebec and Canada.

Chapter 25 Income Distribution 220

The rich get richer and the poor get poorer.

Chapter 26 The Growth of Government 228

We need big government to deliver the services Canadians want.

Chapter 27 The New Economy 239

Job security is a thing of the past in the New Economy.

Chapter 28 The Brain Drain 245

Canada is (or is not) suffering a brain drain.

Glossary 253

Preface

The basis of *Economic Myths: Making Sense of Canadian Policy Issues* is an effort to convey to readers that an understanding of markets, and how they work, is vital to a better understanding of the economy and the role of public policy. This third edition includes an extensive introduction and five new chapters, along with updates from the previous edition.

NEW TO THIS EDITION

The new introduction covers a number of key economic themes that underlie most chapters. In the section "The Proper Role for the State in the Economy," the student is introduced to the difference between positive and normative economics, as well as the concepts of equity and efficiency. "The Power of Economic Thinking" deals with the choices we must make about how to allocate scarce resources and addresses the role of incentives, whether negative or positive, in helping governments pursue specific objectives. This section also discusses how "thinking marginally" relates to public policy. The introduction ends with a brief look at how the media can mislead or distort our perceptions of economic problems and solutions.

As in the previous two editions, each chapter is introduced as a myth. Many people form their opinions about how the economy works based on faulty reasoning and incomplete knowledge of economic principles. The use of myths is also a way of provoking students to question conventional wisdom about common economic problems. And although students are encouraged to question the conclusions reached by the author, they should do so by defending their opinions with logic and an intelligent use of data.

The new chapters cover five more contemporary economic issues. Chapter 5, "Education and Wages," conveys the point that getting more education is still the best way to a good job and a higher income, despite the notion that many people think that staying in school isn't as valuable as it once was. Chapter 6, "Banking and Money", is an attempt to help the reader understand better the concepts of profits and return on investment. The main point in Chapter 25, "Income Distribution," is that poverty is a relative, not an absolute, concept; being poor today is radically different from being poor even a generation ago. Chapter 27, "The New Economy," examines a basic misunderstanding about job security and the relationship between employees and employers; while many tend to believe that employers shed labour more easily than in the past, the data show that jobs are more stable today than is commonly thought. The final new addition is Chapter 28, "The Brain Drain," which clears up some basic misunderstandings of this common economic problem.

AREAS OF STUDY

The reader will notice that the 28 chapters aren't grouped into neat macro or micro categories. It's not always easy to decide under which heading an issue falls. Instead, the chapters are grouped intro five general sections.

Part 1, "Myths About the Market and Price Controls," attempts to highlight that, when governments intervene in the market with regulations to help one identifiable group of citizens, they invariably do so at the expense of another group. Regardless of the good intentions of many public policy programs, there are costs to society; in some cases, the costs are borne by the very group the programs were intended to help.

Part 2, "Myths About Trade and Competition," exposes a number of myths about trade. This section introduces competitiveness, comparative advantage, and the benefits of trade specialization. Without an understanding of these ideas, it is difficult to fully understand the debate surrounding free trade and globalization. The myths that we are losing our manufacturing base and that immigrants steal jobs from others are also examined in this section.

Part 3, "Myths About the Role of Government," looks at a number of issues including the consequences of an aging population, the role of taxes (including the GST), and the national debt.

Part 4, "Myths About Growth and the Environment," contains four chapters on economic and environmental issues. For example, some policies to protect the environment, such as recycling, may not always be beneficial, and greater economic growth isn't incompatible with a cleaner environment.

Finally Part V, "Other Economic Myths," includes chapters covering such topics as the accuracy of government statistics, the costs of Quebec separation, job security, and the brain drain.

FEATURES

Each chapter includes a number of learning aids:

Key Terms used within the chapter are listed at the end. A brief definition of each term can be found in the **Glossary** at the back of the book. The Glossary also acts as an index by including page references pointing to the main discussions of the concepts within the text.

A list of **Weblinks** guides students to interesting Web sites for further research and reading on the issues raised in the chapter.

Review Questions further emphasize the key learning points, and **Discussion Questions** encourage further debate among students or between students and their instructor.

The **Notes** not only provide sources for the information in the chapter but also offer further examples and suggested readings.

Acknowledgements

Even though only one name appears on the cover, books are seldom written alone. This project is no exception. With that in mind, I want to thank the reviewers of this edition for their many useful and constructive comments and suggestions. They include Brian Coulter, University College of the Fraser Valley; Peter Dungan, University of Toronto; John A. Farrugia, Mohawk College; John Henderson, Lambton College; Harvey King, University of Regina; Aron T. Martens, Red Deer College; William Scarth, McMaster University; and Andrew Stark, University of Toronto. I am also deeply grateful for the excellent editorial work of Gail Marsden. Finally I want to thank Suzanne Schaan, development editor at Pearson Education Canada, for her patience and perseverance in keeping this project on track.

INTRODUCTION

Why bother studying economics? That's a good question. To anyone who has leafed through an introductory economics textbook, it seems a jumble of charts, graphs, and indecipherable equations. If that's not enough to turn you off, then just listen to two economists debating an issue, any issue, and you're sure to hear three opinions. And as many believe, economists are always using models that oversimplify assumptions about human, government, or business behaviour. And when they do reach a conclusion, it's so full of qualifications and hedging that their answers hardly seem worth the trouble. Why bother when one opinion seems no better than any other? That view of economics is not only distorted but simply wrong. Granted, economics isn't always easy or intuitive, but with some effort, it provides insights not only about how the economy works, but about how to make it work better.

We can go through life with little or no understanding of the hard sciences or the liberal arts, but we would be poorer for it. But to be a fully participating citizen in a democracy, knowing little or nothing of economic reasoning leaves us at a disadvantage. We aren't expected to be familiar with quantum mechanics in our daily lives, but every time we vote, we're implicitly making decisions about how to use society's resources. Improving economic literacy makes us less vulnerable to bad policy decisions and less susceptible to economic myths and poor economic reasoning. The famous economist Frank Knight summed it up when he said, "It's not what we don't know that's the problem, it's that so much of what we know isn't so." Too many of us believe that Canada can't compete with low-cost developing countries, that immigrants steal jobs, that the only way to fight pollution is to pass tougher laws against polluters, or that rent controls are effective in keeping housing costs down. All of these are economic illusions that prevent us from thinking clearly about public policy issues. But to think clearly, we need to improve our knowledge of some basic economic principles.

It's important to understand that economics isn't about getting at the right answer; in many cases, there aren't any right answers. The challenge is to learn to think logically about economic problems and choose the best answer from an array of possible solutions. That's the essence of economics, making choices. Do we increase the minimum wage? What are the costs? Are there better alternatives in helping the working poor? Should we protect farmers from cheaper imports? If we do, are the benefits worth the higher costs to consumers? And what should governments do about increasing the wages of women? Is pay equity the answer? If society believes that the poor should receive help through welfare payments or subsidized housing, how does one determine adequate welfare levels without discouraging some work-

1

ers from entering the job market? People with no economics background may think they have the answers, but their solutions often unwittingly make situations worse. The dominant theme in this book is that regardless of which option is followed, policymakers should always be mindful of the role of markets and how they function. Any public policy that ignores the role of markets and relies on the ability of governments to set prices and solve economic problems is bound to make things worse.

Health care is a perfect example of fuzzy thinking by Canadians. It seems we all want a first-class health-care system that's both universal and free (in the sense that we don't pay directly), but that we're frustrated and dismayed when we find long waiting lists for surgery and overcrowded emergency wards. Economics tells us that when the price of a good is effectively zero, we shouldn't be surprised when demand outstrips supply, regardless of how much money we throw at the problem. The environment is another area where muddled thinking can make matters worse. Is forcing people to recycle an effective way to protect Canada's renewable and non renewable resources? In many of these issues we actually end up doing the opposite of what we intended mainly because we didn't understand some basic economic principles at work. Economics gives you a set of tools for approaching a problem, not a pat answer to each and every public policy problem.

THE PROPER ROLE FOR THE STATE IN THE ECONOMY

Positive and Normative Economics

All of these issues have one thing in common: they deal with public policy issues. To many, this is a confusing term, but public policy is simply the interaction of the government with the economy. In a democracy we expect the government to address a number of issues, everything from creating jobs, educating the young (and old), and providing health care to distributing income between the rich and poor (whether they are people or regions of the country). But how far should the government go in each of these areas? If we think that those out of work should receive help through employment insurance, how much and to whom? If we want to provide universal health care, again the question is: What kind of health care and who decides how much? We all recognize that there's a role for the state in the economy, but how far should it go? At this point, we should make the distinction between *positive* and *normative economics*.

Positive economics refers to value-free statements about what is happening in the economy. If gas prices increase, an economist can tell you that less will be bought or demanded. How much less and at what price level is a matter of study and analysis. If instead of asking how much will demand drop if prices go up, we state that "we should not allow prices to go up," then we're making a value or *normative* judgment. Statements such as "something should be done about the homeless," "tuition fees should be reduced or frozen," "women should earn as much as men" are all normative statements that reflect our own desires and preferences.

Equity versus Efficiency

No one can argue with the above normative statements. The challenge is to find the best possible solution to these problems. And that's what this book is all about: how do we deal with normative or value judgments through public policy decisions? If we all come to the conclusion that child poverty is an important issue, do we deal with it through universal day-care provisions, or by increasing the incomes of parents or caregivers through, for example, tax reductions? These aren't academic questions: coming up with the best answer means using society's resources as efficiently as possible. The fewer resources we use, the greater the overall economic wealth we have to meet other wants of society. And efficiency means using the economy's resources wisely at the lowest cost with maximum benefit.

But while we're trying to achieve efficiency, equity (or how we share those resources) is also a priority for policymakers. Equity doesn't mean equality or that we all have the same incomes, but that resources are shared according to some level determined by society. Both of these concepts, equity and efficiency—often referred to as the big tradeoff—are central to the theme of *Economic Myths: Making Sense of Canadian Policy Issues*. However, more efficiency often means less equity and vice versa. Efficiency essentially means allowing markets to create as much wealth as possible. Tilting the equation in favour of greater income distribution or equity means less efficiency.

That's the paradox of economic policy making: too much equity, or an attempt at greater income redistribution, can often lead to less economic efficiency, and too much of the latter can lead to a greater discrepancy between the haves and have-nots. The trick for policymakers is to strike the right balance between the two. Those on the political left tend to overemphasize the equity side of the equation, supporting higher taxes to meet the normative needs of society. But if taxes are too high, businesses and individuals react by investing and working less. Those on the political right are criticized for concentrating too much on wealth creation and overplaying the role of markets to distribute wealth and underplaying the role of the state. The role of good public policy is to come up with ideas that increase the benefits of both efficiency and equity without necessarily sacrificing one for the other. A good part of this book is dedicated to trying to explain circumstances where we can have more of both. For example, in the area of trade, removing quotas that protect industries from cheaper imports will increase efficiency by forcing more competition and letting comparative advantage work better. At the same time removing import quotas reduces higher profits in the industry and redistributes them in the form of lower prices for consumers. Now we have the best of both worlds, a combination of more efficiency and more equity.

THE POWER OF ECONOMIC THINKING

Throughout *Economic Myths*, a number of key themes are emphasized in the various chapters. These concepts are at the heart of what is called economic thinking or reasoning. By understanding them, readers will have at their disposal concepts that will help them think clearly about most policy issues regardless of whether they choose to pursue further economic study. For those willing to read and think about the lessons, absorbing these ideas will go a long way in helping make sense of many of today's policy concerns.

Scarcity, Choice, and Opportunity Cost

The trade off between efficiency and equity is at the heart of all public policy making. It also is at the core of how economists think about the economy and policy issues. The economic way of thinking is based on how to use logic in selecting the best choices to solve economic problems. Why choose? For the simple reason that we only have access to limited resources in the world. Scarcity means that at any given time, all factors of production, land, capital, and raw materials are limited. Even knowledge and technology are limited in the short run. Even time is a resource limited by its scarcity. Without scarcity there wouldn't be a need for the study of economics. For without scarcity there'd be no need for economizing any resource.

But where there's scarcity, choices have to be made about how best to use limited resources—whether in the manufacturing of goods and services or the choices we make about how we spend our money or allocate our time. Scarcity makes economizing necessary. Even the rich have to keep in mind the limitations of their resources, although they have more choices than the poor. A week spent skiing in the Rockies means a week not spent on the beaches in the Caribbean. In other words, the cost of spending a week skiing costs a week not spent doing something else. Even getting an education involves the *opportunity cost* of lost wages versus staying in school. Three years of college means foregoing three years of earnings. The economic way of thinking helps us to clarify the economizing process, the act of choosing under the restrictions imposed by scarcity. That's what economists mean when they talk about opportunity cost: the things we give up when we choose to do something else.

The same principle applies when policymakers choose to allocate resources between competing economic choices. Given limited tax revenues, putting resources into education means lower welfare transfers or health-care spending. Protecting the incomes of farmers means giving up lower food prices for consumers. Subsidizing professional sports stadiums means less money to support day care or the arts. Obvious as this seems to anyone with some economic background, it's less than obvious to the layperson. Many suffer under the illusion that we could have it all if only politicians and policymakers knew what they were doing and managed our money better. Although we can improve the latter, the iron law of economics still applies: there's *no free lunch*. All decisions entail costs: the only question that remains is how much and who pays.

Incentives Matter

A second theme of *Economic Myths* is that incentives matter. The concept of incentives isn't difficult to understand. Reward people for certain behaviour and they'll do more of it; punish them and they'll do less. Incentives are the key principles behind why the demand curve slopes downward and the supply curve slopes upward. If the price of a commodity goes down, the demand goes up. If prices rise, people generally respond by buying less. People react to changing incentives after they have done some rough calculations of the costs and benefits. Rational choices involve balancing the costs and benefits of any activity, whether we sit down and do the numbers or roughly estimate what a decision will mean. That, in and of itself, isn't terribly interesting or insightful. What is interesting is that incentives often have unintended consequences. When the NDP government of Ontario increased the levels of welfare payments after the party was elected in 1989, its intention was to improve the lot of the poor. What they didn't intend was the sharp increase in the number of welfare recipients. To be fair, many new welfare recipients were victims of a deep recession in the early 1990s. Yet many people were simply making rational decisions about the trade-offs and benefits between work and reward.

Before the federal government reformed the employment insurance program (EI), formerly known as unemployment insurance (UI), the plan called for eligible unemployed workers to collect up to 50 weeks of UI. Numbers clearly showed that many workers miraculously found work just as their benefits ran out—again, incentives at work with clear unintended consequences. Here are a few further examples. If municipal government charges a flat fee for water regardless of how much is consumed, don't be surprised if water is wasted. Or if governments insist on subsidizing the construction of roads and sewage systems in suburban areas, then people will migrate out of cities where costs are higher. When drivers aren't charged the full cost of building and maintaining the roads, more people will be encouraged to drive and crowd our highways. If governments cover a greater share of the cost of education, more will go to school as the opportunity cost of getting an education is reduced. When gas prices rise, as they did in the energy crisis of the early 1970s, people react by buying fuel-efficient cars. On the other hand, if we pay doctors by the number of patients they see, in too many cases doctors turn their offices into revolving doors, seeing as many patients as they can in a working day. In short, incentives work and are a powerful tool to change human behaviour. But they have to be designed to address the problem at hand. If not fully thought out, incentives can backfire, producing the opposite of what was intended.

The Importance of Thinking Marginally

So far we've said that people make decisions in their own best interest based on the incentives offered. But how much should we buy or consume as prices, or incentives, change? The answer is found in what is called marginal analysis—one of the most important, and useful, concepts in economic thinking. Don't let the jargon bother you. Once understood it will give you insight into most personal, business, and policy decisions. Marginal thinking allows you to make decisions that will maximize the value of any resource you have, including your time. All that matters are the marginal costs that are affected by the decision at hand. The term "marginal" simply means incremental or additional. For example, if you are deciding to replace your old car with a new one, you have to assess whether the marginal benefit of a new car is worth the extra or marginal cost of getting that new car. (Of course with cars, many factors come into play, such as status or simply wanting a cool vehicle. These have to be factored into the benefits you receive.) A question we should all be asking is, "Is the exchange worth it?" That's where marginal analysis comes in. If the marginal benefits are greater than the marginal costs, then we do it; if not, we walk away. This applies whether we are talking about personal issues (studying, working, shopping), running a business, or deciding on public policy issues.

Another example of marginal thinking is the decision to wait in line to renew your driver's licence after you've already been there for an hour. Forget about the hour spent so far: that's a sunk cost. If you estimate that you'll have to wait another hour, but if you returned later that day the wait would only be five minutes, then you leave. If the wait later would be greater than half an hour, then you stay. Your decision should be based on the time and effort of having to return and wait again, and not on how much time you've already spent waiting in line. That's marginal thinking.

Now consider a policy issue such as fighting crime. The question is, how much of society's resources—read taxes—should be spent fighting crime? If a 10 percent increase in the police budget could eliminate 20 percent more crime, it would be a wise investment for the city to approve an increase in the police budget. Would it be wise to increase the budget by 100 percent to eliminate only 5 percent more crime? Probably not, given that those resources could be more efficiently used elsewhere in society where the *marginal benefits* are greater than the *marginal costs*. That's why we don't allocate all of society's resources to any one thing, whether it's subsidized housing, education, health care, or crime. Would society be willing to eliminate all crime if that meant no spending on health and education? There comes a point where the marginal costs outstrip the marginal benefits. Marginal costs increase rapidly as we try to eliminate that last crime, or educate that last student, or cure that last patient. In a perfect world of unlimited resources, we could afford to accomplish each one. In a world of limited resources, choices and compromises have to be made based on opportunity costs (what we're giving up) and the marginal benefits and costs of our decisions.

Faulty Reasoning

Too often, when people see two events happen at the same time, they automatically assume one causes the other. For example, the fact that unemployment rises at the same time that Canada reaches a trade deal with the United States does not mean that that deal caused job losses in Canada. A decline in women's wages is not necessarily caused by discrimination. One point every student should remember is that correlation is not causation. Economists work long and hard trying to disentangle what is cause and what is effect. One way they do this is by changing one variable while holding others constant. This is referred to by the Latin term *ceteris paribus*, meaning "other things being equal." Only by isolating various factors can we get at the truth of what variable really impacts on another. Unemployment may have gone up for reasons wholly unrelated to the new trade agreement, or women's wages may have declined due to factors other than discrimination. But we can only find out by scientifically assessing all other possibilities.

ECONOMICS AND THE MEDIA

This book was inspired mostly by the need to give the beginning student in economics some basic tools to think logically and rationally about events recorded in the media every day. The lessons learned here will be useful for any student, whether continuing in economics or not. The main focus is to concentrate on popular public policy issues too often confused by the media. Reporters are often more interested in controversy than in clarification or education. The debate on free trade and its benefits to Canada is a case in point.

In fact about 93 percent of all economists believe that restrictions to freer trade reduce economic welfare and efficiency. Economists are also in general agreement that rent controls reduce the availability of housing (93 percent), minimum wages increase unemployment among the young (79 percent), and pollution taxes are more efficient than setting pollution limits (78 percent).[1] Economist Alan Blinder once said that economists have the least influence on policy where they know the most, and have the greatest influence on policy where they know the least. What he meant was that people don't pay enough attention to economists where they (economists) know a lot about a topic such as rent control, yet depend on economists where they know little, such as predicting the direction of interest rates. Too often the media is more interested in generating debate and controversy under the guise of reporting both sides of the story. What often passes for objective reporting is simply the spreading of myths and illusions about the economy, further clouding the picture for average citizens looking for understanding. *Economic Myths* was designed to help students not only understand the key concepts in economic thinking, but identify faulty thinking and reasoning in the popular media, a skill that will serve them well beyond the classroom.

NOTE

1. Source: Richard M. Alston, J.R. Kearl, and Michael B. Vaughan, "Is There a Consensus Among Economists? *American Economic Review*, May 1992.

I

Myths About

the Market and

Price Controls

RENT CONTROLS AND HOUSING

MYTH ***"Rent controls are needed during a housing shortage."***

Rent controls are a price ceiling on rental housing. Their intention is to protect poorer apartment dwellers by keeping a lid on rising rents, particularly during a time of high demand for rental accommodation. Unfortunately, they have proved to be a failure wherever they've been tried. Instead, they have had the perverse effect of diminishing supply, subsidizing those who can afford free-market rents, and hurting the group rent control legislation was intended to help. But governments seem to be learning from their mistakes.

Anyone who saw the demolished and abandoned buildings in the Bronx, New York, in the 1980s can't forget the images. The scale of the devastation was overwhelming. Landlords were abandoning thousands of housing units, leaving the city with approximately 200,000 derelict units occupied only by rats and small-time drug dealers. This damage wasn't caused solely by migration to the suburbs, vandalism, or the race riots of the 1970s, but by the attempt to control prices; that is—by rent controls.

It has been said that next to bombing, rent controls can best destroy a city's rental housing. Even if the damage imposed by rent controls isn't as overwhelming as that of bombing, the effects are just as striking. Wherever rent controls are in force, for example, in London, Paris, and Rome, the results are similar—a shortage of rental accommodation; and Canada's big cities aren't immune. Yet many of us believe the myth that rent controls are needed during a housing shortage, despite the theory and evidence that controls are inefficient and self-defeating.[1]

HOW RENT CONTROLS WORK

Before we analyze the cost of rent controls, let's look at how they work. Rent control legislation is usually enacted during a time of rapid economic growth when a housing shortage occurs. As with a shortage of any commodity, prices go up in the short term until more of the commodity, in this case more rental housing, can be supplied. Rent control is a **price ceiling** that freezes or moderates the price increase of rental units. Prices are set below what the market would otherwise allow in the absence of controls.

It is important to note that without market interference a supply shortage can't last forever. Prices will eventually moderate as supply catches up with demand, but rental housing can't be brought on stream overnight. With some products that can react to shortages quickly, prices hardly change. For example, if there's a shortage of ice cream during the summer, manufacturers simply increase production without any effect on prices. Housing, however, takes time. There are investors to find, building permits to arrange, and contractors to hire. In the meantime, the need for more housing increases while the supply stays constant. If the economy experiences inflationary pressures, as happened in 1975 when Ontario introduced rent controls, rents start rising rapidly. Moreover, when the price of housing goes up too quickly, pressure builds on politicians to do something about it.

POLITICAL REASONS FOR RENT CONTROLS

Governments don't normally step in to stop prices from rising. The price of cars, for example, is determined by supply and demand. Housing, however, is considered an essential commodity and because of that is treated differently by governments. Gas is also a sensitive commodity politically. When gas prices were rising sharply in the spring of 2000, truckers and drivers were quick to demand action from their governments. Governments are pressured to act quickly on politically sensitive issues such as gas and rental housing.

Rent controls are introduced for a number of explicit or implicit reasons. Explicitly, governments want to be perceived as helpers of the poor, seniors, and other groups on fixed incomes who are vulnerable to rent hikes. It's politically unsavoury to allow images (whether accurate or not) of unscrupulous landlords taking advantage of people or making windfall gains at the expense of the disadvantaged.

Implicitly, governments see rent controls as a form of redistributing income from the rich to the poor. Although rarely stated that bluntly, keeping rents down is thought to be a form of subsidizing the income of the poor.

Another reason for rent controls is that they are expedient in the **short run**—that is, politicians get credit for solving a perceived problem quickly. Also, let's not forget raw politics. Rental dwellers make up a sizeable group of any major city's population. In Metropolitan Toronto, for example, renters account for over 40 percent of all households. The political power of the tenants is such that few politicians are willing to advocate getting rid of rent controls. Renters are an identifiable group that can bring considerable political pressure to bear on government and, as such, benefit from controls. The victims are those who will need housing in the future and who will have to deal with shortages; obviously, this "unidentifiable" group has no political power. The cruel irony is that those most hurt by controls believe that controls are a benefit rather than a problem.

Such is the distortion of misguided government policies. As with most economic policies, nothing is free. Rent controls are no exception. In this case, not only are they expensive for society and completely inadequate in meeting the needs of the poor, they have also been a public policy disaster in every city where they have been used.

ECONOMIC CONSEQUENCES OF RENT CONTROLS

Economic theory shows us that any form of price control creates shortages. Rent controls not only diminish the stock of private rental construction, they also lower the quality of existing rental units.

The reasons for control-induced shortages are simple. At artificially low prices, or price ceilings, more of a commodity will be demanded, but with price restrictions, the market can't respond to fill the need. Governments have removed profits, the most important incentive for private investors to supply more housing. Once profits are removed, or lowered, by holding down prices, supply will always be less than demand (see Figure 1.1). If supply is constant or shrinking as demand increases, something has to give. In this case, it's a continuing shortage of rental housing. It's that simple. That alone is bad enough, but the story doesn't end there.

If landlords can't make a suitable return on their investment, they start taking existing units off the market for other more profitable uses. Apartments are converted to condominiums, shopping malls, or even parking lots. Governments then set up expensive regulations and bureaucracies to prevent landlords from converting their units. In response, landlords go through a lot of trouble circumventing new legislation, which in turn wastes their own and society's resources. Rent controls don't make the housing shortage problem better; they make it worse. With rent controls, governments spend millions of dollars just in regulating them; money that could be better spent helping the poor. In 1995, Ontario spent about $40 million regulating rent controls.

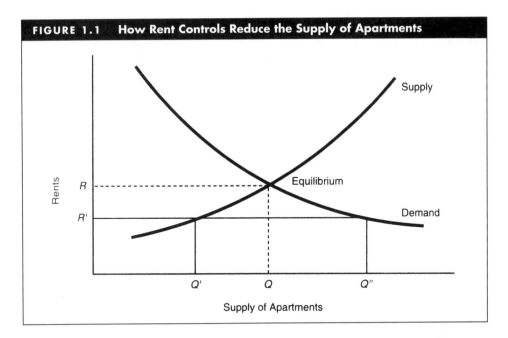

FIGURE 1.1 How Rent Controls Reduce the Supply of Apartments

Note: The market for rental apartments is in equilibrium when rents are at *R*. At *R* the number of units for rent is *Q*. If rents are held down at *R'* by rent controls, the rental price ceiling, the number of units provided by the free market falls to *Q'*, but the demand at this lower rent is *Q''* leading to an excess demand for apartment units and a chronic shortage.

Let's examine one province's experience as an example. Ontario built about 27,000 apartment units each year in the six years before rent controls were introduced in 1974, and that dropped to around 4,200 units per year after rent controls were introduced. By the early 1990s, when rent controls were tightened, the private supply of rental units plunged again. Toronto had higher vacancy rates before controls than after.[2] Rent controls break the housing market's natural ability to correct the housing supply problem. And when the private sector doesn't fill the housing void, governments step in with expensive nonprofit housing. In 1993, Ontario had 110,000 units of nonprofit housing, and 86,000 of them were allocated to tenants that needed some subsidy.[3] Nonprofit housing turned out to be so expensive that the newly elected Conservative government stopped all new construction when it was elected two years later.

Builders and landlords can't be blamed for the housing shortage. They are only responding to the incentives (or lack thereof) created by government policy. Apartments are needed, but they are not being built by private business because there is insufficient profit to be made.

If a landlord can't tear down a building, build a mall, or convert existing premises to condominiums, the only alternative left, if existing rents are insufficient to cover rising costs, is to allow the building to deteriorate. After all, governments freeze rents, not the costs of upkeep.[4] Here we have the worst of all possible worlds: a shrinking supply of rental units, a growing wasteful bureaucracy that pits landlord against tenant, and rundown buildings. In the final analysis, the burden of providing new affordable housing falls on the shoulders of government—in other words, the taxpayer. With a shortage of rental units available, governments are forced to provide accommodation in the form of nonprofit housing. Before rent controls were introduced in Ontario, the provincial government helped subsidize 27 percent of all rental units; by the early 1990s, it was over 75 percent. The cost of rent controls, housing subsidies, and other social housing costs taxpayers hundreds of millions of dollars. And because landlords no longer had the incentives to keep up their properties, it was estimated that 16 percent of Ontario's rental stock was lost in the 1990s through physical deterioration.

But the problem doesn't end there. As the shortage worsens, a **black market** for apartments develops as substandard units come on the market at prices higher than allowed by the controls. People have to live somewhere, so they aren't anxious to complain if they are overcharged or their accommodations don't meet safety standards. Many tenants are happy just to have a place to stay.

More obvious abuses are things such as landlords demanding **key money** as a form of rent increase. Although illegal, this practice is widespread during a housing shortage. There is also the waste of time and resources in looking for a place to live. In some cities, such as Rome and Paris, the shortage is so acute that people inherit apartments from one generation to the next. It's not unknown for apartment hunters to track the obituary columns to see if a unit has been vacated because of a death. The situation is so out of hand in New York City that rent controls created the anomaly that some people pay more for their parking spaces, which are unregulated, than they do for rent.

What about the poor and low-income families this legislation was supposed to help? How are they faring through all of this? There's no denying that there are some winners. They are the ones lucky enough to have been in an apartment before the controls were enacted. Many of these renters are low-income earners. But the poor aren't the only ones who rent. Those who could afford to pay higher rents are now being subsidized by those who can't find proper accommodation. Rent controls have the effect of trading off the benefits of those lucky enough to be living in rent-controlled buildings at the time the legislation was passed at the expense of those looking for accommodation at a later date.

Studies have found that the bulk of the benefits of rent control do not go to low-income rental dwellers. It's not uncommon, for example, to find a single mother paying $900 a month for a basement apartment in Toronto while an executive earning six figures lives in a $1,000-a-month rent-controlled apartment. Thirty percent of Ontario's subsidized housing will go to those who can afford to pay market rents. It is estimated that high-income earners spend less than 20 percent of their income on rent, whereas over 50 percent of low-income earners have to spend over 30 percent.[5] Often those in the upper income bracket hold onto rent-controlled units while investing in real estate. In this case, taxpayers are subsidizing the rich to further build their equity base at the expense of the poor.[6]

The tragedy of rent controls is that politicians know the damage this type of legislation can do, but they can't seem to avoid the temptation of a temporary solution to a long-term problem. Economists can't tell the decision makers what to do, but they can make them aware of the consequences of their actions. The adverse effects of rent controls are well documented.

SOLUTIONS WITHOUT THE SIDE EFFECTS

The obvious question to ask at this stage is: Is there a better way? Can we house the poor and low-income families at a lower cost to society? The answers are, yes, to the above questions.

Economists are a stingy lot by profession. They want to implement the least expensive way to reach society's objectives (in this case properly housing low-income groups and the poor) without wasting resources. A better way is to allow the market to make decisions about where resources should be allocated. In other words, investors normally go where the returns are the highest. One solution is to eliminate rent controls and replace them with a **voucher system** or a shelter allowance. How much each family or individual received in vouchers would be determined by an income or means test. A simple voucher system would allow the market to increase rental housing, moderate rents in both the short term and long term by improving profitability, and help those who need it most—the poor. To those who object to a means test, it should be pointed out that they are already in place and working for those who collect welfare and employment insurance. Besides, vouchers are preferable to waiting in line at a food bank because all your money has gone to pay the rent. However, one thing is clear: there's no free lunch. Whether through rent controls, government-subsidized housing, or direct help to the poor with vouchers, someone pays.

A voucher system is cheaper and more efficient for society in the **long run** because it leaves intact the incentives to private investors to supply more rental accommodation; it doesn't require as expensive a bureaucracy to administer; and it helps the poor without subsidizing those who don't need it.

If a solution is known, why is there no action? The answer is that once vested interests are entrenched, it's difficult to dislodge them. Those who gain from rent controls, those who now live in rent-controlled buildings, have an interest in keeping their rents below market values. Moreover, as long as vested interests hold the ear of politicians, the situation worsens. The longer politicians avoid the problem of eliminating rent controls, the worse the housing problem becomes. But there is evidence that politicians are coming to learn the costs of rent control. In New York City, for example, rent controls have been removed for those who move or die. Rents have also been deregulated for accommodations over $2,500 (U.S.) per month.

In 1998, the Ontario government introduced the Tenant Protection Act. With some exceptions, units that become available when tenants leave are no longer subject to rent controls. Tenants are still protected under the old rules as long as they continue to rent. However, landlords must still get permission for rent increased above a certain level. Whether this change will eliminate the rental housing shortage has yet to be seen. In large cities, such as Toronto, the construction of condos far exceeds new rental units at the turn of the century.

KEY TERMS

Price ceiling	Black market	Voucher system
Short run	Key money	Long run

REVIEW QUESTIONS

1. Explain, using supply and demand diagrams, why a shortage of beer in the summer could be eliminated without a large increase in price, whereas a rental apartment shortage will only disappear with a large increase in rents. (Remember the concept of elasticity of supply.)

2. What are the pressures on governments to introduce rent controls rather than directly help renters with vouchers in a time of rising prices and increased demand for rental housing?

3. How do black markets develop when government policy creates a shortage of rental accommodation? What determines the amount of key money demanded by landlords for rent-controlled apartments?

4. With rent controls, explain the economic dynamics that can actually shrink the supply of housing.

5. Even if governments don't resort to rent controls when demand for housing is high, what other factors could restrain the construction of new apartments, in the short run, and prevent the market from supplying more housing?

DISCUSSION QUESTIONS

1. Why are rent controls tough to get rid of once they are in place? When would be the best time to get rid of rent controls?

2. Why do governments try to control rents but not the costs of private housing?

3. During times of high demand for housing and high inflation, landlords get a reputation for price gouging and taking advantage of the poor. Is this reputation generally deserved?

4. When the Ontario government partially deregulated rents in 1998, do you think this was an adequate measure to substantially increase the supply of rental housing?

NOTES

1. Anyone who wants a better idea on rent control waste should read W.T. Standbury and John D. Todd, "Landlords as Economic Prisoners of War," *Canadian Public Policy* (Fall 1990), pp. 399–417.

2. Before rent controls were introduced in Ontario in 1975, Toronto had a vacancy rate of 3 percent. After controls the vacancy rate seldom rose above 1 percent. In the early 1990s, more apartments became available, but that was a function of the recession and not rent controls.

3. Lawrence B. Smith, "Ontario Housing Policy: The Unlearned Lessons," *Home Remedies* (Toronto: C.D. Howe Institute, 1995), p. 123.

4. In some cases rent controls have made tenants better off than their landlords, especially small investors who have put their savings into small apartment buildings only to find that they cannot maintain their buildings or recover costs.

5. George Fallis and Lawrence Smith give a good account of how the poor are affected by controls in "Rent Control in Toronto: Tenant Rationing and Tenant Benefits," *Canadian Public Policy* (Summer 1985). Another valuable source of information is Report of the Commission of Inquiry into Residential Tenancies (Toronto: Ontario Ministry of the Attorney General, 1987).

6. In New York City before rents were deregulated, the wealthy singer/songwriter, Carly Simon, was renting a nine-room apartment in Manhattan's posh Upper West Side for $3,000 (U.S.) a month. On the open market the rent would have been $15,000 (U.S.).

WEBLINKS

www.straightgoods.com/item383.asp
The rental situation in Toronto with a focus on poverty.

realtytimes.com/rtnews/rtcpages/19990921_cmhc.htm
How the new act affects return on investment for landlords.

realtytimes.com/rtnews/rtcpages/19990921_cmhc.htm
Success of the voucher system.

www.cyberessays.com/Politics/79.htm
Repealing the rent control act in Ontario.

PAY
EQUITY
AND THE
LAW

 **MYTH** *"Pay equity should be backed by law."*

Canadian women earn less than men. For many this difference is explained by systemic gender discrimination by employers. To eliminate the wage differences between the sexes, governments have introduced pay equity legislation. But is legislation the best way to raise women's salaries to the level of men's? Economic theory and evidence suggest that education and not legislation is the best way to increase women's earnings.

Canadian women have traditionally earned less than Canadian men. This fact comes as no surprise to women who, on average, earn two-thirds of what men earn, ignoring occupational differences. Traditionally, women have been paid lower wages than men for doing the same kinds of work and have been concentrated in lower-paying jobs. This is a situation women are no longer willing to tolerate. Gone are the days when women passively accepted wages less than they deserved. The trend towards pay equalization has become stronger as women enter the labour force in greater numbers and go into professions once dominated by men.

If women cannot satisfy their wage demands in the marketplace, they are determined to get them through legislation.[1] To get rid of the wage difference between the sexes, women have been advocating not only **equal pay for equal work**, but

equal pay for work of equal value.[2] Women argue that it is not enough to earn the same wage or salary as men within occupations that are dominated by women such as nursing, but that they must do so between occupations as well if justice in the workplace is to prevail. There is no reason male janitors should earn more than female office cleaners when they both do essentially the same work. But what about jobs, such as clerical work, that are dominated by women? How does one value this work? Is legislation the best way to guarantee that women are properly compensated for their work? What are the costs of passing such laws for employers, women, and society at large? Or, is the most effective option to guarantee that women have equal opportunity in education and employment and leave the market to set wages? Let's examine the issue more closely to see which method makes more sense.

THE PROBLEM

When it comes to wage rates, there are two schools of thought. The first view holds that wages in a free market are set by what economists call the **Marginal Revenue Product (MRP)** of labour. In other words, wages are set according to the productivity and direct value of labour. The more productive the labour, the more value it has to the employer, and the higher the wages. In a market where the employer doesn't discriminate between male or female workers, there is no reason that wages should be different for either sex. What an employer pays is based on a whole range of criteria, such as education, experience, working conditions, occupational mobility, and so on. If female wages are lower, it's because the market, for whatever reason, values the work of women less than that of men. A second view holds that women's choices are not free and that wage differences cannot be explained by productivity differences alone. Because of social discrimination, what is called systemic discrimination, women are channelled into less productive and, therefore, lower-paying jobs. Proponents do not suggest this is overt, or even intended. Rather, it is explained as the product not of individual prejudice, but of collective bias of which we are wholly unaware. This second position has some merit. Even when productive characteristics, such as education, skills, and experience are taken into consideration along with the fact that women are segregated into lower-paying occupational groups, there still remains about a 10 to 15 percent wage difference that can only be explained by sex discrimination.[3] It is this differential that legislation is geared to eliminate. The argument is that since the market cannot do the job of equalizing wages and salaries, legislation is needed to correct the imbalance.[4]

One way is by introducing laws that compel employers to pay their workers the same wages and salaries not only for identical jobs, but also for jobs of equal value. The designers of "equal pay for work of equal value" or pay equity legislation were more interested in compensating women who went into lower paying jobs where few men work. This, then, introduces a new problem into the equation. Who determines the definition of "jobs of equal value"? Outside agencies are now determining how to evaluate jobs where there is no comparable job done by men. Someone who favours such legislation may consider this a small hurdle to overcome, but the costs of implementing pay equity laws may not be as trivial as first assumed. A whole new bureaucracy is needed just to evaluate the differences and similarities between occupations. It's one thing to say women and men should be paid the same for jobs that are the same, but how can unrelated jobs be compared? Under pay equity, wages are a matter not merely for negotiation between employers and employees, but for adjudication by tribunals. The work of these tribunals is proving a tricky problem indeed.

In order to evaluate two totally different jobs, pay equity legislation relies on a point system assigned to various criteria, such as skills, effort, experience, responsibility, and working conditions. These points are added up to see which jobs are comparable and then wages are set accordingly. For example, in the case of hospitals, what jobs are comparable with nurses, physicians, or stationary engineers working in the boiler rooms? In the end all evaluation techniques are fundamentally arbitrary and can at best only estimate the value between one job and another. This task is difficult enough in large firms where there are a number of jobs that can be compared, but what about small firms where job categories or responsibilities are not that clearly drawn? Some have argued that the administration costs don't have to be permanent and that the pay equity laws can be used to change the perceptions of employers about undervaluing the work of women. Experience shows, however, that once imposed, rules and regulations are tough to dislodge.

WHO PAYS?

As with any government policy that entails setting prices, there are winners and losers. Pay equity legislation is no exception. The winners are those women who will benefit from the legislation with higher wages. Society might benefit from the increased job satisfaction and productivity of these women. However, these benefits do not come without costs.

First are the costs that economists attribute to the misallocation of resources, or **allocative inefficiencies**. What this means is that even if two jobs require the same skills, education, and experience, the market still might value one more than the other. One job might be riskier (for example, welding), while the other requires fewer skills (for example, cashier). Welders earn more than cashiers, but their salary difference can be explained by factors other than skills and experience. The reason the two jobs pay differently is that the market knows that to entice workers to go into welding, usually a tough, dirty, and cyclically unstable job, they have to pay more not only in absolute terms, but also in relation to other jobs. Let's say cashiers formed a strong union and started earning more money. People would tend to move out of welding and start working at grocery stores, all things being equal. Employers hiring welders will now have to pay higher wages to attract the necessary number of workers and increase the costs of products which they produce. Unemployment will increase among cashiers as more are now willing to work at the higher wage. In short, we now have a situation of too many cashiers and not enough welders. Governments can set the wages of a certain profession, but they cannot compel employers to hire all those who want to work at those new and higher wages. No one can measure precisely the costs in terms of the misallocation of resources, but no one can deny that they exist and are substantial.

Another allocative cost to society caused by pay equity is the cost of stifling mobility between occupations by changes in supply and demand. If the pay for engineers, for example, goes up because of an increase in demand for their services relative to college professors, this acts as a market signal that there is a shortage of engineers. If those signals are concealed because pay equity arbitrarily erases the wage differences between these occupations, then society loses crucial mobility and flexibility when economic conditions change.

Second are the added expenses to the employer of the entire program. One study estimates the cost at between $2,200 and $3,300 (in 1986 dollars) for every worker to close the wage gap by 10 percent between men and women.[5] Companies that have to implement pay equity legislation are concerned about the effects of higher costs on their businesses. Most programs allow for some form of program phase-in over a period of time, but that doesn't alleviate the problem that someone, either the firm or the customer, has to pay. These costs are exclusive of the millions paid by taxpayers to set up commissions to monitor and administer the program.[6] Although the concept of pay equity implicitly allows for the increase in wage for females in certain jobs, and a decrease in wage in other male-dominated ones, few, if any government agencies or private companies, will reduce wages paid to men who may be identified as overpaid.[7] That is one reason employers are so opposed to the legislation.

Finally there is the cost to women themselves. In any form of government control that tries to regulate prices either by setting a floor price, as in minimum wages, or ceiling prices, as in rent controls, someone pays, and it's usually those people the legislation was intended to help. Laws to correct a wage difference are no exception. If the wages of women are increased, then fewer women will be hired regardless of whether sexual discrimination existed in the first place. As already mentioned, some women will benefit from higher wages, at the cost of others losing their jobs.[8] These factors do not take into consideration that more expensive female labour may be substituted with more capital, or that men may now compete for the higher-paying jobs in the sectors once dominated by women.[9] Pay equity laws cannot by themselves eliminate wage differentials without costs. As with any policy designed to compensate one group over another by interfering with the market, the benefits do not come free.

GOOD NEWS FOR WOMEN

If economics tells us that pay equity comes only at a price for society in terms of less efficient use of resources and higher unemployment of women, how can the wage differential be eliminated? As with most government policies that try to improve the lot of one group over another, there are no short-term or easy answers. In the case of equal pay, the most effective means to increasing women's earning potential is to encourage them to go into jobs and occupations that pay higher wages, and that means going into jobs dominated by men. Here education and training are key.

In 1996, Statistics Canada reported women between the ages of 25–44 working full time earned 73 percent of what full-time working men earned: $33,500, compared to $44,200. But that was quite an improvement from 1967, when the female–male ratio was just 59 percent. The surprising news is that while women's wages have increased by 21 percent from 1980 to 1996, men increased their real wages by only 7.5 percent over that time. There were similar improvements for younger women in their 20s compared to their male counterparts.[10] At the same time women have been entering the labour market at historically high rates. Since 1980, male full-time employment hasn't changed, while the number of women entering the work force has increased 45 percent, or over 1 million. The 73 percent figure is also misleading because women working full time put in, on average, 12 percent fewer hours than men: 38.7 hours a week compared to 43.8 hours for men. Experience may well account for a good share of the remaining wage difference because men, on average, still have more experience. That will change in time. In other words, the closer one examines the numbers, the more the wage gap begins to disappear.[11]

One major factor dissolving wage differences between the sexes is education. One federal government study showed that the earning gap between male and female university graduates working full time was 82 percent in 1987.[12] By 1994 single female university graduates working full time were earning more than their male counterparts. The conclusion seems to be that the more education women have, the higher their earnings in relation to men.[13] The message is getting through. In the early 1960s only one-quarter of all undergraduates were women; today they receive more than half of all undergraduate degrees. And women between 25–44 have one-third more degrees than men in that age group (*The Globe and Mail*, April 19, 1999). Fifty-five percent of all university students in Canada are women, and they are going into fields of study once dominated by men such as pharmacy, law, and engineering. In pharmacy alone, women now receive 62 percent of all degrees compared to only 38 percent in the early 1970s. Women who crossed over to nontraditional jobs earn more and are more likely to work full time than those in "traditional" jobs.[14]

In other words, education has virtually eliminated the wage gap between men and women. Under these conditions, pay equity legislation will have little effect on women with higher levels of training and education. If society wants to increase women's salaries, public policy should channel its resources to encourage women to get the education they need to enter more job areas once dominated by men. The occupational segregation of women accounts for the earnings gap, rather than outright discrimination.[15] In that case, then, women need more educational and employment opportunities rather than pay equity legislation.

Pay equity treats the symptom rather than the cause of wage discrimination. The problem starts outside the labour market before women enter the labour force. Policies should be directed not at employers, but at the source of the problem: there should be greater employment opportunities for women and attempts to change the attitudes of parents, teachers, and children about proper occupations for men and women. Changing people's ideas before they enter the labour force is crucial to changing market behaviour. A radical change is needed in cultural values and attitudes towards women. Without these changes, pay equity legislation won't do women much good.[16]

KEY TERMS

Equal pay for equal work

Equal pay for work of equal value (pay equity)

Marginal Revenue Product (MRP)

Allocative inefficiencies

REVIEW QUESTIONS

1. After accounting for skill differences, training, and experience, it has been estimated that women still earn 10 to 15 percent less than men. What are some of the traditional reasons for this discrepancy?

2. One of the costs of pay equity legislation is that it distorts the wage differential between occupations. Using supply and demand analysis, explain how this distortion leads to allocative inefficiencies in the economy.

3. Assume that if things were left to the market, welders would earn $25.00 an hour and grocery store cashiers would make $10.00 an hour. Using demand and supply diagrams, illustrate what happens in the markets for welders and for cashiers if pay equity laws impose a wage rate of $20.00 an hour for both welders and cashiers. Explain the outcome in a brief comment.

DISCUSSION QUESTIONS

1. "Unequal wages between men and women are more complex than simply passing pay equity laws." Discuss.

2. Ontario's Pay Equity Commission claims that pay equity laws are narrowing the difference between what men and women earn. Does the evidence and theory support this claim?

3. Pay equity legislation doesn't come free. Who are the winners and losers when such laws are enforced to bring men's and women's earnings into line?

4. Economists argue that wage differentials between people, regardless of gender, are a function of occupational choice and not discrimination. Do you agree? Defend your answer with examples.

NOTES

1. Twelve of Canada's jurisdictions have already introduced some form of pay-equity legislation.

2. Equal pay for work of equal value is the same as the terms "pay equity" and "comparable worth."

3. R.E. Robb, "Equal Pay for Work of Equal Value: Issues and Policies," *Canadian Public Policy* 13, no. 4 (Winter 1987): 445–61. The wage differential is based on full-time employment. These studies were also based on census data from 1971 and 1981. This is much less than the 25 to 33 percent gap estimated by the Ontario Pay Equity Commission due to systemic discrimination.

4. Some economists argue that there is no real wage gap between men and women that cannot be explained by factors other than sex discrimination. If a true wage differential exists between men and women based solely on sex discrimination and not on ability, then a smart employer would exploit that difference and hire more women and less men. It is no different for a broker to deal in the arbitrage of an undervalued bond, currency or stock. The question is, why hasn't this happened in the labour market?

5. Robb, "Equal Pay for Work of Equal Value," p. 453.

6. The Canadian Federation of Independent Business estimates that the administration costs for large firms could be as high as $500 per worker, and $300 per worker for small firms.

7. Problems can arise in certain cases where municipal governments may be compelled to raise the salaries in certain jobs. If budgets won't allow them to raise taxes, services or staff could be cut.

8. Robb states that from the preliminary studies based on U.S. census data, a wage adjustment of 20 percentage points in the public sector will lead to a 2–3 percent decline in female employment. The results in the private sector would likely be larger because the wage gap is wider. Given that employment in the private sector is also more "elastic," that is, the demand for labour is more sensitive to wage increases, any increase in female wages would lead to even higher unemployment for women.

9. In the mid-1970s Australia introduced a pay equity law. As a result women's wages went from 65 to 93 percent of men's wages from 1970 to 1980. What were the impacts on women's employment? One study found that pay equalization slowed the growth of women's employment by one-third and increased unemployment by 0.5 percent.

10. *Source:* "Women gaining ground in labour force," *The Globe and Mail*, 19 April, 1999.

11. Andrew Coyne, "Why We Don't Need Pay Equity," *The Globe and Mail,* 14 June 1995. Coyne makes the interesting point that there is virtually no wage gap between single women and single men working full time and that the wage gap is not between men and women per se, but between married men and everyone else.

12. Ted Wannell, "Male–Female Earnings Gap Among Recent University Graduates," *Perspectives on Labour and Income* (Ottawa: Statistics Canada, Summer 1990), pp. 19–27.

13. The Wannell study found that for Ph.D. graduates, the wage differential between men and women was virtually nonexistent. In certain occupations, there was little wage difference in 1987: law (5 percent), sociology/anthropology (3 percent), political science (0 percent), biochemistry/biology (5 percent), and mathematics (7 percent). Nevertheless, there remains an unexplained differential in wages regardless of education and profession. One possible explanation can be found by "statistical discrimination." This means that some employers prefer hiring men because women tend to interrupt their working careers for marriage and children. In the higher occupational categories, this seems less of a factor.

14. Karen Hughs, "Trading places: Men and Women in Non-traditional Occupations 1971–86," *Perspectives on Labour and Income* (Ottawa: Statistics Canada, Summer 1990). This is consistent with evidence in the U.S., where women were closing the wage gap with men in the 1980s. One reason for this change is that women are getting the education they need. See Sylvia Nasar, "Women's Progress Stalled? Not So." *The New York Times,* 18 October 1992, section 3, p. 1.

15. That was a major conclusion of Professor Morley Gunderson in his study "Male–Female Wage Differentials and Policy Responses," *Journal of Economic Literature* 2 (March 1989): 67.

16. That has been the experience in Australia where there has been pay equity since the early 1970s.

WEBLINKS

www.goav.on.ca/lab/pec/
Overall view of pay equity from the Pay Equity Commission of Ontario.

www.realwomenca.com/html/equal_pay.html
Statement on equal pay for work of equal value.

www.stanford.edu/dept/news/report/news/march17/canadaedu317.html
Better education policies help Canada keep narrower wage gap than U.S.

www.capitalresearch.org/LaborWatch/lw-1299c.htm
The cost of implementing pay equity.

www.weq.gov.bc.ca/economic-equality/topics.stm
Discussion papers on women's economic security and pay equity, focusing on British Columbia.

PRESERVING THE FAMILY FARM

 **MYTH** *"The family farm should be preserved as a way of life."*

Governments have long treated family farms differently from other industries by stabilizing incomes using quotas, tariffs, and subsidies. Support programs amount to billions of dollars in transfers to farmers, both directly and indirectly, by consumers and taxpayers. Although some farmers have done well under these programs, many are in financial trouble. Instead of helping, government programs have made Canadian farming less efficient, raising costs for consumers and producers. Coupled with international demands for greater access to our markets, farming must become internationally competitive to survive, which means less support for family farms.

Few things engender such emotional attachment as the notion of preserving the values, traditions, and history of Canada's family farms. To maintain this way of life, governments have historically intervened to protect the interests of farming regardless of the cost to taxpayers and consumers. Even though the economic circumstances surrounding agriculture have changed, the myth persists that farming is different from other industries and must be protected come what may.

As with any public policy that distorts free-market prices, someone pays the bill. With regard to agriculture, there is no exception. How much do we pay to preserve the family farm and the income support system for our farmers? The answer is plenty. In 1990, taxpayers supported the Canadian farmer in the amount of $7.5 billion through direct assistance alone. These amounts have increased steadily over the last decade. In addition, consumers had to pay $3.5 billion in higher food costs. That translates into over $100,000 for every job saved in agriculture compared with $13,000 to $20,000 in the United States.[1] Despite federal cutbacks in the 1980s and 1990s to trim the deficit, spending on farm support continued to climb. Farmers get the equivalent of over 40 percent of their income from government support systems as measured by **Producer Subsidy Equivalents (PSE)** (see Figure 3.1). Yet the more farmers receive, the worse off they are. Of Canada's 276,000 farms, 98 percent are family farms, and many are in financial trouble without any relief in sight. In 1996 over 190,000 of a total of 276,000 farms produced less than $100,000 in sales; and only 10,000 farms produced more than $500,000. And these financial pressures are revealed by the drop in the number of farmers. In 1981 there were 320,000 farms in Canada; in 1996 there

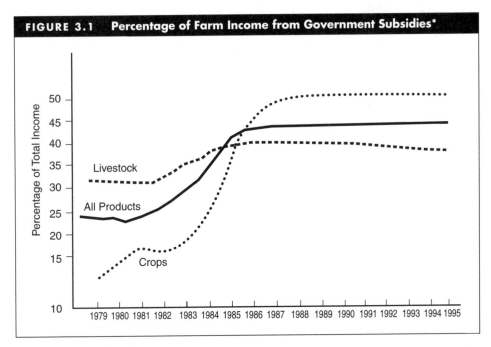

FIGURE 3.1   Percentage of Farm Income from Government Subsidies*

Note: 1995 estimates by author

Sources: J.C. Gilson, *World Agricultural Changes* (Toronto: C.D. Howe Institute, 1989); OECD, *Monitoring and Outlook of Agricultural Policies, Markets and Trade* (Paris, May 1988).

* Producer Subsidy Equivalents (PSE)

were 276,000.[2] Today, only about 3 percent of total employment is directly employed in primary agriculture. The current farm problem is so large that it may be beyond the fiscal capacity of the government to solve with subsidies and public aid.

What happened to farm policy in Canada that seemed to make everyone worse off including the taxpayer, consumer, and farmer? A good part of the answer lies in how governments get involved in supporting farmers, not only in Canada but around the world.[3]

WHY AND HOW GOVERNMENTS GET INVOLVED

Government has always been interested in securing adequate supplies of food for its citizens. On that basis alone, it has been considered in the best interest of a country for governments to intervene in agricultural production by protecting domestic farmers from imports. A nation's dignity has been defined by its ability to feed itself and become self-sufficient. In line with this, another reason for involvement has to do with securing farm incomes. It has long been known that in agriculture, incomes can fluctuate wildly from year to year, caused mainly by large shifts in supply. Weather conditions, for example, have a lot to do with how much wheat, corn, or fruit is harvested. Bumper crops tend to depress prices, while crop shortages push them up. It is one of the ironies in agriculture that good harvests don't always coincide with good incomes. Agricultural commodity prices are very sensitive to small changes in supply, and this is one of the strongest justifications for government intervention: the stabilization of farm prices and incomes. Finally there's the practical matter that farmers have traditionally carried a lot of political clout and for that reason demand special attention.

There are a number of ways governments intervene in agricultural markets. The Americans and the French, for example, prefer to provide **price support programs** in which they buy, at a price above that dictated by supply and demand, as much as the farmer can produce. The farmer now has the incentive to increase profit and income by producing as much as possible. At these artificially higher prices, or **floor prices**, farmers farm more intensively to raise yields. But as a result of these higher prices, less is demanded by consumers. The governments now have the added expense of storing this excess production, or selling it in international markets at below the cost of production. In the United States, taxpayers pay the cost of buying the produce in the first place, plus the cost of literally paying farmers billions of dollars not to produce.[4] Price support programs are so out of hand in the United States that, by the late 1980s, there was enough grain in storage to make seven loaves of bread for every man, woman, and child on earth! Even today price support systems create similar surpluses. At the same time, there was a shortage of oats because the price supports for wheat are so much higher. European farmers have also become rich under their **Common Agricultural Policy (CAP)**, where farmers sell as much as they can to the state at prices above those set by the market.

MARKETING BOARDS: THE CANADIAN WAY

Canadians have chosen another way to help their farmers. For seasonal crops such as fruits and vegetables, the government provides straight subsidies and tariff protection. But for the big cash crops such as grain and dairy products, governments use a uniquely Canadian institution, the **marketing board**.

In the case of grain and oilseed, where the bulk of production is exported, the Canadian government acts as the selling agent for the farmer. The most famous board of this type is the **Canadian Wheat Board (CWB)**, which pays the wheat farmer 75 percent of the world price and then sells the wheat on behalf of the farmer. When the wheat is sold, the farmer gets the difference. In the event that prices on the world markets collapse below the original 75 percent level between the time the government buys and sells the wheat, the loss is absorbed by the federal treasury. By providing 75 percent of the estimated average selling price over the year, the government ensures that farmers do not have to worry about short-term fluctuations in price and can be assured of a set price at time of delivery.[5]

Marketing boards for dairy, poultry, and eggs work differently. Their objective is to control the price of these commodities by restricting their supply with **quotas**. Without a quota, farmers cannot sell their produce. Quotas control how much is produced, which in turn determines the price. If prices are stabilized, so are incomes for farmers. National quotas for Canada's supply-managed commodities are aimed at making the country self-sufficient and are enforced with strict controls on imports and foreign competition. Only by buying an existing quota can someone farm in those areas controlled by supply-managed marketing boards—and the quotas don't come cheaply. The price of the quota reflects the value of the profits or income generated by the restricted supply.[6] The higher the profits in, say, the production of eggs, the higher the cost of purchasing a quota. It is not surprising that the entire system is popular among farmers who hold quotas because it guarantees them a stabilized income above what they could get in a free market.[7]

WHAT WENT WRONG?

In the case of grain marketing boards, everything works well when world prices are either steady or are going up. That is what happened in the early 1970s when world grain prices went from $70 per tonne to over $200 per tonne as grain shortages began to appear around the world. Along with the rise in grain prices, the cost of farmland went up. Farmers who were "just getting by" a few years before were now borrowing heavily and growing rich overnight (on paper at least). By 1981, farm property values topped $103 billion, two-and-a-half times their value of a decade earlier, much of it supported by farm debt that banks were more than willing to provide. Then things slowly began to sour.

As farmers brought more marginal and less productive land into production, costs began to rise. That didn't seem to matter as long as the price of wheat kept rising. Farmers also invested more in high-yield, disease-and drought-resistant crops, which helped yields more than double in North America in the 1960s, '70s, and '80s. However, these developments were taking place everywhere, and countries we once exported to were becoming self-sufficient themselves. World grain production was steadily increasing. This was bad news for Canadian grain farmers who were mortgaged to the hilt when the inevitable price collapse finally occurred. What followed was traumatic: European and American wheat producers started competing madly for a shrinking world market. By 1987, grain farmers were getting $60 per tonne where they had received $186 just a few years before. The real price (adjusted for inflation) for Canadian wheat in 1986 was less than 50 percent of that received during the Great Depression of the 1930s. Despite the price increases in the early 1970s, the long-term trend for wheat prices was down. Canadian farmers had gambled and lost.[8]

Grain farming was a victim of its own success. Better farming techniques and advances in genetic engineering and biotechnology has increased yields to the point where farm production in developed countries has more than kept pace with world population growth. Canada produces 70 percent more grain than it needs to be self-sufficient, compared to Japan, which only produces slightly more than half of its national food requirements.

Ottawa's high interest rate policy in the early 1980s did not help matters. Farmers were struggling to hold on as land values dropped and **equity** disappeared. As if that wasn't enough, the droughts in the Prairies made a bad situation worse. All Ottawa could do was wait for better times and hand out more subsidies. Throughout the 1990s droughts in Western Canada resulted in billions of dollars flowing to farmers in Southern Alberta, Saskatchewan, and Manitoba. By the early 1990s, grain farmers were getting 10 percent of the cash receipts from government programs. In the end, the federal government and taxpayers were victims of poor planning, cutthroat international marketing, and bad luck.

Under this environment, the Wheat Marketing Board is quickly losing its power and relevance. Grain farmers are now demanding that they have greater control over the sale of their output. The CWB, with its large bureaucracy, can no longer respond to the changing nature of grain farming (Carter and Loyns).

Where grain producers have no control over world prices, marketing boards for dairy, eggs, and poultry are designed to get back that control from the vagaries of supply and demand. But where the costs are obvious to everyone, as is the case in grain subsidies, the support for **supply-management** programs is more subtle but just as damaging.

As with any scheme by governments to stabilize incomes by restricting supply, the consumer pays a price higher than would exist under a free market and consumes a quantity less than dictated by the free market. It's not surprising that Canadians pay 20 percent more for their chickens and eggs than they would without supply-management programs. Even food producers are compelled to buy their inputs from marketing boards, thus raising the cost for consumers. Perhaps more important, however, is the fact that marketing boards distort production efficiency and actually reward the least efficient producer. Once a farmer has a quota, there is little or no incentive to compete and cut production costs. The younger, more efficient farmers also pay a price because many find the cost of quotas prohibitive. When chicken quotas were about $35 a bird, that meant that anyone who wanted to buy a modest 6,000 chicken farm would need $210,000, and that was even before taking into consideration land and capital equipment. Anyone lucky enough to have a quota hangs on to it as long as possible. The result is that there are too many small, inefficient producers. Because of these price distortions, Canada has about as many egg producers as does the entire United States.

All farmers do not benefit equally from supply management. For the 40,000 poultry, egg, and dairy producers, or approximately 14 percent of Canada's farms, they account for 21 percent of the cash receipts in Canada. Most of that went to the farmers in Quebec and Ontario, who have considerable political clout. Those two provinces hold 80 percent of the industrial milk quota, 55 percent of the egg quota, 68 percent of the turkey quota, and 66 percent of the chicken quota. Dairy farmers receive over 80 percent of their incomes from higher prices paid by consumers through supply-management programs. It's understandable, therefore, that Ontario and Quebec farmers are strong defenders of supply-management. Farmers protected by marketing boards argue that these costs are worth paying because extra taxes are not needed to prop up farm incomes. That's true, but higher prices hit the poorer consumer more than the rich, given that the poor spend a higher proportion of their income on food. Taxes are more equitable if they are progressive and more open to scrutiny by taxpayers.

The ultimate irony is that despite decades of government protecting the family farm with massive transfers of money and income-support systems, the farmer is under growing pressure just to survive. The entire system worked well when prices and demand for food products generally moved upward, but in periods of prolonged price declines, overproduction, and greater international competition, the economy is left burdened with over capacity, an inefficient network of trade-distorting income-support programs, and the prospect of greater shifts in income to the farm sector. Although marketing boards protect jobs in farming, thousands of potential jobs are lost in food processing because of the higher costs of production.

THE IMPACT OF REMOVING SUPPORT PROGRAMS

What would happen if we simply got rid of all the subsidies and programs that stabilize farm incomes? How much production would be lost in Canada from farms going out of business? One estimate was that farm output would drop by 16.7 percent compared to 13.6 percent for all countries in the **Organization for Economic Co-operation and Development (OECD)** countries if they in turn did the same thing, However, because taxes from the industrial and service sectors would fall, nonfarm output in Canada would increase along with real household incomes.

Another concern is that prices would climb if we got rid of the subsidies. Perhaps some would climb, but not by much. In many cases, such as poultry, eggs, and cheese, they would come down. There is an abundance of world agricultural production that would keep farm prices low. Canadians could take advantage of lower food prices from U.S. producers. (Canadians living close to the United States already take advantage of lower food costs by shopping south of the border where dairy, eggs, and poultry prices are considerably lower than in Canada.) But if we got rid of the subsidies, consider what Canadians could do with the billions saved on propping up farms that have little or no prospect for surviving in a more competitive world. Realistically, such dramatic changes in income transfers to the agricultural sector are not about to happen any time soon, but world pressures are clearly moving away from guaranteed income support for farmers and towards a system of greater market-oriented trade. Even the banks are seeing the writing on the wall and are discounting the value of farm quotas as collateral.

HARD CHOICES AHEAD

The government now faces a dilemma: whether to sacrifice one group of farmers to save another. The demand from some farm groups that no farm should be allowed to go under is simply not feasible. If Canada wants greater access to international markets, it cannot argue for import restrictions to help dairy farmers. Eventually taxpayers and consumers will refuse to carry the growing burden of agricultural income-support programs. Food manufacturers have been warning governments and farmers for some time that billions of dollars of investment will be lost if ways are not found to get input costs down. Governments cannot indefinitely justify bailing out farmers while they allow other small businesses to compete without government protection. Farming is seen more as a business rather than a way of life to be protected by expensive government support systems.

That reality was manifested with the signing of the Canada–United States Free Trade Agreement (FTA) in 1989. The FTA eliminated barriers for cattle, hogs, and red meat. The removal of a few border irritants, such as tariffs and health regulations, makes it easier to move products between countries. The agreement also phased out restrictions and discrimination against the importation of American wine and liquor, although these restrictions were already being removed under the **World Trade Organization (WTO)**.[9] However, farmers managed to keep Canada's supply-management programs off the negotiation table, protecting dairy, poultry, and eggs. Even the North American Free Trade Agreement didn't change that. In the end, the choice may be out of the hands of the federal government as pressure builds in the WTO to reduce agricultural trade restrictions worldwide. The WTO has already put Canada on notice that they won't allow our supply-management programs to exist if we hope to gain greater access to foreign markets. Although the federal government has gone on record supporting supply-management programs, it seems unlikely Ottawa will go to the wall to defend them indefinitely, given Canada's support for trade liberalization in general. The successful farms of the future will be those that can compete internationally. The transition to freer markets for agriculture won't be easy, but the days of keeping the family farm going at any cost are at an end. For farm policy to be successful, we can no longer view farming in the twenty-first century with the sentiments of the nineteenth century.

KEY TERMS

Producer Subsidy
  Equivalents (PSE)
Price support program
Floor price
Common Agricultural
  Policy (CAP)

Marketing boards
Canadian Wheat Board
Quotas
Equity
Supply management

Organization for
  Economic Co-opera-
  tion and Development
  (OECD)
World Trade
  Organization (WTO)

REVIEW QUESTIONS

1. Even though supply management or marketing boards for dairy or egg production do not create surpluses, why do economists find them inefficient?

2. Using supply and demand curves, show how large changes in supply (bumper crops) can actually generate less revenue for farmers.

3. Price support systems tend to encourage excess production if the floor price is set too high. What are the implications of such a policy? How are taxpayers penalized more than once because of it?

4. Why have governments traditionally come to the rescue of farmers with income-support programs?

5. To a great extent, agriculture is a victim of its own success. How does this explain the crisis in wheat production in Western Canada?

DISCUSSION QUESTIONS

1. What makes agriculture different from other industries? Should family farms be treated any differently from other small businesses?

2. How can governments help family farms in the transition to a more free-market economy?

3. "Without support for farmers, we'll be at the mercy of foreign producers." Discuss this statement in light of current world agricultural developments.

4. Has the Canadian Wheat Board outlived its usefulness? Should grain farmers be allowed to sell their own products?

NOTES

1. OECD estimates as reported in *The Financial Post,* 9 April 1990, adapted from Michael Parkin and Robin Bade, *Economics: Canada in the Global Environment* (Don Mills: Addison-Wesley, 1994).

2. Colin Carter and Al Loyns, "The Federal Government and the Prairie Grain Sector: A Study of Overregulation" (Toronto: University of Toronto, Centre for Public Management, 1998).

3. Canadian and American farmers aren't the only farmers getting help. The Japanese farmer gets 68 percent of income from subsidies, while the Swiss farmer gets 78 percent. In 1990, OECD countries transferred around US$300 billion to farmers from consumers and taxpayers.

4. In the United States about 78 million acres, an area the size of New Mexico, are covered by acreage restriction programs. Farmers often get around these restrictions by increasing yields on available land.

5. Federal marketing boards are not the only way farmers receive assistance. Grain farmers receive billions of dollars in an array of subsidies covering transportation, insurance, irrigation, and bailouts. Farmers also got lump-sum payments when world prices collapsed in the late 1980s and early 1990s.

6. Canada is close to self-sufficiency in most agricultural products, including those products covered by supply-managed commodities. Although there are some provisions for marginal imports such as cheese, it's vital that foreign competition is controlled so that prices can be maintained in the domestic market.

7. To anyone who is noticing, the milk, egg, and pork marketing boards are particularly aggressive advertisers. As with any commodity, this advertising is necessary to forestall declining demand or increase overall sales.

8. J.C. Gilson, *World Agricultural Changes: Implications for Canada* (Toronto: C.D. Howe Institute, May, 1989), p. 64.

9. The WTO was formerly known as **GATT** (the General Agreement on Tariffs and Trade). The change came in 1995. Where GATT dealt mainly with tariff restrictions, the WTO is a vastly more comprehensive institution that deals with all aspects of trade including services, subsidies, and intellectual property to name a few.

WEBLINKS

www.nfu.ca/welcome.htm
National Farmer's Union.

www.cwb.ca/
Canadian Wheat Board.

www.agr.ca/aida/
Agriculture and Agri-Food Canada, a government body that supplies disaster relief to farmers.

www.agr.ca/policy/epad/english/pubs/adhoc/98067r/appa.htm
Impact of selected federal cost recovery initiatives on the agri-food sector.

www.oecd.org/
Home page of the OECD.

MINIMUM WAGES AND THE WORKING POOR

**"Higher minimum wages are a good way
to help the working poor."**

*Economists have long known that minimum-wage legislation destroys
jobs by raising labour costs. But politicians see it as a quick fix to raise
the incomes of the working poor. Unfortunately, the poor and young are
hurt most by minimum-wage laws. There are better ways to help the
working poor, but they require longer-term solutions such as social policy reform and better educational opportunities for young people.*

Imagine trying to make ends meet, in any major Canadian city, on a weekly salary
of $274 or $1150 a month, before taxes and Employment Insurance (EI) (formerly
Unemployment Insurance—UI) payments. That's what someone working at the
minimum wage of $6.85 per hour earns for a 40-hour work week in Ontario. After
paying for rent and food, not even a financial wizard living on a diet of macaroni and
cheese can scratch out a decent standard of living. It is hard enough for an individual, but compound the problem by adding a spouse and children. By anyone's definition, earning the minimum wage means poverty, pure and simple. In fact, Statistics
Canada estimates that, in order to escape being classified as poor, a family of four
had to earn $25,000, or about twice the amount provided by the minimum wage,
whether through work or social assistance.[1]

Some studies estimate that the working poor in Canada make up over 50 percent of the poor in our society. Thus, having a job is certainly no guarantee of escaping poverty, although that's exactly what minimum-wage legislation was designed to cure. It attempts to make sure that if people work, they will not be earning wages so low that they cannot provide the essentials of life.

As with many public policy programs, minimum-wage legislation is designed to correct an "equity" problem in the system. Most of us would argue that it is only right that the working poor make a decent income, and it's this **equity principle** that drives policy makers to distribute income from the haves to the have nots, because we intrinsically believe that the poor are needier than the rich. That's why we have a **progressive income tax** system that requires those who earn more to pay a higher percentage of their income to taxes. But what about a policy that pretends to help the working poor by increasing their wages, but in fact hurts the very group it was intended to help? By anyone's standards, that would be totally unacceptable. Odd as it may seem, that's what minimum-wage legislation actually does; it kills jobs.

HOW MINIMUM WAGES HURT THE POOR

To begin with, minimum wages are a form of price control for labour. In this case, there is a **floor price** under which wages can't fall. There is interference with what the cost of labour would normally have been without government intervention. The theory works something like this: if the forces of supply and demand in a free-market economy determine that wages in a given sector are $6 per hour, and the government dictates that they should be $8 per hour, then there is a problem. At $8 per hour, more people are willing to work, but fewer businesses are willing to hire. The result is an **excess supply of labour** or an increase in unemployment at the new wage rate (see Figure 4.1). What happens when employers are legislated by law to pay the higher minimum wage? Businesses have a number of choices: pay the higher labour costs; begin substituting capital or machinery for labour as the cost of labour goes up relative to capital; cut expenses by laying off some workers or cutting back on employee incentives; or, in more drastic cases, shut down operations and close up shop. Another alternative open to business is to pay workers illegally (under the table), in which case the taxpayer pays the higher costs of taxes foregone. In each situation, someone pays for the higher wage: either the worker by losing his job or having his hours or incentives cut back, or the employer who absorbs the higher costs. In the more drastic case where the business closes down, everyone suffers. This is the classic case of a **zero sum game** where you can only better one group by making another worse off.

As with any government tampering with the price system, whether it involves commodities or wages, there are winners and losers. The winners still have jobs at the higher wage. However, there are several types of losers. The first is the

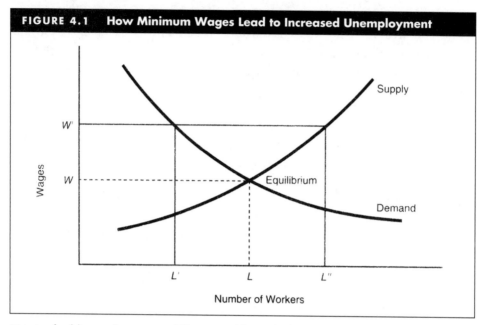

FIGURE 4.1   How Minimum Wages Lead to Increased Unemployment

Note: In a free labour market, wages would be at *W* and the supply of labour at *L*. If the minimum wage by law goes to *W'*, the supply of labour now goes to *L"*. The demand for labour drops to *L'*, leaving an excess supply of workers, or a higher level of unemployment.

employer who has to pay higher wages. One way or another, employers will try to get someone else to "foot the bill." Employers will either pass on the costs (in which case the consumer loses out by paying higher prices) or will have the employees themselves take on the burden of the higher labour costs. As already mentioned, employers can decide not to hire an extra worker or can cut back the hours of those already employed. They can get their employees to work harder, thereby making the workers "earn their keep." Some employers have other ways of getting around the legislation, from hiring family members (who are often exempt from the legislation) to paying for labour in cash and thereby eluding detection and taxes altogether.

The second loser is the unemployed worker. If an employer makes the decision to let someone go or not to hire an extra worker in the future, the victim is likely to be a young, inexperienced worker who needs training. Typically, when workers enter the labour market, their productivity is low and consequently they earn low wages. However, employers use this low-wage period to train their workers. This, in turn, allows workers to get a better foothold in the labour market. But if the minimum wage exceeds that paid to workers while they are being trained, employers tend to cut back on-the-job education. In the end, society ends up with fewer trained workers and a reduction in human capital. The third, and final victim, is the taxpayer.

For workers who can't find work because of the minimum-wage law, the alternative is usually some form of social assistance.

Not surprisingly, research confirms what theory tells us: raising the minimum wage actually causes more unemployment, particularly among the young with the least job experience. An increase of 10 percent in the minimum wage increases unemployment by about 1.4 percent for women and 1.5 percent for teenagers.[2] Once the young lose their jobs, there is little immediate prospect of finding more work. Therefore, it should come as no surprise that the unemployment rate in the 15-to 24-year-old age group is always 5 percentage points higher than the rate for the entire labour force; teenage unemployment is traditionally twice the national level. Yet despite the evidence that this antipoverty theory does not work, the Left continues in its pursuit to "outlaw poverty."

POLICIES OF THE LEFT

When Ontario's New Democratic Party (NDP) was elected in 1990, they made it clear they were going to boost the minimum wage from $5.40 per hour to 60 percent of the average industrial wage over the next five years. By 1995, Ontario's minimum wage was up 26 percent. But, as we have already seen, someone has to pay for the higher wage. In a study designed to measure the effects of Ontario's legislation, the Institute for Policy Analysis at the University of Toronto estimated that the NDP plan could cost the province almost 55,000 jobs.[3] Even a study commissioned by the Ontario Ministry of Labour estimated that a 10 percent increase in the minimum wage would cost Ontario about 25,000 jobs.[4]

The group most affected by the NDP proposal was young, single women. According to the Ontario Ministry of Labour figures, of the 160,000 workers collecting the minimum wage (about 4.1 percent of the labour force), 57 percent of these were women, while 22 percent were heads of households. So we see that in order to raise the wage of less than 5 percent of the labour force, the Ontario government was willing to jeopardize the jobs of thousands of workers. Is the benefit worth the cost?

What of the businesses that are required to pay the higher wages? It is important to keep in mind that it is not General Motors, IBM, or Northern Telecom that pays minimum wage; rather it is small businesses, the ones that have less leverage to begin with. Low wages are paid in the more marginalized and competitive sectors of the economy, such as fast-food restaurants, retail outlets, and a whole range of low-skill operations. Only about 10 percent of workers earning minimum wages work in manufacturing. The remainder work in areas such as retail trade and the hospitality industry. If these businesses are compelled to pay higher wages, someone has to pay. Poor wages can't be legislated out of existence without significant costs to the worker, the employer, and society.

There are those who make the case that jobs lost to higher minimum-wage legislation were not worth keeping anyway, that society is better off without them, and that we can live without jobs like security guards, cleaning staff, and retail sales clerks. But these jobs are not completely without value. These are the jobs that allow the young to enter the labour market and gain the experience and responsibility that they carry into adulthood. Many new immigrants rely on these jobs to get a foothold in the labour market and acquire the skills to better their lot in society. Besides, if the intention of minimum-wage laws is to ban or discourage certain types of jobs, it would be more effective to do so directly rather than as the side effect of laws that are supposed to improve the wages of the working poor.[5]

If the public policy of imposing minimum-wage legislation is so costly for society, why do governments bother? One answer is that it's simple and initially costless for governments. Simply legislating higher wages, gives the impression that governments are doing something to help the working poor. It doesn't take much to pass legislation, even though it ends up creating enormous problems down the road. It's no different from the motivation that drives politicians to implement rent control. For governments, it's an expedient short-term solution to a long-term problem. Besides, it is politically harmless to trade off the benefits of the few known beneficiaries against the jobs of those yet to come into the labour market. The former group are a known quantity with political clout, while the latter, who bear the cost of the legislation, are not yet identified and will be looking for jobs sometime in the future.

It is not surprising that trade unions are the main supporters of minimum-wage laws. Unions, essentially, want to identify themselves as defenders of the working poor and present a united front when negotiating higher wages. It would not be in their best interest if nonunion workers were willing to perform identical services as union members at lower wages. The higher the minimum wage, the greater the wage bargaining influence of labour. Another reason for trade unions' support of the minimum wage is that various occupations or trades maintain a constant wage difference between skill groups. For example, if, as a guide in wage negotiations, electricians earn four times the minimum wage, the higher the minimum wage, the higher the wages for electricians. Minimum-wage legislation was a hard-fought victory for labour that goes back to the 1930s, and they won't give it up without a fight.

Despite the evidence that minimum-wage laws only make the working poor worse off, politicians insist on using them to raise incomes. They seem to see the problem of low income in its most simple form. They think that by passing a law, they will automatically improve the circumstances of the poor. Politicians have to learn the difference between the intent of the law and its actual effects. Minimum-wage laws have exactly the opposite impact from that intended: more working poor and higher unemployment. In short, higher labour costs reduce employment.[6]

HELPING THE WORKING POOR

If legislating higher wages is not an effective way to help the working poor, what is? First of all, helping the working poor cannot be addressed simply as a wage problem. Poverty is a social, educational, and economic problem. As most low-wage earners are young, part of the solution lies in helping workers before they reach the labour market. That means keeping students in school as long as possible in order for them to get the skills they need for gainful employment. More than one-third of all high-school students never graduate, and the resultant low literacy rates are affecting Canada's ability to compete at home and abroad. Another solution is to revamp the entire apprenticeship program to help workers get the best on-the-job training possible. These solutions aren't new; governments have known about them for years. Social programs such as employment insurance and welfare must not be deterrents to work. Provincial and municipal governments have to cooperate to encourage welfare recipients to supplement their incomes by working part-time without endangering their welfare status. Minimum-wage laws are not a remedy, only a palliative.

Another alternative is for Canada to move towards a **guaranteed annual income (GAI)**. Our current system, designed to eradicate poverty, is a confusing assortment of social security and income-support programs that inefficiently transfers income from the rich to the poor. Under these programs, it costs society more than $1 in administration costs for each dollar provided to the poor. It's long been advocated that one way around this dilemma is to provide the poor with a positive incentive to enter the labour market by allowing them to earn more without jeopardizing their social assistance payments. The argument against a GAI is that it will be a disincentive to work, but that doesn't seem to be the case. One government study found little evidence that people generally worked less when they received a minimum guaranteed income. In any case, governments should seriously consider eliminating programs such as minimum-wage laws that indirectly hurt the poor and distort market incentives.

KEY TERMS

Equity principle
Progressive income tax
Floor price

Excess supply of labour
Zero sum game

Guaranteed annual income (GAI)

REVIEW QUESTIONS

1. The B.C. Federation of Labour wants the minimum wage increased to 75 percent of the average industrial wage, which would put the minimum wage at $10 an hour as opposed to the current $6 an hour. Describe how the proposed increase in the minimum wage would affect the labour market in B.C. Use supply-and-demand diagrams to illustrate your answer.

2. Identify the winners and losers when governments interfere in the free market by setting a floor price for labour.

3. When the minimum wage goes up, describe ways both workers and employers may get around the legislation.

DISCUSSION QUESTIONS

1. Why do politicians turn to legislation that mandates higher wages for the working poor?

2. Why has organized labour traditionally supported higher minimum-wage laws?

3. Describe some methods, other than higher minimum wages, that could increase the incomes of the poor while leaving the free market to set wages for labour.

NOTES

1. Defining poverty is not as easy as it first appears. Some argue that poverty is a relative concept rather than an absolute one and that Statistics Canada's method for measuring poverty is poor. For a discussion on the topic see Christopher A. Sarlo, *Poverty in Canada* (The Fraser Institute, 1992).

2. Jean-Michel Cousineau, David Tessier, and Francois Vaillancourt, *The Impact of the Ontario Minimum Wage on the Unemployment of Women and the Young: A Note,* Policy Study 91-6 (Toronto: Institute for Policy Analysis, University of Toronto, 1991), p. 5.

3. Ibid.

4. Peter Dungan and Morley Gunderson, *The Effect of Minimum Wage Increases on Employment in Ontario* (Toronto: Institute for Policy Analysis, University of Toronto, 1989).

5. Another odd side effect of minimum-wage laws is that they may be helping the wrong people. Although 30 percent of minimum-wage earners had family earnings below the poverty line, 37 percent of those collecting minimum wages were in families with high average incomes. It seems minimum wages were going to part-time, teenage workers of wealthier families.

6. One famous study in the United States, done in 1994, attempted to show that employment grew with increases in the minimum wage in the fast-food industry. Professors David Card and Alan Krueger, two economists at Princeton University, surprised many with their results. Their work has not gone unchallenged. Gary S. Becker, a Nobel laureate in economics, found their work to be flawed and says the overwhelming evidence still shows that higher minimum wages destroy jobs.

WEBLINKS

www.bc.ndp.ca/News/Newswire/000629_CCPAminimum.htm
Minimum wage increase as good public policy.

www.self-gov.org/cox02.html
The ugly truth about the minimum wage law.

www.cupe.mb.ca/minwage.html
Minimum wage brief: comparison of minimum wage by province.

www.caledoninst.org/speaking/spkg01.htm
Policies of the left.

EDUCATION
AND
WAGES

 *"A university education is losing its value."*

There is a general perception that higher education is no longer the route to higher wages and job stability that it once was. However, the data show that those with either a college education or higher not only earn higher wages, but also tend to have lower rates of unemployment. It is important to understand that more education alone does not guarantee a better life. Work habits, talent, and personal effort are also important contributing factors. One must also factor in opportunity costs when making a decision to earn a college diploma or a university degree. But all things considered, those who stay in school beyond a high school diploma fare better than those who don't.

After the recession of the early 1990s, there was a general perception that a university education wasn't as valuable as it once was. Members of **Generation X** were convinced that the baby boomers from the previous generation had taken all the good jobs leaving them with poor employment prospects. There were the proverbial stories of Ph.D.s waiting tables and driving cabs, unable to find proper employment, while younger entrepreneurs with only a secondary education were earning more than college graduates. After all, even Bill Gates was a college dropout. In many ways, there was some truth to the perception that spending four or five years in college or university wasn't paying off. In the recession of the early '90s, employment offices were full of job seekers with or without college or university educations. In short, it appeared to many that more schooling doesn't always guarantee a better life. Besides many argue that in the New Economy, firms tend to value creativity and adaptability, attributes that don't readily come with more post-secondary education.

On the surface it appears that staying in school and getting that degree or college diploma isn't always the wise choice. Or is it? Is investing in **human capital**, getting more education and training, worth the effort?

WHY MORE EDUCATION IS STILL BETTER THAN LESS

Although there is plenty of anecdotal evidence that staying in school isn't a guarantee of higher pay and lower unemployment, in most cases the rewards are worth the effort. Let's start by looking at the evidence to see who is most likely to be unemployed. The National Graduates Survey (NGS), which followed the activity and employment rates of three cohorts of college and university graduates from graduating classes of 1982, 1986, and 1990, showed that more education means lower unemployment. (Each cohort was followed up with interviews two and five years after graduation.) For example, in 1995 the general rate of unemployment for the Canadian economy was around 11 percent. The rate for college graduates was 7 percent, 5 percent for those with a bachelor or masters degree, and around 4 percent for those with a Ph.D. The survey clearly showed that unemployment rates were lower for graduates at all levels (college through Ph.D.). Some of these rates were as low as 2 percent and nowhere were they above the average rate of unemployment in the Canadian economy.[1] Even among younger workers, who often experience higher levels of unemployment, those with more education have a much higher probability of finding work.[2]

The NGS also showed, rather surprisingly, that those with post-secondary education experienced no significant general deterioration in employment opportunities from the early 1980s to the mid-1990s. This means that the perception by members of Generation X, that they were losing out to the baby boom generation, was generally unfounded. The data also showed that the unemployment rates among male and female graduates were pretty much the same; however, female graduates tended to hold a higher share of part-time jobs. This was the case regardless of how much education women had compared to their male counterparts. For example, for the 1990 cohort, 13 percent of females with a bachelor's degree had part-time work compared to 6 percent for men with the same level of education. This can be explained mainly by the decision of women to have and raise children rather than any discrimination of the labour market against women.[3]

Now let's turn our attention to the other benefit of more education: remuneration. Again the evidence is clear: someone with a college or university education makes more money than someone with just a high school diploma. In 1984, a male high school graduate working full time, between the ages of 35–44, earned on average about $29,800. By 1992, that same worker, with no further education, earned $30,300, a mere $500 more than eight years before. (Keep in mind that these numbers are 1986 dollars, which eliminates the effects of inflation.) Now let's examine a male worker over the same years who has graduated from college. In 1984, he was earning $45,400, and by 1992, $46,900. Not only was the college graduate earning more, his relative earnings increased at a faster rate.[4] The same differentials apply to women with a high school diploma and those with a college education, except that the average earnings of women were lower. A woman in the same age category with a high school education earned, on average, $18,650 in 1984. By 1992, that same person earned $20,580. However, a woman with a college education increased her earnings from $32,450 to $35,140. Although women earned less than men with the same education, their wages tended to increase at a faster rate: 8 percent over that period for women compared to 3 percent for men. The earnings picture gets even better for men and women who earn a master's degree. In 1995, the average wage for a male with a master's degree was over $56,000 and around $50,500 for women. The data are quite clear that earnings increase given higher levels of education.

WHEN MORE EDUCATION IS LESS

However, it isn't the case that increasing amounts of education mean ever increasing wages and income. For example, those who earned a bachelor's degree in 1990 increased their average incomes by 23 percent from 1992 to 1995, while the increase was only 12 percent for those with a master's degree. If a person had earned a Ph.D. in 1990, her or his overall income would be roughly the same as someone who had earned a master's degree.[5] In other words, it appears that the more education the better when it comes to earning power, but only to a point. It seems that the labour market values education attainment below the levels of a Ph.D. One lesson from these observations is that unless you need a Ph.D. to get the job you want, such as teaching at a university level, the **opportunity cost**, what you have to give up in terms of time and foregone income, may simply be too high.[6] And in economics, most things are measured in what has to be given up in order to acquire something else. For some, the psychic benefits of more education may be worth the cost, but each one of us has to assess overall costs and benefits. There are those who put a high value on earning a Ph.D. even though the benefits are not measured by greater earnings. For others the **marginal cost** of more education may not be worth the marginal benefits. Even in education and increases in human capital, the **law of diminishing returns** applies.

But not all education is created equal when it comes to earnings and employment, and most students instinctively realize this before beginning their studies. One recent study has shown that graduates in computer science and health sciences have done very well when it came to finding jobs and earning potential. However, the news wasn't as good for those pursuing jobs in applied sciences. Comparing the average earnings of graduates with a bachelor's degree or diplomas in applied sciences in the 1980s, they were the lowest when compared to occupations in engineering, computer, and health sciences. In 1991, the average salary for someone in the health sciences, who graduated in 1988, was $41,000 compared to $28,000 for someone in applied science and $33,000 in computer science. Not surprisingly, these figures also predicted levels of job satisfaction. Those enjoying the highest levels were those with undergraduate and graduate degrees in computer science and health occupations. This isn't surprising given the fact that graduates in the applied sciences were often found to be overqualified for the jobs they held. There was a greater mismatch in skills among this group than in other occupations.[7] This brings us back to the question of the opportunity cost of earning a degree rather than a diploma. Given this information, a wise choice for some students in applied science would be to acquire a diploma at a community college rather than spend the extra year or two earning a university degree.

But what are the reasons that an applied science background would be less valuable? This result is surprising especially given that all the market signals, at least the informal ones, indicate that science-based occupations are the place to be in our knowledge-based economy. There are a number of possible explanations. One is that we've been oversold on the importance of science and technology as potential occupations in the New Economy, therefore increasing the supply in these fields. Another possible explanation is the tendency for firms to make shortsighted decisions about their need for more scientifically trained workers leading them to underinvest in this area. A third explanation may have to do with public policy and the incentives offered for students to study in certain fields. The Canada Scholarship Program offered financial incentives by the federal government for students, especially women, to study science and engineering. Could these programs be partly to blame for causing an oversupply of jobs in an area the labour market didn't need and therefore driving down the average earnings in these occupations?[8]

Another explanation is that the New Economy requires workers with flexible, general education backgrounds, such as in the arts. And there's growing evidence that those with backgrounds in these areas are doing well when it comes to getting jobs, even though most Canadians believe that more technically-based jobs are the way of the future. In one key study, those with backgrounds in education, social sciences, and humanities fared just as well, if not better, than more specialized occupations in technical and vocational courses.[9]

A key lesson to learn is that education is not a homogeneous commodity. Consumers have to be aware of which fields offer the greatest benefits. This isn't to suggest that students should only enter those fields with the highest potential earnings if they truly want to pursue other studies. Job satisfaction demands that one pursue a field of study that is compatible with one's talents and interests. But the student should be aware that the labour market, in the final analysis, will determine whether a good secure paying job is waiting at the end of the road.

As a rule, we've seen that the **return on investment** in education pays off in lower unemployment and higher wages. In general, it's always better to get more education than less. However, that's not the complete answer. If someone completes high school and finds a job, the costs of going back to school, and foregoing the job in the first place, comes at a cost. Going to college or university means not earning any money in the interim. The opportunity cost of acquiring a college education means foregoing the income that could have been earned by being employed. Only when the benefits of getting more education surpass the opportunity cost is it worth making the decision to invest in more education. Then again, some people's ability to acquire more education is limited by their innate abilities and backgrounds. We are all born with different cognitive abilities and talents, which also affect how difficult or easy it is to learn or stay in school. However, it has to be recognized that educational attainments are not the only factors determining the level of wages and salaries. Intangibles such as hard work, perseverance, and experience often determine our capacity to earn a living. Education can help us get a foot in the door when starting our careers, but education takes a back seat to experience and performance in the long run.

APPENDIX: WHO SHOULD PAY?

If it goes without saying that more education is a benefit to those who avail themselves, then society also benefits by having a more educated labour force. These benefits are called the **social returns to education**: the excess return on education over and above any extra earnings obtained from being educated. That has been the justification for the government to pick up most of the costs of educating Canada's youth. Currently, provincial governments pick up the majority costs of higher education. However, with the general trend for provinces to control their spending, more of these costs are being transferred to the students themselves through higher tuition fees. Is this wise public policy?

The proportion of Canadians aged 25 to 29 with a university education is very high compared to other countries. In 1998, those with a university education in this age group rose to 26 percent from 17 percent in 1990. Compared to the OECD average, almost twice as many Canadians have post-secondary education. Canada also spends more on education, 7 percent of GDP, than other OECD countries.[10] Although about 50 percent of students borrow to finance their education, a proportion that hasn't changed over the years, they are leaving school with higher debt loads. In 1990 the average debt carried by students was $8,600—by 1998 it had increased to $25,000.[11]

It has been argued that those who benefit from education should pay a higher proportion of the costs, especially since those in higher income brackets use the post-secondary system more than lower income Canadians. The children of those in the higher socio-economic group go to university at a greater rate than those in the lower or middle income groups. In 1995, 40 percent of university students were from the highest income group compared to 18 percent from the lowest.[12] And those in the lower and middle income classes must make a relatively greater financial sacrifice to send their children to college or university. That is, their opportunity costs are higher.

But some students in different subject areas benefit more than others. Although tuition fees have gone up, they haven't increased the same amount for all students. Some economists have argued that tuition should be low because those who earn post-secondary education more than pay for their education through higher taxes, given Canada's progressive income tax system. The question remains, however, what is a fair share for taxpayers, given that the students will benefit most from their education. Are the externalities to society worth the cost?[13] And is it right that lower income Canadians should subsidize post-secondary education if the wealthier in society make greater use of the system? And is it really beneficial for society to subsidize the education of students studying for their MBAs, for example, where the benefits will accrue mainly to large corporations?[14] These aren't easy questions to answer, but they are important to address if we want to make our education system more equitable and efficient.[15]

KEY TERMS

Generation X
Human capital
Opportunity cost
Marginal cost

Law of diminishing
  returns
Return on investment

Social returns to
  education
Income-contingent loans

REVIEW QUESTIONS

1. Earning a college diploma or university degree usually leads to higher wages and higher employment levels. Does this apply to all forms of higher learning? Give some exceptions.

2. The evidence shows that although more education is better than less, going beyond a bachelor's or master's degree may actually be counterproductive in terms of earnings. Give some reasons why this may be the case.

3. Explain how government policy can often distort supply and demand in the labour market through misguided policies. (Keep in mind the incentive programs to encourage women to study science and engineering.)

DISCUSSION QUESTIONS

1. "The longer one waits to earn a degree or diploma, the higher the opportunity cost." Explain.

2. Canadian students complain that they are leaving school with higher debt loads than in the past. Are their complaints well founded?

3. It has been proposed that students should pay back their loans based on income earned after graduation. Those who earn more should pay their loans over a shorter time period. What are your thoughts?

NOTES

1. Ross Finnie, "Post-secondary Graduates: Holding Their Own in Terms of Employment Rates and Earnings Patterns," *Canadian Business Economics*, December 1999. The NGS files are longitudinal based on information gathered during interviews two and five years after graduation for each cohort (1984/87, 1988/91, 1992/95).

2. Susan Crompton, "Employment Prospects for High School Graduates," *Perspectives*, Statistics Canada, Autumn 1995. These figures are for 1993.

3. Another clear lesson is that more education also means more job stability and security. Workers with 11 years or more of education have average job lengths almost twice that of those with 10 years or less. With 11 years or more of education, that is from grade one, the average job tenure is 47 months compared with 24 months with 10 years or less of education. (*Source:* "Changes in Job Duration in Canada," Andrew Heisz, *Industrial Relations*, Vol. 54, No. 2, 1999.)

4. Statistics Canada, *Earnings of Men and Women*, 13–217.

5. Ibid., "Post-Secondary Graduates," p. 55.

6. It should be remembered that the opportunity cost of education is lower when unemployment is high. That's why many choose to return to or stay in school longer during recessions.

7. Marie Lavoie and Ross Finnie, "It It Worth Doing a Science or Technology Degree in Canada?", *Canadian Public Policy*, March 1999.

8. One way that workers can increase their skills is through government-sponsored training programs. Unfortunately these programs have turned out to be a great disappointment. In a growing body of research, economists have compared groups of unemployed that enter government training programs with similar groups who don't. These studies have found that the schemes failed to improve either wages or employment prospects. (*Source:* "What Works?" *The Economist* (6 April 1996), p. 19.

9. Robert Allen, "The Employability of University Graduates in the Humanities, Social Sciences and Education: Recent Statistical Evidence," University of British Columbia, August 1998. (http://web.arts.ubc.ca/econ/dp9815.pdf)

10. "School costs more, pays less, study says," The *National Post*, 22 February 2000.

11. Canadian Association of University Teachers Bulletin, October 1998.

12. *Education Indicators in Canada: Report of the Pan-Canadian Education Indicators Program, 1999,* © Canadian Education Statistics Council, Catalogue #81-582-XP3, February 2000.

13. At the University of Western Ontario, dentistry students' tuition is $3,278 per year compared to $2,620 for a student in social sciences. Yet the social science student pays 45.8 percent of the program cost, compared to only 8.2 percent for someone in dentistry.

14. There is a trend for business schools to increase tuition rates. Queen's University has effectively privatized its business school by charging students in their Masters of Business Administration program full tuition.

15. One solution that has been suggested entails using **income-contingent loans**, where students pay back their education loans based on their level of income after leaving school. This way higher earners would pay back their loans at a faster rate than those with lower incomes.

WEBLINKS

www.statcan.ca/english/freepub/81-582-XIE/Chapter5.pdf
Labour market outcomes: the flows between formal education and work.

www.cirpa-acpri.ca/halifax94/don/don.html
Earnings and labour force status of 1990 graduates.

www.hrdc-drhc.gc.ca/student_loans/
Canada student loans program.

C h a p t e r

6

BANKING
AND
MONEY

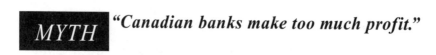

MYTH *"Canadian banks make too much profit."*

*Banks have always had a special place in the economy. That's one reason
the financial sector is one of the most regulated industries in Canada.
Although domestic banks are slowly becoming more deregulated and profitable compared to those in other countries, they aren't as profitable as
they could be. Yet there's a general perception that banks are too profitable.
Banks make big absolute profits because banking is big business. As world
financial institutions become more global and competitive, consumers will
come to see banks as any other business—profit-making enterprises that
will succeed or fail based on the services they offer the public.*

At the end of each year when bank profits are reported, the media gets into full
gear reporting on the enormous revenues of Canada's financial institutions. In 1998,
for example, the Royal Bank, CIBC, Bank of Montreal, and Bank of Nova Scotia each
reported profits in excess of $1 billion. These reports attract considerable attention
because of the big numbers involved. Yet according to many Canadians, there's
something unseemly about high bank profits, usually in the billions, especially if
banks are downsizing and laying off workers as was the case in the late 1990s. Part
of the problem is that banks now charge for services they once provided free. (Of

course, in economics, nothing is free.) Now consumers are charged for writing cheques, withdrawing money from automated bank machines (ABMs), using their debit cards, and receiving monthly statements. To add insult to injury, banks charge high rates to borrow money and pay modest interest for customers' chequing or savings accounts. So it's not surprising that when banks report their profits, consumers feel they're being ripped off.

Before answering the question of whether bank profits are too high and banks are overcharging their customers, we have to keep in mind that, although heavily regulated, banks are businesses that want to maximize profits for their shareholders like any other business. And just as in any other business, whether restaurants, auto companies, or software firms, profits are a sign that they are doing something right and providing customers with services they want. In a market economy, profits are a signal that risk is being rewarded. The banking industry is no exception. The more efficient a firm, the higher its profits or the lower its costs. This chapter is not so much about banking per se (any good economics text will outline the role and function of banks) but about how to think about profits and profitability in the financial sector.

BANKS AS A SPECIAL INDUSTRY

Banks have always held a special place in the economy. They are one of the few institutions that, as consumers, we can't avoid. Eventually everyone needs banking services. And because we rely heavily on them, we worry about the integrity of financial institutions, and therefore demand that they be closely regulated by the government. In fact, we are obsessed with making sure that they don't fail and jeopardize the savings of Canadians. So far the policy has worked. In the United States, thousands of banks failed during the Great Depression of the 1930s, while in Canada only two small chartered banks, in Western Canada, failed in the 1980s. In fact, we care so much about our savings that the federal government guarantees them up to $60,000 through the government-owned Canada Deposit Insurance Corporation (CDIC), even though the banks contribute to the insurance corporation. The irony is that insurance has its downside by making banks greater risk takers. Knowing that depositors' assets are protected, banks are free to make riskier investments knowing that the federal government insurance will rescue its customers. In economics this is called **moral hazard**. Moral hazard simply means that if the banks themselves aren't responsible for their depositors' savings, then they have a tendency to take risks they might otherwise avoid. That was the case in the late 1970s and early 1980s when banks lent freely to South American and East European countries, losing hundreds of millions in the process. This is the sort of direct protection other businesses don't enjoy. The same principle applies with all forms of insurance. If a person's house is insured against fire, there's a tendency for the owner to be a bit more careless about installing smoke detectors.

What makes banking different from other enterprises is that banks are interme-
diaries in the flow of financial resources in the economy. For example, a retailer
makes money by charging a spread between wholesale and retail prices. Banks
make money by the spread between the interest they pay individuals and firms that
keep their money in banks on a short-term basis, and funds they lend out on a longer
term basis to other firms and individuals. Banks also make money by providing a
range of financial services to their clients and customers.[1]

We shouldn't forget just how highly regulated banks are in Canada. Bank pow-
ers are set out at the federal level in the Bank Act, which is updated at least every five
years. The Bank Act recognizes and governs two distinct types of chartered banks.
Schedule I banks must be widely held—no one party may own more than 10 percent
of a bank's shares. Schedule II banks include all foreign and Canadian-owned banks
whose shares are closely held—one party may hold more than 10 percent of the
outstanding shares. As of May 1999, there were eight Schedule I banks, three domestic Schedule II banks, and 43 Schedule II foreign bank subsidiaries operating in
Canada. And the whole operation is overseen by Canada's banking watchdog, the office of the Superintendent of Financial Institutions.

HOW PROFITABLE ARE BANKS IN CANADA?

Given the special place in public policy that banks enjoy, they also generate high levels of *absolute* income and profits. According to the Canadian Banker's Association,
the after-tax earnings of the six major chartered banks in Canada was $7.1 billion in
1998, while the total asset base of the industry was around $1.3 trillion.[2] By any
estimate, that's a considerable sum. One also has to remember that banks are large
compared to other industries—making up about one-fifth of the Toronto Stock
Exchange's total market value. So the big profit numbers should come as no surprise.
But if one wants to assess whether profitability is high, average, or low, it has to
be measured against some objective criteria. One way is to compare the **return on
investments** with other banks around the world. It isn't enough to say banks are
making billions in profits, and leave it at that. Only by comparing profitability by
these objective measures, does one get an indication of whether banks, or any enterprise, are making a fair return on their investment.

Based on recent studies, it appears that Canadian banks are profitable when
compared to banks around the world, despite the fact that banks in Canada are relatively small compared to other international banks. And Canada certainly does
not have large banks when it comes to those in the United States, Europe, and
Japan. Canada's largest bank, the Royal Bank of Canada with assets totalling $178
billion in 1997, ranks only 49th in the world. Currently the largest bank in the
world is The Bank of Tokyo Mitsubishi with assets of $654 billion. However, based

on ROI, it seems that Canadian chartered banks rank at the top of the international heap. From 1981 to 1995, when compared to U.S. and British banks, Canadian banks ranked as the most profitable. How was it that Canadian banks were making so much money? Part of the profitability of the banks can be explained by the fact that government regulations protect them from too much foreign competition. Another explanation is that banks are doing a better job at becoming more efficient. These profits came essentially from two sources: earned income from investments and lending, which represented 52 percent, and the other 48 percent from "fee for services" derived mainly in the financial services sector. Based on ROE, over that period of time, Canadian banks averaged an annual return of 7.6 percent—a full percentage point above the average of banks in all English-speaking countries.[3] And banks in English-speaking countries outperformed those in the G7 and 16 other industrial countries.[4][5]

Many Canadians, however, were convinced that banks were simply making money by overcharging for their services coupled with low interest payouts on short-term deposits. The reality suggests otherwise. Although the main source of income for banks comes from accepting deposits and making loans, this part of their business income was falling. Average spreads between the interest cost of liabilities and interest income on assets were declining throughout the 1990s, from 3.2 percent in 1989 to 2.2 percent by 1997.[6] These spreads are low compared to those in other countries in Europe according to the World Competitiveness Report.[7] It would be logical to assume that the difference was more than made up by higher bank service charges, such as maintaining a banking account, writing cheques, ABM fees, and so on. As it turns out, deposit service charges were almost twice as high for U.S. banks as they were for Canadian banks.[8] Compared to American consumers, Canadians were getting a deal when it came to paying for services.

The reason for Canadian banks' higher revenues and greater profitability can be found in the growth of non-traditional sources of income related to securities businesses. Since 1993, securities-related income made up for over 50 percent of all non-interest sources of income. Part of the reason is that banks, in the second half of the last decade, were allowed to engage in a whole array of other business by taking advantage of relaxed government restrictions on their activities. For the first time, banks could compete by offering their customers full security and mutual fund management services by buying out independent securities firms. However, Canadian banks are limited still in providing comprehensive insurance and leasing services as they can in the United States. One could argue that government policy to deregulate the industry was partially responsible for higher bank profits. In the final analysis, banking is a high-volume, low-margin industry. In percentage terms, profit margins are slim. For every $100 of assets (including loans) in 1998, banks earned 57 cents on average, a drop from 71 cents on average in 1997.[9]

BANKS COULD DO BETTER

Now we know that Canadian banks are profitable not because they overcharge their customers compared to other financial institutions around the world, but because they're providing more services that earn them higher incomes. One could argue that their profitability would suffer if Canadian banks were forced to face more open competition at home. That's partly true given that Canadian law restricts foreign ownership of Canadian banks. If banks are profitable for good reason, is that the end of the story? Not necessarily. We should not confuse profitability and income with efficiency. Profits are simply a measure of income after accounting for all expenses. Efficiency measures how well a company or industry utilizes its resources. There is considerable evidence that banks are not that efficient and could earn greater profits if they maximized their resources better. In the early 1990s, the five largest banks' market value was below the **opportunity cost** of the capital employed. That means that bank shareholders could have made more money investing their money elsewhere in the economy.

For example, in 1995, the Bank of Montreal and the Bank of Nova Scotia had almost identical market value at $12.15 billion and $12.12 billion respectively. The Bank of Montreal was much more efficient and profitable because it was able to maintain its market value with 30 percent fewer workers. In the same year, the Bank of Nova Scotia was actually eroding its shareholder wealth to the tune of $1.7 billion. Despite the high nominal profits, these numbers disguised the fact that Canadian banks suffered from inefficiencies and a misallocation of resources.

WHY WE LOVE TO HATE BANKS

The question still remains, why are we so suspicious and angry when banks report making money? Surely no one gets excited when General Motors, Nortel, or BCE report their earnings figures. Part of the answer is the unique relationship Canadians have with their banks. Despite the many changes in the financial industry since the early 1990s, Canadians are extremely loyal to their banks. Even when it seems that banks are overcharging for their services, we are reluctant to move our accounts.[10] Another reason is that we don't appreciate that banks provide products that are tangible when compared to some other industries. And we also tend to resent the multi-million dollar incomes and bonuses paid to bank presidents for work that is essentially that of a corporate bureaucrat and not a true wealth-creating entrepreneur. In the end, we view banks the way we would a public utility—with obligations not only to provide services, at below cost if necessary, but as a means to create new jobs. In no other industry is the move to automate business, and thereby increase efficiency, met with such ambivalence. On the one hand, while we enjoy the convenience of ABMs and 24-hour service, we simultaneously mourn the loss of jobs because of the technology.

In the final analysis, where do all those profits go? Who actually owns the banks? Given that there are tight restrictions on how much any one party can control, banks are widely held by Canadians and Canadian institutions. Millions of Canadians own shares in the country's chartered banks, either directly or indirectly through RRSPs, pension plans, and mutual funds. It's estimated that the equivalent of one in every two adult working Canadians owns bank shares. In the final analysis, Canadians themselves are the beneficiaries of greater bank profits.

In 1998, shareholders received more than $2.9 billion in common- and preferred-share dividends from the banks, representing approximately 42 percent of the banks' net after-tax income. Among the largest holders of bank shares are the Ontario Teachers Pension Plan, PEI Civil Service Fund, Caisse de dépôt et placement du Québec, the Nova Scotia Public Service & Teachers Pension Plan, the Alberta Public Service Pension Plan, and the Newfoundland Government Employees Fund. The irony is that a good portion of bank profits, whether high or not, may go to the very people who complain about them. Nevertheless, this chapter isn't a defence of high bank profits or how banks currently operate. In many ways it is a critique of banks that could be even more efficient, thereby returning to their shareholders even higher returns.

THE CHANGING FACE OF BANKING

Banking and financial institutions have come a long way since the days when banks were open from 10 a.m. to 3 p.m., giving their customers the impression that banks were doing them a favour. Today we can do our banking around the clock seven days a week at ABMs, by telephone, or on the Internet. The financial world is now consumer driven responding to the needs of the customer. And banking will only get more convenient in the future. It was unimaginable just a few years ago that one could arrange a bank loan online and get an answer within the hour. Today that kind of service is routine.

These changes are taking place around the world, forcing mergers and creating larger banks and financial institutions. That reality was the driving force behind the proposed merger in 1998 between the Royal Bank and the Bank of Montreal, which was eventually rejected by Paul Martin, Minister of Finance. The banks argued that only by becoming bigger could they compete in the international markets, where Canadian banks are relatively small. A year later the Department of Finance approved the merger of the TD Bank and Canada Trust. But at the heart of these changes will be more competition and consumer choice. Even though some argue against mergers because banks are already profitable, in time, the special status now enjoyed by banks will evaporate, making them look no different from any other industry that has to compete to survive.

There's no question that the banking business will look radically different over the next decade as consumers demand more services from their financial institutions. Banking as a brick and mortar operation, with large buildings as a symbol of substance and dependability, is quickly disappearing.[11] With the **globalization** of technology and information, governments can no longer influence domestic and international capital markets as they did just a few decades ago. Financial markets are too global for that to happen. To see how banks are taking advantage of this trend, consider that large corporate customers only need transaction balances while the banks in their area are open. Overnight, banks move billions of dollars around the world where these deposits can earn greater returns. These sorts of transactions were unthinkable before the computer and the advent of information technology. And the loyalty that Canadians feel toward their banks will eventually change as they get used to the new technology of banking. It is these sorts of changes that will eventually force governments to further deregulate the financial sector. In the process, we'll also come to see financial institutions, whether domestic or foreign, not as public utilities to be regulated, but as businesses that will be judged by the quality and cost of their services, rather than how much money they make.

KEY TERMS

Moral hazard   Opportunity cost   Globalization
Return on investment

REVIEW QUESTIONS

1. Why are bank profits viewed with suspicion by many Canadians? Are their suspicions justified?
2. Financial services and banking have been highly regulated by governments. What are your thoughts about government regulation as financial markets become more global?
3. Canadian banks have been more profitable than other banks in the industrial world. Can you give some reasons for this performance over the past two decades?
4. Explain why return on assets, or return on equity, are better measurements of financial performance than simple profit information.

DISCUSSION QUESTIONS

1. "In the near future, there will no longer be a need for physical banks." Comment.
2. Make some predictions of how banking will change over the next 20 years.
3. Even though banks are now profitable, do you think that bank mergers should therefore not be allowed?

NOTES

1. This is a highly simplified version of how banks make money. Banks have changed radically since the early 1990s and now offer an array of sophisticated services such as securities brokerage, investment banking, trust and custodial services, and insurance products to name a few.

2. After-tax profit in banking is measured by: Net income = (net interest income) + (other income) – (operating expenses) – (provisions) – (income taxes).

3. R. Todd Smith, "Money in the Bank: Comparing Bank Profits in Canada and Abroad," Commentary No. 124 (Toronto: C.D. Howe Institute, May 1999).

4. Ibid., pp. 8–9.

5. Canadian banks outperforming U.S. banks is relatively recent. Up to the mid-1990s, Canadian bank profits tended to trail those in the United States.

6. For a full explanation of why this spread narrowed, see the above C.D. Howe study by R. Todd Smith.

7. "Canadian Bank Facts," Canadian Banker's Association, 1998/99 edition.

8. C.D. Howe study by R. Todd Smith, p. 19.

9. "Canadian Bank Facts," Canadian Banker's Association, 1998/99 edition.

10. "Banks may make too much money, but it's not enough," *The Financial Post*, 19 October, 1996.

11. Canadians now have the option of banking at such companies as the Dutch based ING, which offers higher deposit rates and operates entirely without branches.

WEBLINKS

www.royalbank.com
Home page of Royal Bank of Canada.

www.cdic.ca/
Home page of Canada Deposit Insurance Corporation.

www.osfi-bsif.gc.ca/
Home page of Superintendent of Financial Institutions.

www.cba.ca/
Home page of Canadian Banker's Association.

www.cba.ca/cba/eng/tools/brochures%5Farchivedaug23/tools%5Fbankfacts%5F 2000%5F2.htm
Comparison of Canadian banks to banks in other countries.

II

Myths About

Trade and

Competition

THE NORTH AMERICAN FREE TRADE AGREEMENT

 **MYTH** *"NAFTA was a bad deal for Canada."*

Since the signing of the North American Free Trade Agreement between the United States, Mexico, and Canada, the dire consequences predicted by the opponents haven't materialized, such as massive job losses and the flight of capital to the southern United States and Mexico. Although there were adjustments as industries adapted to freer trade, the benefits outweighed the costs. The agreement did what it was intended to do, which was to stimulate industrial specialization and increase overall trade between the signatories, especially between Canada and the United States.

Few policies or programs caused as much divisiveness in the country as the **Free Trade Agreement (FTA)** signed with the United States and put into effect January 1, 1989. It became the **North American Free Trade Agreement (NAFTA)** in 1994 when Mexico became the third party included in the deal. Canadians have been arguing about whether we got a good deal ever since. Those who opposed both deals, such as labour groups, Canadian nationalists, political scientists in general, and the New Democratic Party, still claim that Canada got a bad deal. Other groups, made up of big business, free-traders, and academic economists felt that Canada was right to go ahead with the agreements. Even the Liberals, who were against the agreement, are now strong supporters. Both sides can provide numbers defending their arguments. Free trade opponents have claimed that Canada lost hundreds of thousands of jobs in the early 1990s to freer trade. They argued that manufacturing jobs were going south where the cost of production is less expensive.[1] Those who supported the deal argued that the purpose of the agreement was to increase trade among the three countries, creating more jobs in the long run.

Again the average citizen has been left in the dark about whether Canada made the right decision. Although the majority of tariff reductions weren't implemented until 1998, the evidence suggests that the gains are positive, but small. It only stands to reason that if there were no gains to be made on both sides, an agreement would never have been signed. That's the essence of international trade.[2]

If that's the case, why do so many people feel we were "had" by the Americans and Mexicans? Part of the answer lies in politics, rather than economics, and in what people saw the agreement to be in the first place. Another explanation is that the agreements, especially the FTA, came into effect just before the country entered the 1990 recession, and it was inevitable that opponents of the agreement would confuse the hardships of the recession with greater trade liberalization. The Bank of Canada's high interest rate policy in 1990 and 1991 did not make matters any easier. Tight monetary policy had the desired effect of dampening demand and bringing down inflation, but at the cost of lost jobs.[3] To understand the agreement, and whether Canada got a good deal, it's important to understand the main reasons Canada wanted the deal in the first place; then one can judge better whether the effort and years of negotiations were worthwhile.

WHY THE GOVERNMENT WANTED FREER TRADE

The Conservative government under Brian Mulroney wanted an agreement for three main reasons: first, to remove tariffs and reduce the cost of production for the domestic manufacturing industry; second, to secure access to the U.S. market for Canadian goods; and third, as the basis for a new industrial policy to bring about restructuring and adjustment in the Canadian economy. Let's look at each reason in turn and assess whether Canada got what it wanted.

Economists have often complained that Canada's small domestic market made it difficult to achieve what they call **economies of scale**. One way countries can reduce production costs is by concentrating on production in which they have a **comparative advantage**, or where they have lower **opportunity costs**. Countries should allocate their resources in the production of goods or services where they have a comparative advantage and then trade among themselves for the products they do not produce. This way everyone will be better off. That is the simplified theory behind freer trade and the main reason economists support the unfettered movement of goods and resources between countries without interference from tariffs or non-tariff barriers.

But what is simple in theory, is harder in practice. **Specialization** and free trade mean that what a country produces today may not be what it produces tomorrow. It is understandable why some labour groups, especially in those sectors of the economy that face stiff international competition, would oppose freer trade.

However, there are clear advantages for Canadian producers. Free trade with the United States gives them greater access to a market 10 times as large as their own and reduces their costs by not forcing them to pay tariffs for any intermediate goods they import. In time, Canadian firms will learn to adapt. Although this may sound like a risky venture, theory and evidence show us that Canadian producers can survive and prosper with more free trade. A number of economic studies show that if tariffs were removed, domestic production would increase, and so would jobs and our standard of living. That was the same logic that led the Royal Commission chaired by Donald Macdonald in 1985 to recommend that Canada pursue a free trade agreement with the United States. Macdonald said it would be a "leap of faith," but the risks were worth the potential gains in jobs and output.

Many economic organizations and think tanks across Canada supported freer trade. One reason was that over 80 percent of the goods flowing between the United States and Canada prior to the agreement were already crossing the border duty free.[4] NAFTA would get rid of the tariffs on the remaining 20 percent over a 10 year period. Granted, the remaining higher tariffs were then on manufactured goods, such as textiles, food processing, and furniture, but these were coming down in any event given that Canada was a member of the World Trade Organization (WTO). The average tariff on all imports in 1950 was around 12 percent. By the late 1980s it had dropped to below 5 percent. Under NAFTA all tariffs were eliminated in 1998, except for a few products such as fruits and vegetables.

While tariffs had been decreasing, trade between the United States and Canada had been increasing along with jobs, output, and our standard of living. In 1988, Canada had $101 billion of merchandise exports to the United States; by 1999 the figure was around $270 billion. From 1994 to 1999, Canada's merchandise trade increased by 80 percent, reaching $475 billion. U.S. investments also increased 63 percent from 1993 to 1998.[5] Even though Canada's economy is only a tenth the size of the U.S. economy, over 80 percent of all our exports go south making us their largest trading partner.[6]

The majority of economists agreed that before NAFTA, Canadian firms were less efficient because of tariff protection, which encouraged too many firms to produce too many high-cost products. The result was that trade barriers, such as tariffs, led to lower wages, lower productivity, higher costs, and lower exports in manufacturing.

There was also concern that if Canada did not sign a free trade pact with the United States, we would have been the only industrialized country without access to a market of 100 million or more consumers. With this rising tide of U.S. protectionism in the late 1980s, the reasoning was that it was better to be in a formal North American agreement rather than outside it if and when world barriers started going up. Some may argue against such a view of international trade, but before the agreement was signed there was plenty of evidence to support it. To begin with, Canada has what economists describe as an **open economy**, that is, we depend heavily on trade. Over one-third of Canada's GDP depends on trade. These traded goods were not just raw materials and natural resources. Eighty-six percent of total merchandise exports were in manufactured goods. Canada had good reason to worry about American protectionism or any program that would have affected our exports. As the U.S. trade deficit increased, so did the protectionist sentiment in their Congress. Even during the free trade talks with Canada, the United States imposed a 35 percent tariff on Canadian shakes and shingles. Clearly Canada wanted to stop the momentum of trade action, which was based not on economics but politics. A free trade agreement was one way to stop this trend. In the end, the Canadian negotiators got most of what they wanted—improved access to the U.S. market.

Many critics of the deal felt that we never secured a guaranteed access to U.S. markets because Canada is still subject to current and future American trade law. If we had been exempt, the United States would also have been exempt from Canada's trade law, and we would have been restricted in our ability to retaliate against unfair dumping and subsidies. But this was never a realistic or possible goal. What Canada's negotiators really wanted was to rid bilateral trade of any political interference by American interest groups. This was partially achieved by negotiating a **dispute settlement mechanism**. Final decisions about trade disputes are now in the hands of a binational panel composed of two members from each country and a fifth member chosen jointly. Canadians now have a say in decisions previously handled only by Americans. In addition, Canadian business people now have easier movement in the United States as well as the ability to bid on equal terms with Americans for government contracts.

Another reason for the deal had to do with industrial policy. NAFTA effectively binds the government's hands in subsidizing certain industries. For many economists, the government was doing a bad job helping out certain sectors of the economy and hampering real industrial and international adjustment. The best solution was to get the government out of the business of regional and industrial development by reducing subsidies and allowing the market to determine what would be produced and where. This side effect of the agreement did not rest well with Canadian nationalists who believed that the government has a role, if not an obligation, to intervene directly in helping Canadian businesses. Some saw the condition of **national treatment** (which means both countries must not discriminate against each other's products or set limitations on investment on each other) as a clear loss in the negotiations. In any case, the agreement still allows for some flexibility to determine industrial policy, but it makes direct government intervention more difficult.[7]

As with any negotiated deal, Canada did not get everything it wanted. One of the major shortfalls was the failure to reach an agreement on a definition of what constitutes a "government subsidy." To have worked out the issue during the talks would have broken down the negotiations. In order to save the negotiations, the question of subsidies was left to be worked out over a five-to-seven-year period after the agreement went into effect. Unfortunately that deadline has come and gone with little progress on subsidies. In many ways, subsidies go to the heart of the agreement and determine how governments interact in the economy. Another deficiency of the agreement is the lack of worker mobility. In the European Community, workers are free to work anywhere as long as they hold a European passport. Although Canadians can work more easily in the United States and vice versa, there are still many labour mobility impediments.

HOW ARE WE DOING SO FAR?

The first thing to remember is that NAFTA was never intended to produce instant results. Second, it will take some years after the agreement is fully implemented to adequately determine the impact on jobs, output, competitiveness, and productivity. Others have argued that Canada should benefit economically from the agreement, although it will cost the country politically.[8] In the meantime, we will have to be satisfied with incomplete information, regardless of what some of the opponents of free trade argue. However, the evidence indicates that Canada has done well.

Perhaps the most important way of looking at the impacts of NAFTA are changes in trade flows. Export growth was strongest in sectors where tariffs fell the most and trade liberalization was the greatest.[9] The biggest beneficiaries were not in resource-based industries, but in manufacturing sectors such as telecommunications, office equipment, and precision instruments. Even industries such as the box and furniture industry, that were supposed to fare badly, have done surprisingly well under the agreement.[10] As one would expect, imports from the United States rose faster in the sectors where tariffs fell the most. Contrary to the pessimistic projections of many opponents to lower trade barriers, those who benefited the most were Canada's higher-value-added industries—the very sectors that are key to higher wages. This fact should not conceal the seriousness of those who have lost their jobs in the more labour-intensive import sectors. The objective of freer trade is to improve overall productivity which leads to higher future growth and a better standard of living. By that test, NAFTA is meeting its objective.

Many were concerned that Canada would lose jobs and investment to Mexico under NAFTA. Even here Canada has done well. Canada's sales to Mexico have increased five-fold from 1989 to 1999 to $7.6 billion. NAFTA has enabled Canadian companies to gain access to Mexico, a previously highly protected market of 90 million people.

One of the biggest concerns about NAFTA was how we would do under the dispute settlement mechanism. Would it be an effective forum for resolving major trade irritants between our countries? Of the over 100 cases that involve United States and Canadian trade disputes of dumping and countervailing action under NAFTA, between 1989 and 1999, there is about a 50-50 split in cases won and lost ranging from agricultural to manufactured goods.[11] The panel won't diminish the number of trade disputes, but it does provide a system for resolving many of the issues that were once determined by political pressures.

The debate is not over yet. Figures will be distorted by supporters and opponents of the agreement to defend their cases. It is important to remember that the general movement of industrial countries is toward more liberalized trade between nations, either using bilateral or multilateral agreements. As international agreements go, NAFTA is a modest one. However, had Canada stayed out of the negotiations, it could have prevented some industrial adjustments and saved some jobs in the short run. In the long run, the adjustment process would have been much more difficult. These agreements were never intended as a panacea to Canada's economic problems, but rather as a means to an end.

KEY TERMS

Free Trade Agreement (FTA)	Economies of scale	Open economy
North American Free Trade Agreement (NAFTA)	Comparative advantage	Dispute settlement mechanism
	Opportunity costs	
	Specialization	National treatment

REVIEW QUESTIONS

1. Although critics of NAFTA are certain of the ill effects of the agreement, why is it so difficult to measure accurately the impacts of any trade deal?

2. Why do economists, in general, favour the reduction of trade barriers even when it seems that the general public is wary of removing tariffs and nontariff barriers?

3. What do you believe would have been some of the consequences for Canada if we did not sign the free trade agreement? What would the benefits have been?

DISCUSSION QUESTIONS

1. One of the main criticisms of the free trade deal was that Canada lost political sovereignty when it signed a trade agreement with the United States. Was this the case?

2. "In the final analysis, even though we didn't have perfect information about the effects of the deal, Canada was justified in signing a trade deal with the United States." Based on current information, discuss this statement.

3. Why did the government of Prime Minister Mulroney think it necessary to sign an agreement with the United States and Mexico for tariff and nontariff reductions when these were already falling?

NOTES

1. The Canadian Labour Congress and other trade unions claimed that we lost 350,000 jobs because of the deal with the United States. The 1981 recession saw almost 300,000 jobs disappear a decade before the free trade agreement was signed. Canadian nationalists, such as Maude Barlow and Mel Hurtig, in his book *The Betrayal of Canada* (Toronto: Stoddart, 1991), blame free trade for everything from higher unemployment and lower corporate profits to declining investments and lower merchandise trade surpluses with the U.S. To blame free trade for these problems is both simplistic and misleading.

2. What's often overlooked in the free trade controversy is how modest the agreement is in its impact on the economy. When the agreements were signed, an increase of a couple of percentage points in interest rates would easily swamp the benefits of the FTA in terms of jobs and output.

3. There are those who accused the Mulroney government of making a secret deal with the Americans to keep the Canadian dollar artificially high as a condition for the United States to sign the agreement. No evidence has ever come to light to support such a conspiracy.

4. One study that received considerable attention during the negotiations was done by Professor Richard Harris at Queen's University, Kingston, Ontario. He estimated that, in the long run, real income would rise 5 percent in Canada. In fact, Canada would gain from removing trade barriers according to most economic studies, including reports by the Economic Council, the C.D. Howe Institute, and Informetrica, an Ottawa consulting group. What most of these studies have in common is that the benefits would be positive, but modest.

5. "Free Trade 10 Years On: Good or Bad for Canada," *The Globe and Mail*, 28 May 1999.

6. Some Canadian nationalists want us to become less dependent on the U.S. market and diversify our exports. This was tried in the late 1970s under the *Third Option* in the Trudeau government. It not only failed to increase our exports to Europe, as a share of total exports, but it made us more reliant on the U.S. economy today than ever before.

7. The western provinces saw this provision in the agreement as a victory, because it would prevent future governments from setting discriminatory export prices for energy, such as the much hated National Energy Policy.

8. G. Bruce Doern and Brian W. Tomlin, *The Free Trade Story: Faith and Fear* (Toronto: Stoddart, 1991), p. 291.

9. Richard G. Lipsey, Daniel Schwanen, and Ronald J. Wonnacott, *The NAFTA: What's In, What's Out, What's Next* Policy Study 21 (Toronto: C.D. Howe Institute, 1994).

10. Kimberly Noble, "Box Industry Stands Up to Heavy Odds," *The Globe and Mail,* 7 September 1992, p. B1. Instead of losing market share, this $1.5 billion industry is holding its own, despite predictions by analysts that it could not survive without tariff protection.

11. NAFTA Secretariat, Ottawa, July 1999. "Free Trade 10 Years On," *The Globe and Mail*, 28 May 1999.

WEBLINKS

www.infoexport.gc.ca/docs/101224-e.htm
Overview of NAFTA from Canadian point of view.

www.cargill.com/today/bulletin/t041997.htm
Support of NAFTA.

wwwsbanet.uca.edu/docs/proceedingsII/98sri267.txt
Free trade of the Americas by 2005: Is it working?

www.dfait-maeci.gc.ca/tna-nac/doorsworld/04-e.asp
Canada's market access priorities for 1999 under NAFTA.

www.infoexport.gc.ca/docs/impact-e.htm
How NAFTA affects the FTA.

8

THE STATUS
OF CANADIAN
MANUFACTURING

"Canadian manufacturing is disappearing."

Many believe that manufacturing in Canada is dead or dying, and that our economy is being deindustrialized. The reality, however, is that manufacturing is just as important to the economy today as it was in 1960. Today fewer workers are required as manufacturing becomes more capital intensive. Part of the perception that manufacturing is declining is caused by the blurring between jobs in goods and services as we move into the "information age."

There is a common anxiety among Canadians that our economy has feet of clay. The argument goes something like this: the structure of the Canadian economy is built on an unstable service sector with too many government jobs, retail outlets, banks, fast-food operations, and foreign-owned companies that are glorified warehouses for goods produced outside the country. The idea is that we have become rich simply by "taking in each other's laundry." In other words, we really don't produce anything, we just move things around. Furthermore, as the argument goes, the whole operation does nicely when the North American economy is booming, but during a recession this tenuous structure comes crashing down like a house of cards.

Although most of us work in the service industry, and the majority of jobs are in that sector, we somehow feel that they are less valuable than the "real" jobs found in manufacturing and resources. We believe that an economy's wealth is based on output in the goods-producing sector and we feel that the country could use more manufacturing jobs in autos, aerospace and computers, and we know that we could certainly get along with fewer lawyers, civil servants, and personal services. This general unease about services is aggravated by the sense that Canada's economy is suffering from **deindustrialization**, and that the "real" jobs are moving south of the border or off-shore altogether.

Is that the reality? Is Canada moving from a nation once based on resources and manufacturing to one of fast-food outlets and video arcades? The simple answer is no. This myth has two misconceptions: first, that the more valuable manufacturing jobs are being lost at an alarming rate; and second, that the service jobs replacing them are inferior and less useful to society. The truth is manufacturing isn't dead in Canada, and our economy is not being "hollowed out" and replaced with second-rate jobs.[1] What *has* changed is the nature of manufacturing as it becomes more **capital intensive**. Also, there has been a greater blurring of the line between goods and services. Nevertheless, many believe that manufacturing jobs are somehow more valuable than service jobs and that governments should do what they can to save them.

MANUFACTURING STILL MATTERS

Canada's transition from a goods-producing economy to a service-oriented one is similar to its switch from an agricultural to an industrial economy at the turn of the century when almost 40 percent of the labour force was in agriculture. Today only 3 percent work in farming and primary industry. A similar labour shift has occurred from the goods-producing sector to the services sector. In 1958, there was an equal share of jobs in services and goods production. Today almost 70 percent of the jobs are in services and 30 percent in goods. Just as there was concern about too few farmers to grow food for a growing urban population working in factories, today we worry that our goods manufacturing jobs are going off-shore. But North America became an industrial economy largely because of the rapid productivity growth in agriculture. The same type of transformation is taking place today, as we move from goods to services because of the rapid productivity growth in goods production. This growth has allowed employment to shift from the factory to services: a natural transition in the development of any advanced industrial country.[2] The anxiety about the loss of employment to technology is nothing new. In the eighteenth century a group known as the **physiocrats** believed that real wealth came only from the land and not from factories. In 1811, the **Luddites** took to smashing textile machines in northern England because they feared modern machinery was destroying their jobs.

Has manufacturing or the production of goods dropped off as a share of Gross Domestic Product (GDP)? It may surprise some to know that it hasn't. Since the early 1960s, manufacturing continued to account for about 50 percent of all goods produced, which includes agriculture, natural resources, and manufactured products. Manufacturing still makes up about 23 percent of GDP and has remained at that level for decades (see Figure 8.1). Total manufacturing GDP increased from $93 billion in 1990 to $104 billion in 1996—growing faster than overall GDP growth. What has changed is the number of jobs in manufacturing. In 1960, manufacturing employed over 30 percent of the labour force; by 1996, that figure dropped to under 15 percent. Even with the drop in the share of manufacturing jobs throughout the 1980s, the absolute number of jobs increased from 1.5 million in the mid-1980s to over 1.8 million a decade later. Even though jobs were lost in manufacturing from 1990 to 1996, value added per employee increased from $66,000 per worker to $96,000 over that time period.[3] The economic recovery in 1993 that saw the return of thousands of manufacturing jobs was concentrated in southern Ontario. The drop in relative employment was not the result of manufacturing becoming less important to the economy. The decline in the manufacturing share of Canada's total number of jobs indicates the greater use of technology in the manufacturing process and higher productivity. Canadian industry is producing the same level of output with fewer workers. One of the reasons is that virtually all research and development spending is in manufacturing or goods production and far surpasses that in services.[4]

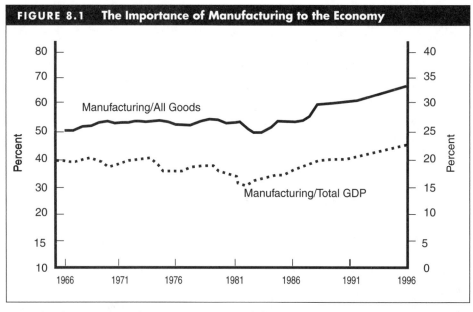

FIGURE 8.1   The Importance of Manufacturing to the Economy

Note: Left scale represents manufacturing as a percentage of all goods produced. Right scale represents manufacturing as a share of total GDP in the economy.

Source: StatsCan.

If anything has changed, it is how the number of manufacturing jobs are expanding and contracting more rapidly in response to economic swings. Employers are reacting to economic changes more quickly by hiring and releasing workers faster than they have in the past. In recessions before 1980, there was an average five-month lag between cuts in output and cuts in employment. That is no longer the case. For the recessions of 1981 and 1990, the production and employment cuts were virtually simultaneous. The high cost of labour and competitive pressures to increase productivity are forcing companies to respond more quickly to downturns in the economy. They no longer have the luxury of holding onto workers as they wait for the economy to improve. This gives the impression that manufacturing jobs are more at risk now than in the past, and that once they're gone, they're gone for good. A more accurate description would be that when manufacturing changes, the jobs associated are changed forever. That does not mean that manufacturing is dead. It signifies that the pace of manufacturing change is now quicker and that the way we employ labour is changing.

THE NEW ROLE OF SERVICES

Even the increase in services has to be understood in the context of a changing economy. Services do not exist in a vacuum. As the needs of the economy change, so does the service sector. Also, the gap between the goods-producing and service sectors are often exaggerated. Many services use tangible goods such as computers and many goods-producing businesses contract substantial service-oriented businesses (such as outside lawyers and accountants) to do work that was once provided by professionals on their own staffs. Manufacturers still need these services, but they no longer retain the people who provide them on permanent staff. It is less expensive to contract the work from outside. With the rapid globalization of industries, firms are under greater pressure to increase their level of specialization and are contracting out more of their work to the service sector.

But not all service jobs are created equally. There is a world of difference between a short-order cook and a highly trained nurse. Not surprisingly, it was high-powered service jobs (e.g., accounting, marketing, and legal) that helped propel the Canadian economy since the mid-1980s. These dynamic, high-paying jobs in business, along with those in health, education, and public administration, accounted for 60 percent of the increase in service sector jobs in Canada from 1983 to 1988, compared to 29 percent in the lower-paying, traditional services, such as personal services, retail, and food services.[5] These trends are continuing today.

Within these services, the fastest growing ones are related directly to business, such as computers, management consulting, and advertising. The service sector provides more than half of the jobs classified as "high-tech." Within this high-tech sector, half were in services to business management and the other half in the finance industries. These jobs are growing because of manufacturing, not in spite of it. A dynamic service sector is essential for maintaining the competitiveness and health of the nation's manufacturing base. It seems irrelevant to ask which is more important: a manufacturing job making a specific product, or the truck-driving service taking it to market. In the final analysis, both are as important in getting the product into the hands of the consumer.

As manufacturing and services become more interrelated, the lines between them are becoming more clouded. For instance, one might ask, does Xerox provide goods or services? In many ways, manufacturing firms are behaving more like services. The level of information technology in an automated car plant is such that services are becoming an ever bigger part of the production process. The growing need for better and faster information on the part of the service industry drives the need for better equipment and hardware, which in turn drives the need for better information. Gone are the days when services and goods were distinct commodities bearing little relationship to each other.[6]

A common criticism of services has been the lower level of productivity, as measured by output per employee, compared to manufacturing. The obvious implication is that we should have more manufacturing if we want to improve our standard of living. However, not all services have been slow in productivity improvement. Productivity in transportation, utilities, and the communications sector grew at almost twice the rate of the manufacturing sector. Some analysts have also argued that service productivity is a statistical illusion and current forms of measurement underestimate the growth of service productivity.

Compounding the problem of measurement is the issue of quality improvements in the service sector. It's relatively easy to measure output in dollars and cents when it comes to goods; it's a different story when quality is being assessed. How do you measure the quality of a day in hospital, the convenience of 24-hour banking, or the satisfaction derived from a good movie? The problem is even worse in non-market services where there isn't even the benefit of an objective market price. How do you measure the value of a good teacher, social worker, the Cancer Foundation, defence, or police protection?

Despite the integration and rising importance of services in the economy, there is one role that goods production plays that is not matched by services: goods still dominate in international trade and allow Canada to maintain a positive trade balance. Ninety-nine percent of manufactured goods and 97 percent of the primary sector (i.e., agriculture and natural resources) compete at home and in the international market, compared with only 3 percent of all business services. Services as a share of total exports is around 15 percent in Canada, the lowest for all the Organization for Economic Co-operation and Development (OECD) nations.[7] The services we do trade are tourism, consulting engineering, and financial services.

The sectors that have no international component are education, personal services, utilities, and government. In 1995, Canada exported about $220 billion in merchandise trade compared to $60 billion in non-merchandise receipts. Canada usually maintains a balance-of-trade surplus in goods production, but we traditionally run a trade deficit in services, mainly because we travel abroad so much. Nevertheless, services and goods production we send abroad depend upon each other. An efficient domestic service sector makes our products more competitive internationally.

KEY TERMS

Deindustrialization   Physiocrats   Luddites
Capital intensive

REVIEW QUESTIONS

1. Why are goods-producing or manufacturing jobs considered more valuable than service jobs? Are these arguments valid? Why is it becoming more difficult to differentiate between a service job and a goods-producing job?

2. What are the possible reasons for the long-term decline of manufacturing employment as a share of total employment, and the increase in service sector jobs in Canada?

DISCUSSION QUESTIONS

1. It is often claimed that once goods-producing jobs are lost, they are gone forever. This implies that we should do what we can to save manufacturing jobs if we don't want them to disappear. Does that line of reasoning make sense in a rapidly changing economy?

2. Information technology has blurred the distinction between goods and service jobs. Give examples where this is the case. Show how computers have changed the nature of work itself. What does this imply for the future?

NOTES

1. The U.S. economy is experiencing a comeback in its "rust belt" states. In a study by the Department of Commerce, it was found that manufacturing has staged a revival since the early 1980s. It seems that fears of deindustrialization were exaggerated. U.S. manufacturing as a percentage of Gross National Product climbed from 21 percent in 1960 to 23 percent in 1990.

2. From 1966 to 1986, Canada saw a decline of 6.7 percent in the share of workers in manufacturing, while Germany's share fell 9.1 percent, the United States by 10 percent, and Japan by 5.7 percent. Source: OECD and Statistics Canada.

3. Industry Canada, 1999. See Industry Canada Web site for more information on Canadian manufacturing.

4. The sectors with the highest growth rates in R and D are electronics, transportation, and chemicals.

5. The Economic Council of Canada, *Good Jobs, Bad Jobs, Employment in the Service Economy* (Ottawa: Supply and Services, 1990).

6. The great economist Alfred Marshall writing almost 100 years ago said that there is little distinction between goods and services in the sense that workers simply readjust matter in order to create a good. Because all commercial activity is a service of one kind or another, one shouldn't exaggerate the distinction between goods and services.

7. Economic Council of Canada, *Employment in the Service Economy* (Ottawa: Supply and Services, 1991), p. 16.

WEBLINKS

www.incan.com/
A sourcing and information tool dedicated to Canada's industrial community.

strategis.ic.gc.ca/
Home page of Industry Canada.

www.the-alliance.com/amecsite/indexe.html
Home page of Alliance of Manufacturers and Exporters of Canada.

9

VALUING THE DOLLAR

 *MYTH* **"We need a lower dollar in order to be competitive."**

To many, a simple solution to a sluggish economy, slow export growth, and a poor balance of trade is to depreciate the dollar. Economic policy is seldom that easy. Experience tells us that currency depreciation may provide short-term relief by boosting exports, but it comes at the price of increasing costs to industries that rely on imported goods. The best solution to improve competitiveness and economic prosperity comes with improvements in productivity and product innovation.

When most people think of currency crisis, Latin American and East European countries quickly come to mind. The Mexican peso, for example, lost about 40 percent of its value to the U.S. dollar at the end of 1994. However, few noticed that the Canadian dollar also was losing against the U.S. dollar. In 1991, the Canadian dollar was worth 87 cents U.S. By January 2000, the Canadian dollar was only worth 64 cents U.S. Canadians travelling to the United States certainly noticed the weakened Canadian dollar. Where the collapse of the peso was seen clearly as an absolute fall in the confidence of the Mexican economy, the gradual decline of the Canadian dollar was also caused by a lack of confidence by international investors in Canada's ability to manage its economy. The two main factors underlying this lack of confidence were a growing public debt and uncertainty in the Quebec situation. These two factors were important in explaining Canada's low dollar in the first half of the last decade, but by the late 1990s the U.S. economy was growing much faster than Canada's. Despite the fact that Canada was being punished by foreign investors as they sold off their Canadian assets, some people think that a weaker dollar is beneficial to the economy. After all, a cheaper domestic currency helps our exports. But is devaluation a good thing in all circumstances to help the economy? The answer is, no.

Few points of economics confuse the layperson more than the workings of exchange rates. Nevertheless, most Canadians know that if our Canadian dollar strengthens (**currency appreciation**), in the sense that it can buy more U.S. currency, American products are cheaper to buy and our domestic goods are more expensive abroad. Cross-border shopping is a testimony to that simple fact. When the Canadian dollar weakens (**currency depreciation**) compared with the U.S. dollar, it has the opposite effect; our goods become relatively inexpensive, while the prices of imports go up. When that happens, we do most of our shopping on this side of the border, and Americans start finding bargains in Canada. Based on that logic, federal government policy should seem fairly obvious: depreciate the Canadian currency by lowering its value in relation to U.S. currency. Our exports would go up; we would decrease our imports by replacing them with relatively inexpensive Canadian products; and we would benefit by having more jobs. The **balance of trade** should also improve with more exports and fewer imports. It seems like the perfect solution to Canada's problems. However, economic policy is not that simple. Exporters tend to support a cheaper dollar to help boost their sales, while companies that rely on imported intermediate products want a stronger dollar. That's why it's a myth that a weaker dollar will solve our balance-of-trade problems and increase employment.[1]

To understand the issue more clearly, let's start with how **flexible exchange rates** are set in the marketplace of currencies. The price of the Canadian dollar in terms of other internationally traded currencies is determined just like any other commodity— by the forces of supply and demand. The higher the demand for the U.S. dollar, the more Canadian dollars it takes to buy it. The number of dollars available are determined primarily by the Bank of Canada. To simplify matters, over time the supply of Canadian-dollar assets is determined by the size of the government's budget. If there's a budget deficit and the government finances it by borrowing from the Bank of Canada, the money supply expands. Conversely, the money supply decreases if the budget is in surplus. The Bank of Canada can also expand or contract the supply of money if it buys or sells foreign securities with newly created Canadian-dollar bank deposits. Confusing as this may seem, the important point is that changing the demand or supply of Canadian dollars has an effect on the exchange rate just as changing the supply and demand has an effect on the price of any good or service.

What determines the demand for the Canadian dollar and hence the exchange rate? Mainly, it is the foreign demand for Canadian goods and services abroad and assets at home, such as stocks, bonds, and capital investments. When the Japanese, for instance, buy our coal or invest in our factories, they need Canadian dollars. The same thing occurs when they buy Canadian government bonds. For example, the strong Canadian dollar in the late 1970s was the result of Hydro Quebec selling billions of dollars in bonds abroad to build the James Bay project. Foreign investment poured into Canada, pushing the Canadian dollar above parity with the U.S. dollar. As soon as these mega projects were completed, the Canadian dollar promptly fell. The greater the demand for our products, services and assets, the greater the demand for our currency. How much other countries buy, however, depends on the price of these goods and assets in Canadian dollars and the exchange rate. The lower the prices of our assets, the more we can sell.

Another important factor to consider is the *expected* or *anticipated value* of the Canadian dollar. People and institutions hold foreign currencies not only to buy goods or to earn a set return on Canadian bonds based on interest rates, but also to make money when currencies appreciate. In short, there are currency speculators who try to buy low and sell high in order to make a profit—a process in economics known as **arbitrage**. If, for example, someone believes that the deutsche mark is undervalued because he expects Germany's exports to increase, that speculator would buy marks today and sell when he thinks that the mark can no longer rise or is overvalued—making a profit in the interim. Because of modern technology, speculators can move billions of dollars around the globe instantaneously to take advantage of small currency differences. To discourage such practices, some have advocated taxing speculative currency transactions. However, speculators instead of being the villains, are actually imposing a market discipline on currencies that have become overvalued, usually through irresponsible government policies.

Although in Canada the weakness of the Canadian dollar is partly the fault of foreign borrowing to meet increasing interest payments on the budget deficit, there's little question that Canada's constitutional uncertainty was also responsible for wide swings in the value of the Canadian dollar. Foreign investors feared that a break-up of Canada would lower the returns on domestic investments and therefore withheld investing in Canada until they were satisfied that separation was a remote possibility.

Just as important as the above-mentioned factors is the sensitivity of the exchange rate to changes in interest rates. If interest rates on dollar assets go up, Canadians holding foreign-currency assets will switch to Canadian-dollar assets to earn a higher rate of return. Foreigners will do the same thing. Even if interest rates change in other countries, they will have an impact on the demand for Canadian dollars as international investors try to earn the highest rate of return on their investments.

NO SURE THING

One of the direct ways that the Canadian government influences the value of the exchange rate is by buying and selling the Canadian dollar to stabilize the Canadian dollar. This occurs when foreign holders of Canadian assets start selling, putting downward pressure on the dollar. If the dollar drops too much, the Bank of Canada usually intervenes in the market by buying Canadian dollars. The Bank also affects the value of the dollar indirectly by affecting the interest rate through the buying and selling of marketable securities, known as **open market operations**. A lower interest rate generally means less demand for Canadian-dollar assets, which leads to a lower dollar. A higher interest rate, however, has the opposite effect. But it doesn't always work that way. From April 1990 to November 1991, the prime interest rate fell dramatically from 14.75 percent down to 8.50 percent: a drop of 57.6 percent. Over the same period, the Canadian dollar appreciated against the U.S. currency. In theory, if capital earns less in Canada as interest rates fall, then there should be less demand for the Canadian dollar, leading to a drop or depreciation in its value. But even with a substantial drop in interest rates, that does not always happen (see Figure 9.1). In other words, the demand for the Canadian dollar remained high. During some months, the Canadian dollar actually appreciated against the U.S. dollar, while interest rates fell.[2] The story was essentially the same for the Canadian dollar against all major currencies.

What happened? Why did demand for the Canadian dollar stay high, while domestic interest rates fell? To begin with, the United States was lowering its interest rates as well, effectively frustrating and nullifying what the Canadian monetary authorities were doing. As a result, even if the **nominal interest rates** were falling in Canada, the spread between the two countries was roughly the same, and it's the spread that makes all the difference. Another factor was that speculators expected stronger economic recovery in Canada and so bought more dollars.

Even when the Canadian dollar depreciates against the currencies of our major trading partners, that does not mean we will improve our balance of trade. An example is what happened to the Japanese yen in the mid-1980s. There was a spectacular depreciation of the Canadian dollar in terms of the yen from 173 yen per dollar in 1985 to 120 yen per dollar in 1986: a drop of 44 percent in the value of the dollar to the yen. One would expect a good boost of Canadian exports to Japan and a decline in imports, but that did not occur. In 1985, Canada ran deficits of $1.7 billion on our current account (goods and services trade) with Japan. By 1986, it was $3.9 billion, and over $4 billion in 1987.[3] To those who argue that perhaps the dollar didn't fall far enough, the obvious question is, how far does it have to fall? In any case, it seemed the Japanese were getting more competitive, even though their yen was getting stronger. This was nothing new. Analysts have been saying for years that a strong Japanese yen tends to improve, rather than worsen, Japan's balance of trade.[4] By the mid-1990s, even though the Japanese economy was clearly going

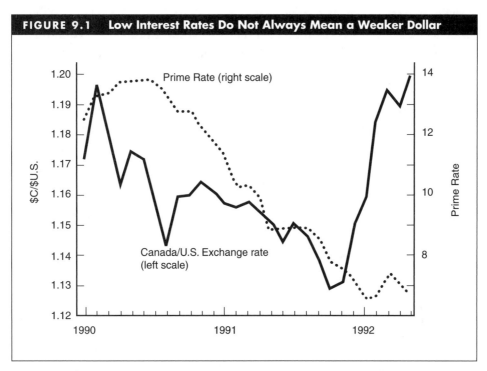

FIGURE 9.1   Low Interest Rates Do Not Always Mean a Weaker Dollar

Source: Bank of Canada.

into recession, the yen didn't weaken in relation to the currencies of its major trading partners. Even in the late 1990s while the Japanese economy was still clearly in recession, the yen continued to be strong. The Japanese government had kept a tight rein on the economy keeping inflation low and the value of its currency strong further aggravating domestic economic problems.

OTHER PROBLEMS

Even if a depreciation of the Canadian dollar means that other countries buy more of our goods because they can afford more, it also means that imports become more expensive. That brings us to the next point—inflation. Canada has what is known as an **open economy**, which means that exports and imports make up a large share of GDP. For Canada it's about 33 percent. When we depreciate our currency, we pay more for imported goods; and if we have to pay more for them because of a weaker, or depreciated currency, it means higher prices and more inflation.[5] That is why the governor of the Bank of Canada, who is in charge of keeping inflation down, doesn't like a weak dollar.[6] That brings us back to a dilemma: a lower dollar may boost exports but it does so at the expense of higher inflation and, eventually, higher interest rates, and no one wants that. What is the solution?

The answer can be found partly in the reason for the need to lower the currency in the first place, that is to counteract the rising costs of domestic producers. If Canada's costs of production rise faster than those of our major trading partners (leading to balance-of-payment problems), two ways of getting back on even competitive ground are to lower costs by raising productivity or to depreciate the value of the Canadian dollar. The latter alternative is more painless in the short term. But that is a prescription for lowering our standard of living. The real test of competitiveness is not simply to sell goods on the world market and achieve balanced trade, but to do so while achieving an acceptable rate of improvement in productivity and standard of living. Trying to get an edge on the competition by depreciating currency may briefly give some relief, but if done too often, other countries may end up retaliating by doing the same thing or by raising tariffs. Few countries would tolerate importing someone else's unemployment simply by allowing them to devalue their currency. Another reason to use depreciation judiciously, is that in the long-run, export-oriented industries come to rely on depreciated currencies as a way of avoiding the real problem of becoming more competitive through innovation and cost cutting.[7]

The trick for Canada is to follow the example of Japan and Germany. Both of these countries were able to maintain strong balance-of-trade surpluses throughout the 1980s even though their currencies underwent remarkable appreciations during that decade. How did they manage to do it when other countries couldn't? The simple answer is that they made goods the world wanted even at a high price, such as cars, electronics, and consumer products. Their key to an improved standard of living was to maintain market share regardless of whether prices were rising. There are no quick remedies, such as getting rich by depreciating a nation's currency. The Japanese and Germans have relied on product innovation rather than devalued currencies to improve their productivity and competitiveness.

But things don't always turn out the way governments want them. In early 2000, economists estimate that the Canadian dollar should be much stronger vis-à-vis the U.S. dollar. Some estimates suggest that the Canadian dollar is underestimated by 23 percent.[8] Despite an economy that is experiencing faster growth and higher exports, the dollar languishes because of the even stronger U.S. economy. Regardless of how well we are doing, if our major partner grows even faster, one result is a relatively weaker currency.

KEY TERMS

Currency appreciation	Flexible exchange rate	Nominal interest rates
Currency depreciation	Arbitrage	Open economy
Balance of trade	Open market operations	

REVIEW QUESTIONS

1. What are the main factors that determine the exchange rates? Why is it difficult to predict, with certainty, what the rate will do?

2. What does it mean when we say that Canada has an open economy? What dilemmas, regarding the exchange rate, face the Bank of Canada when it decides to keep interest rates high?

3. How did the Japanese manage to increase their balance-of-trade in the 1980s even though the yen underwent a massive appreciation in relation to currencies of its major trading partners?

4. What are the consequences for a country that too often tries to gain an economic advantage by devaluing its currency?

DISCUSSION QUESTIONS

1. "Real growth and wealth don't come from currency devaluations." Comment.

2. Some have accused currency speculators of destabilizing world currencies and have advocated taxing such speculation to discourage the practice. Do you agree? Explain.

NOTES

1. The corollary to this myth is that a strong dollar means a strong economy. Just as a lower dollar doesn't guarantee more exports and fewer imports, a strong dollar policy has little to do with a healthy economy.

2. In the first half of the year 2000, the Canadian currency remained weak vis-à-vis the U.S. dollar even though interest rates began to rise.

3. *Bank of Canada Review* (December 1990), p. 119.

4. Robert Solomon, *The International Monetary System, 1945–1981* (Harper & Row 1982), p. 359.

5. What if prices or the rate of inflation differ from one country to another? Under a fixed exchange rate system, one country can import another's inflation. This is not so, theoretically, under a flexible exchange rate system. If prices rise faster in Mexico than Canada, we will buy fewer Mexican products, while our products become relatively cheaper. Flexible exchange rates provide a buffer or mechanism where one country can protect itself from importing another country's inflation. Flexible rates are also a way to keep balance of payments in equilibrium between countries. If German producers are more competitive, their cost of production falls, which means higher exports and less imports. As they run a balance-of-trade surplus, other countries, such as Canada, import more and export less, which means they have a balance-of-trade deficit. As countries buy fewer Canadian products, their demand for Canadian dollars falls, which triggers a depreciation in the Canadian dollar, making our products cheaper to buy. The depreciation of the Canadian dollar, or appreciation of the German mark, carries the seeds of their own reversal.

6. Critics have accused the Bank of Canada of being too vigilant regarding inflation. There's some justification for that view. In mid-1995, when the Bank quickly lowered interest rates, following the United States lead, it became apparent that the economy was weaker than the Bank realized.

7. When Canada's merchandise trade surplus with the United States did improve, rising from $11 billion in 1982 to over $21 billion in 1985, it was because our relative cost of competitiveness was improving and not because of the devaluation of the Canadian dollar. The U.S. economy suffered the same problem as Canada during the 1980s when the Americans found themselves running deficits of over $100 billion. Why didn't the lower U.S. dollar help? According to Paul Krugman in his book *The Age of Diminished Expectations* (Cambridge, Mass: MIT, 1990), the United States just wasn't as competitive as it had once been.

8. "Big MacCurrencies," *The Economist*, 29 April 2000.

WEBLINKS

www.bankofcanada.ca/en/intro-e.htm
Home page of Bank of Canada.

www.bankofcanada.ca/en/monetary/index.htm
How monetary policy works.

www.isuma.net/v01n01/carr/carr.htm
Defending the current monetary system.

www.imf.org/external/pubs/ft/seminar/2000/targets/freedmn2.htm
The Canadian experience with targets for reducing and controlling inflation.

Chapter

BUYING
CANADIAN

 **"Buy Canadian *means more jobs*."**

*It seems only logical that if we buy Canadian-made goods, we also pro-
vide jobs for Canadian workers. But as with many myths that seem to appeal to common sense, this one is also wrong. Even though protectionist
arguments have been discredited for hundreds of years, new variants
crop up all the time. "Buy Canadian" policies are no exception. The
gains from international trade come not from keeping imports out or
erecting trade barriers, but by keeping our markets open to competition.*

"Buy the cars your neighbours build" became a popular slogan for the Canadian
Auto Workers (CAW) when the domestic auto industry began losing market share
to the Japanese. The argument seems to make sense. Buying cars from Windsor or
Oshawa does provide jobs for Canadian workers. But should it be used as an argument for restricting imports? The answer is a clear no.

Few myths die harder than the notion that "if we produce it in Canada, we'll
keep the jobs," and few economic arguments have less validity. This variant of the
antitrade position that "we can't compete with inexpensive labour" is equally as
fallacious as the idea that "we can't compete with inexpensive imports." These arguments still have appeal today, even though many similar arguments have been

discredited over the centuries.[1] Just like any justification to protect domestic indus-try, the **Buy Canadian** argument is usually couched in helping the interests of the na-tion when in fact it is protecting the interests of a particular industry or labour group.[2]

On the surface Buy Canadian policies appear to make sense, but digging below the surface reveals that the argument doesn't hold. To begin with, if the argument ap-plies to the auto industry, why not to all industries? After all, by keeping all im-ports out we can produce everything here, keeping all the jobs for ourselves. To carry the analogy one step further, why not protect Ontario grape growers from British Columbia farmers? If that sounds absurd, it is exactly what **interprovincial trade barriers** were doing before we slowly started taking them down.[3] In the end, keeping out imports under the guise of protecting jobs at home leads to higher prices and a lower standard of living.

When a country decides to use tariffs to protect a given sector of the economy from foreign competition, it is, in effect, redistributing income from one sector of the economy to another. Just as tariffs turn out to be an expensive way of protecting jobs and distributing income, Buy Canadian policies have the same effect by ap-pealing to our sense of nationalism.[4]

Argentina is a perfect case of what can happen when special interests sabotage trade and **competition policy**. Half a century ago Argentina and Canada both had promis-ing economic futures. Since then Argentina has nearly collapsed under a massive misallocation of resources, high unemployment, crippling budget and trade deficits, loss of investment, and hyperinflation in which prices rose an annual average of 450 percent throughout the 1980s. By 1990, what was one of the richest nations on earth 60-odd years ago had a GDP per capita that was 10 percent of the OECD average. It is not hard to see what happened. Governments channelled resources into unpro-ductive sectors, while import barriers protected inefficient industries. It was no secret that powerful trade unions, little competition, and runaway budget deficits made it im-possible to check inflation. Now Argentina is scrambling to open its markets to com-petition and undo the damage of decades of protectionist economic policies.[5]

Another problem with restricting imports to encourage employment is that other countries will not stand idly by taking our exports while we restrict theirs. Before long everyone starts implementing these **beggar-my-neighbour policies**. In the end, it makes everyone worse off. That's what happened during the Great Depression of the 1930s as countries tried to export their unemployment by keeping imports out. But we don't have to go back 70 years to see the effects of these policies. Every time there is a recession or a surge in imports, governments come under pressure to protect jobs and companies by restricting these imports.[6] That is exactly what is happening in the case of grain production. Canada cannot sell its wheat because too many countries are busy protecting their grain farmers, even though Canadian producers are among the most efficient in the world.

THE NEW MERCANTILISM

The desire to restrict imports comes from the basic notion that imports are bad and exports are good. Despite the obvious drawbacks in the impulse to keep imports out, there is no denying that policies to protect domestic companies from competition do provide immediate (if not lasting) relief. It seems to make sense that if we buy a Japanese car, we get the car but they get the money; but if we buy Canadian, we get the car and the money. This is an extension of **mercantilism**, the sixteenth-century philosophy that propounded that European colonies should be used mainly for exporting to and not importing from. Therefore, according to this notion, a country should always strive for a positive balance of trade (exports exceed imports), but such a policy is illogical. We can always sell more goods by lowering the price of exported goods, subsidizing those industries that export, or devaluing the currency, but should we? Do exporters need subsidies because they belong to some underprivileged group? If we encourage exports by pricing below the cost of production, Canadians end up subsidizing foreign buyers. No one would argue that American consumers should be encouraged to benefit at the Canadian taxpayers' expense. But that's exactly what happens when we make our exports less expensive than they would normally be without subsidies. There is another problem as well: the higher export subsidies are, the higher the profits in the export sector, which means that more resources will be taken out of domestic production, resulting in a misallocation of resources from domestic products to exports.

Another misconception about increasing exports at the expense of imports is that when we buy imported goods, other countries then hold Canadian dollars. The Japanese or Germans don't hold Canadian dollars for the pleasure of holding them, but for buying Canadian goods. We demand foreign currency for the same reasons. In the long run, a country's exports are determined by how much it imports; otherwise, how would we get paid? If we restrict the buying of imported goods, other countries end up with fewer dollars to buy *our* exports. The more exports we want, the more we have to import and vice versa.

In simple terms, the process of adjustments works as follows. A Canadian vintner delivers a shipment of wines to an importer in Britain, who pays for the shipment in British pounds. But the Canadian wine maker can't pay his Canadian suppliers and labour with any currency other than Canadian funds. Where does he get it? The answer is from a build up in Canadian-dollar credits from British exports to Canada. In other words, if it weren't for imports from Britain, the British would not have been able to import the wine from Canada. Foreign exchange is a clearing transaction in which British pounds and Canadian-dollar credits are cancelled against each other. There is no mystery about it. On a more immediate and local level, each of us must sell something, even if it's our own labour, in order to have purchasing power. Just as internal trade is conducted by cancelling cheques through bank clearing houses, the same process applies in international trade.

This is obviously an oversimplification of the complex rules that govern international trade, but the basic principle holds: if we want to export more, we have to import more. If a country runs a trade deficit for too long, it restricts its long-run ability to import indefinitely. However, running surpluses brings its own problems.[7] One way or another, those credits will be run down because they cannot be used to buy domestic products.

VARIATION ON A THEME: MANUFACTURING MATTERS

Despite the various and discredited arguments for protecting domestic producers, new arguments are always being created to defend the indefensible. The latest version falls under the category that "manufacturing matters" and therefore must be protected with import restrictions if necessary.

The argument goes something like this: Western nations are undergoing a process of **deindustrialization** in which services are replacing manufacturing as the dominant source of economic activity. Those who advocate this position claim that a modern society cannot sustain a service-driven economy without manufacturing. Stephen Cohen and John Zysman, who advocate protection on this assumption, state that "there are ... other kinds of linkages in the economy, such as those which tie the crop duster to the cotton fields, the ketchup maker to the tomato patch, the wine press to the vineyards. Here the linkages are tight and quite concrete."[8]

What this means is that if a country loses one link in the production process, it jeopardizes all the links. But if one takes a quick look at how things are made in a world that is becoming more integrated (and not less), the opposite is true. It's not unusual to have a garment designed on Queen Street in Toronto with cotton grown in the southern United States, cut in Hong Kong, and sold in London.[9] According to Cohen and Zysman, anything to do with cotton should be done in the southern United States.

DUMPING AND PREDATOR PRICING

If buying Canadian isn't a good enough argument for keeping out imports, perhaps one should look at imports that are sold at below the cost of production or at prices lower than those offered in the home market. This is one case where government intervention is justified. **Dumping** is universally condemned, and it is the only time that the WTO allows countries to defend themselves with special tariffs. However, dumping *alone* is not viewed as sufficient reason for **countervailing duties**. In Canada, for example, it must be shown after study by the Department of National Revenue that material harm has been done to the domestic industry, otherwise no protection is allowed. In most cases, the government decides to monitor the situation. If little or no harm is done, then dumping is a bargain for the importing country. Although the situation can't be allowed to go on forever, the practice is not always condemned, especially when the consumer is the winner. And it must be remembered that it is the interests of the consumer that come before those of the producer.

Predator pricing is a different situation. The objective of the producer is to drive the price low enough to eliminate competition and to increase market share, with the purpose of extracting higher prices later on. The most adamant free marketer would not justify such practices, even if consumers were to benefit for a short time. The cost of adjustment to the companies and workers affected are usually greater than any benefits that consumers receive. In such cases, governments should do what they can to prevent expensive disruptions to their markets.[10]

When all arguments for greater protection are dismissed by logic and reason, Buy Canadian policies are defended on the grounds of national pride and honour. Even the federal government has run ads encouraging us to check labels to make sure we are buying Canadian. It may make good politics, but it's bad economics. We are reproached, on the basis of our fellowship with other Canadians, for allowing other countries to provide us with the necessities of life. Just listen to the farmers trying to protect the marketing boards or the auto workers defending their jobs. When unions and industry appeal to our sense of nationalism on the grounds that it protects jobs, it's time for consumers to watch their wallets.

It has to be recognized that justifications for protectionism are few and far between, and that governments should resist calls to protect certain workers or firms at the expense of the consumer. That does not mean that governments are helpless to provide protection and relief to the import-sensitive industries and their workers. Help should come in the form of adjustment assistance and re-training programs that anticipate and encourage change with well-considered programs. The bulk of assistance should come from the proper management of monetary and fiscal policy that steers the economy to fuller employment. Canadian consumers would be doing themselves and their country a favour if they bought goods and services based on price and quality rather than whether they are Canadian. Otherwise, we all end up poorer.[11]

KEY TERMS

Buy Canadian	Beggar-my-neighbour	Dumping
Interprovincial trade	policies	Countervailing duties
barriers	Mercantilism	Predator pricing
Competition policy	Deindustrialization	

REVIEW QUESTIONS

1. How are Buy Canadian policies different from other nontariff barriers that restrict imports? Whose interests do they serve? What are their impacts on the economy?

2. What would be the implications to the Canadian economy if everyone were to follow the logic of a Buy Canadian program?

3. How are Buy Canadian policies just another variation of the sixteenth-century economic doctrine of mercantilism?

4. "The ultimate irony of Buy Canadian and other import-restraining policies is that the export sector invariably pays the price." Explain this statement.

5. Under what conditions are restrictions on imports justified? Does this always apply to foreign companies dumping their products on the Canadian market?

DISCUSSION QUESTIONS

1. When France keeps out Canadian wines to protect their own wine producers, what should our reaction be?

2. Should farmers out West complain when Canadian trade policy protects the manufacturing industry in Ontario and Quebec?

NOTES

1. Over a century ago, the French economist Frederic Bastiat satirized the French candle makers for asking the government to protect them from the sun's light by passing a law forcing everyone to shutter their windows, dormers, and skylights. They argued that during the day the sun's cost of production was zero, and they certainly couldn't compete at those prices. See Blomqvist, Wonnacott, and Wonnacott, *Economics,* 1st Cdn. ed. (Scarborough: McGraw-Hill Ryerson, 1983), p. 632.

2. Economist David Freedman tells of an interesting way to look at international trade. Assume two technologies to produce cars, one is to make them in Oshawa, and the second is to grow them in Saskatchewan. Everyone knows the first, but not the second. First you plant the seeds, which are the raw material for producing cars. Then you harvest the wheat, put it on ships and send it to the Far East. After a few months the wheat returns as Hondas and Toyotas. International trade is nothing but the second form of technology to produce cars. The fact that there are factories and workers in Japan or Korea is irrelevant to Canadian car buyers. Any policy that favours the first technology, favours Canadian autoworkers over car producers in Saskatchewan. In other words, if you protect Oshawa car producers from competition, you will hurt grain farmers out West because they *are* the competition. Supporting workers in Oshawa not only transfers income from farmers to autoworkers, it also raises the total cost of cars to Canadians. The efficiency loss comes with no offsetting gains making us all worse off. This delightful story is told by Steven Landsburg in his book *The Armchair Economist* (New York: The Free Press, 1993).

3. Within Canada, until 1992, Canadian beer could only be sold in the province where it was brewed. That led to the absurd anomaly that a Canadian brand, such as Moosehead, could be found in New York, but not Toronto.

4. Policies to protect jobs in the United States were even more expensive for society. One study concluded that trade protection in 31 industries cost consumers $53 billion in 1984. Protecting a single job in the auto industry cost $105,000; in television manufacturing $420,000; and $750,000 for every job saved in the steel industry. See Gary Hufbauer et al., *Trade Protection in the United States: 31 Case Studies* (Washington, D.C.: Institute for International Economics, 1986).

5. See "Nearly Time to Tango," *The Economist,* 18 April 1992, p. 17.

6. Opposition to imports comes not only from organized labour and some industries but also from the Canadian Conference of Catholic Bishops, which has come out against labour-destroying technology and an industrial policy to encourage labour-intensive manufacturing. That position is reminiscent of the Luddites, who destroyed the textile machines for the same reason in eighteenth-century England. The truth is, technology isn't the destroyer of jobs, and manufacturing can only remain competitive if it uses labour-saving technology. Otherwise, the only way to maintain employment, and only in the short run, is to limit imports. That puts the bishops in the awkward position of favouring jobs for Canadian workers at the expense of jobs abroad, and often in countries with higher levels of unemployment. See Gregory Baum and Duncan Cameron, "Ethical Reflections on the Economic Crises," *Ethics and Economics* (Toronto: James Lorimer and Company, 1984), p. 185.

7. It's important to realize that trade surpluses aren't a sign of a healthy economy. Some countries that ran surpluses in recent years were Poland, Venezuela, Hungary, Mexico, Gabon, and Chile.

8. Stephen Cohen and John Zysman, *Manufacturing Matters: The Myth of the Post-Industrial Economy* (New York: Basic Books, 1987).

9. The famous international economist Jagdish Bhagwati was amused as he read these lines while eating some British Crabtree and Evelyn vintage marmalade. "It surely never occurred to me that England grew its own oranges." See Bhagwati, *Protectionism* (Cambridge, Mass.: MIT Press, 1988), p. 114.

10. What about the situation in which countries, such as Japan, price their products abroad at lower prices than they charge at home? On the face of it, this isn't always dumping or justification for imposing countervailing duties. Firms always charge a lower price in markets where the competition is greater. That is usually the case when Japanese cameras and camcorders are cheaper here than in Japan. We do not have to go to the Far East to find examples. The "grey market" is an example of how firms charge different prices in different markets. Office products, computer disks, batteries, and film are products that companies ship at various prices around the world. The problem arises when grey marketeers make a profit by buying in one country and shipping to another market where prices are higher. This technique is called "arbitrage" and companies fight hard to prevent it, though it's usually tough to stop.

11. As mentioned in Chapter 7, one of the prime reasons for NAFTA was to prevent the three signatories from unfairly subsidizing domestic industries. Under NAFTA rules, programs that encourage Buy Domestic policies can be challenged by the affected country.

WEBLINKS

strategis.ic.gc.ca/sc_mrkti/iptrade/engdoc/iptrd_hpg.html
Industry Canada's site concerning interprovincial trade barriers.

www.imf.org/external/pubs/ft/issues10/
Deindustrialization—its causes and implications.

www.ccra-adrc.gc.ca/agency/fairness/97-262-e.html
Ensuring fair customs and revenue administration in Canada.

strategis.ic.gc.ca/SSG/ct01656e.html#1EconPred
Anticompetitive pricing practices: predatory pricing.

IMMIGRANT
EMPLOYMENT

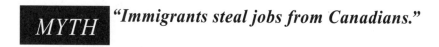

MYTH *"Immigrants steal jobs from Canadians."*

Many people worry that immigrants steal jobs, pay less taxes than they receive in social assistance, and lower the incomes of Canadians. All of these concerns are ill-founded. By definition, immigrants are both consumers and producers, and the evidence shows that they more than earn their keep. That's not to say there aren't concerns about Canada's immigration policy. Canada does better when there's a greater emphasis on encouraging immigrants with skills and training, and less emphasis on family reunification.

One of the more common myths heard in Canada is that immigrants steal jobs from Canadians and reduce wages, especially during times of high unemployment and economic slowdown. The implications of more immigration are obvious: there is less to go around for all residents in Canada. Those who hold this view also tend to believe that immigrants are a burden to the taxpayer because new Canadians are perceived to be using more than their share of employment insurance, welfare, and other social programs. Some environmental groups also oppose more immigration on the grounds that having more people damages the environment. A more sophisticated criticism is that too many immigrants reduce the per capita income of the country's residents. This view is based on the assumption that there is an optimal population size and that beyond some point per capita incomes start falling as the economy becomes less efficient.

Given that Canada is a land where immigration has played a crucial role in economic development, there is surprisingly little information about its social and economic impact. But from what we know we may ask, do recent immigrants steal jobs, reduce income, and take more from the system than they contribute? The answer, on all counts, is no. Studies done in Canada cannot find any evidence that immigration has adverse effects on the employment and earnings of Canadians.[1] Before we examine the available evidence in more detail, let's take a look at the changing role and history of immigration in Canada.

THE CHANGING FACE OF IMMIGRATION

Canada has always been known as a country of immigrants, but during the latter part of the nineteenth century, Canada actually had more people leaving than arriving. Immigration reached the astounding number of 401,000 new immigrants in 1913, but only 25 percent of those who came stayed. The rest went to the United States. There was another net loss of people in the 1930s and early 1940s, but after that things started to pick up. From 1946 to 1957, 1.1 million immigrants arrived. They came mainly from Europe and for the purpose of finding better jobs and higher wages. Those who arrived in this wave often had few skills, but a strong desire to work and better their lives. After 1957, Canada changed its immigration focus by recruiting those with skills or money. By the late 1960s, professionals made up 25 percent of all immigrants. With the adoption of the point system, Canada emphasized skills and education, and downplayed immigrant sponsorship or family reunification. However, that trend has changed. By the 1970s only one in ten immigrants was a sponsored immigrant. Now the family reunification category covers three in ten immigrants. In addition, there are the spouses or dependants who are not joining relatives but accompanying immigrating skilled workers and businesspeople. By 1998, this category made up 38 percent of all immigrants.

The countries from which immigrants came also began to change with the new rules for entry. Before the 1960s, over 85 percent of all immigrants came from either Europe or the United States. By the late 1960s and early 1970s, 40 percent arrived from the West Indies, the Middle East, Asia, and Africa.[2] Today, the majority of immigrants arrive from developing countries. These changes have transformed the face of Canada: it's no longer predominately white and European. The English and French Canadians are now minorities in their own country. With each generation, Canadians are again debating the question of an appropriate level of immigration: how many can we afford to take in, and what are the economic consequences for Canada?

IMMIGRATION: BURDEN OR BLESSING?

What has been the impact on the Canadian economy? To help answer this question, we can look at immigration in three ways: first, its contribution to the per capita income of Canadians or those already living in Canada; second, the immigrants' use of federal and provincial social immigration programs in relation to taxes paid; and third, the question as to whether recent immigrants actually create work or displace resident Canadians from jobs, thereby raising the rate of unemployment.

Economic Efficiency

The question of economic efficiency centres around the idea that there's some ideal or optimal level of population, and that after that level has been reached, per capita income levels begin to drop. Economists call this the **law of diminishing marginal returns**. This economic law simply means that the more people there are, the less contribution the last one makes to national output. There comes a point when, regardless of how many people are added, output and income won't increase any further. In fact, it may actually decrease as population grows. That is what we mean by reaching our maximum efficiency point. Have we reached that point? The answer is, no, and we probably never will. Economists enjoy trying to calculate some optimum population point where adding any more people would make the economy work less efficiently. One estimate by the Economic Council of Canada puts Canada's optimal population size at 100 million, but that is only sophisticated guess work.[3] Besides, output depends on more than just worker population. Machines, tools, and technology are also important and those inputs are always changing, making labour more productive. In many cases, immigrants bring considerable **human capital** in the form of education and skills not available to the host country. That's why there is no clear relationship between population size and economic efficiency.

Social Programs and Taxes

Another important question deals with the dependence of recent immigrants on welfare and other social assistance programs. A common perception is that immigrants use the system more than those already in Canada. The data shows that 12.5 percent of the immigrants who arrived between 1981 and 1986 used the welfare system at some point, compared with 13.8 percent of people already living in Canada. Among those who immigrated to Canada from 1976 to 1980, only 6.7 percent were on welfare. It seems the longer immigrants are in Canada, the less they rely on welfare. Contrary to conventional wisdom, only a small share of immigrants ever go on welfare, and certainly no more than Canadian residents.

It would follow that if immigrants do not overuse the welfare system, they must have jobs to go to; and in fact, they do. Immigrants, in general, have lower unemployment rates than those already settled in the country. In 1986, immigrants had an unemployment rate of 8.2 percent compared to 10.8 percent for nonimmigrants. These lower rates of unemployment are not instantaneous. Recent immigrants do have higher rates of unemployment as they adjust to their new country.

Do immigrants pay their fair share of taxes, or do they use more social services than they pay for? One study has found that immigrants do indeed pay more in taxes than they take out in services. In short, immigrants carry more than their share of costs, and, in the process, transfer income through their taxes to established residents. The study further found that the younger the immigrant, the higher the contribution. By paying taxes, the immigrant makes a net contribution to society for up to 35 years. The implication is that if we are going to bring in immigrants, then we should do it when they are young.[4] Another plus is that in 1986, 27.5 percent of adult immigrants who had to qualify under the point system to gain entry into the country entered with university degrees, saving taxpayers considerable educational expense. This compares to 22.6 percent of Canadians who had university degrees.

If immigrants do make a positive financial contribution to the country, why not allow more into the country? The case has been made that as the Canadian population ages, the country will need more workers to pay for the soaring costs in health, education, and social security. The Economic Council of Canada has found that we can reduce the per capita tax burden of administering these services per person if we have higher immigration levels. But these savings would be very small.[5] Even if we add the benefits of economies of scale, in other words the reduced per capita costs of a higher population, the benefits to the host population would still be small. What the evidence seems to show is that immigrants do not pose a burden to the host population in higher taxes, but they do not substantially alleviate the tax burden to the rest of the population.

It would be wrong to assume that immigration, including refugees seeking asylum in Canada, does not have its social and economic costs. Canada spends hundreds of millions of dollars on programs for immigrants ranging from language training and social assistance to counseling and job placement. But these costs, which have been rising with the increase in immigration and refugee-status claims, do not capture the added burden on the three major destinations of immigrants (Toronto, Montreal, and Vancouver) in terms of higher housing, educational, and social costs caused by growth in population. Immigration has not been a national phenomenon, but one highly focused on Canada's three major urban centres.

Jobs, Wages, and Immigrants

Now we come to the belief that immigrants steal our jobs. People who believe immigrants displace resident Canadian workers base their reasoning on three assumptions: first, that immigrants displace jobs on a one-to-one basis; second, that immigrant and domestic labour are perfectly interchangeable; and third, that immigrants are willing to work at lower wages than most Canadians. Such assumptions are usually not based on evidence but on the view that there are a fixed number of jobs in the economy. We know this isn't true by the fact that as the population grows through immigration, the demand for goods and services increases along with the demand for new jobs. In many ways immigrants create their own jobs and increase the level of **aggregate demand** by buying cars, houses, and everything else that Canadians purchase.

At the same time, more recent immigrants spend a higher portion of their income on food, shelter, and transportation, and because of their spending patterns change the nature of aggregate demand in the economy. In this regard, immigrants cannot steal jobs from resident Canadians since their purchases create exactly the need for the jobs they fill. In other words, immigrants are both consumers and producers. On the supply side, immigrants also tend to contribute more to the labour force. When adjusted for age, the **participation rate** for male immigrants is around 78 percent and is essentially the same for resident Canadians. Also, where once Canada gave preference to immigrants with technical skills that were in short supply domestically, there's a greater tendency today for immigrants to find jobs in professional and administrative occupations.

In reference to the idea that immigrants are willing to work at jobs refused by Canadians, this view sees the economy having primary and secondary jobs, the first being high-paying ones preferred by Canadians and the latter poorer-paying jobs preferred by immigrants. This black-and-white approach to the labour market is flawed because it depends on unfounded assumptions. For example, if Canadians didn't want to work in secondary jobs, it would soon become apparent—crops wouldn't get picked, and houses would go uncleaned. In a market economy, a labour shortage would dictate that wages in these secondary occupations would go up. There is no theoretical reason that Canadians wouldn't work in these occupations. A possible explanation why wages haven't gone up is that immigrants possess many of the same skills as the resident population. As the number of immigrants increases, they compete for the same number of jobs at lower wage rates. This is a possible scenario, but there is little evidence to support it. If this were the case, Canadian wages would drop. But there's no evidence that this happens either. Immigration doesn't seem to affect the wages of resident Canadians. Most studies show that a 10 percent increase in immigration reduces wages, at most, by 1 percent.[6] This can be explained partly by the fact that immigrants and Canadians are not perfect substitutes or completely interchangeable. How immigrants and Canadians interact economically is not well understood and needs more investigation and research.

The skills of immigrants vary greatly among and between the immigrants themselves and their countries of origin. Persons migrating under one set of economic and political conditions have different impacts on the labour market; and it is difficult, if not impossible, to predict what these impacts will be. Having said that, there are signs that immigrants who have come to Canada after 1978 tend to have lower levels of education and have more difficulty finding work.[7]

Even though the evidence suggests that immigration does not increase unemployment, the federal government acted to reduce target levels of immigration during recessions. Until 1990, under the point system an immigrant could not apply for landed immigrant status, other than under the family unification program, unless there was a need for their occupation. Although it might appear to the layperson that it would be an easy matter to determine whether immigration causes unemployment to rise, in reality it is not all that straightforward. The Federal Government has looked at this question from various angles to find the answer. Simply looking at the data and seeing if unemployment rates increase with immigration levels is unsatisfying. It isn't enough to look at immigration flows to see whether the unemployment rates go up or down. A quick examination of the data shows that immigration tapers off as the unemployment rate increases. After all, immigrants generally do not want to come here unless there are jobs waiting (see Figure 11.1).

What about population growth and unemployment, are they closely related? If we assume that immigration is just another way of increasing population size, we might find a relationship between unemployment and population growth; however, no such correlation can be found between the two. Another way to increase unemployment may be to increase the labour force beyond the capacity of the economy to produce jobs, but do countries with high labour-force growth rates have higher levels of unemployment? Comparing the experience of various OECD countries, again, there is no relationship to be found between unemployment rates and the growth of the labour force. Canada had a lower unemployment rate than France and Italy throughout the 1990s, even though our labour force grew at a faster pace. Given Canada's falling fertility rates, the welfare of Canadians could be increased if immigration levels are chosen to assure a long-run population growth rate of two percent per year.[8]

Another supporting piece of evidence that immigrants do not cause more unemployment is that they tend to create their own jobs through self-employment. Over the 1990s, a greater proportion of immigrants were self-employed compared to the general population. Finally there is the question of who fares better under our immigration policy. Again there is the problem of inadequate information and data. On average, immigrants not only have jobs to go to, but they also tend to earn about 3 percent more than resident Canadians, adjusting for factors such as educational levels. Immigrants also tend to save more than Canadian-born citizens.

What we conclude from the studies and analyses of immigration in Canada is that first, immigrants do not steal jobs; second, there's no evidence that immigrants lower the earnings of resident Canadians; and third, immigrants are not a burden on the welfare system. Finally, immigrants pay more than their fair share of taxes for social programs. But if there's no evidence that they are a burden to society, it should also be said that there are no compelling reasons for assuming that immigrants are an overwhelming benefit to the country in terms of increasing Canada's per capita income. This means that to understand the costs and benefits of immigration, one has to look beyond economics and assess the contributions of a society that has a diverse mix of cultures and provides a haven for many on humanitarian grounds. If anyone persists in believing that immigrants steal jobs, they cannot count on the evidence to make their case.

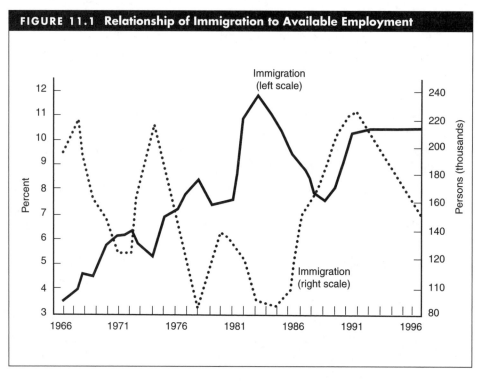

FIGURE 11.1 Relationship of Immigration to Available Employment

Source: StatsCan.

KEY TERMS

Law of diminishing
  marginal returns

Human capital
Aggregate demand

Participation rate

REVIEW QUESTIONS

1. If the evidence suggests that immigrants do not steal jobs, why not increase the level of immigration beyond the current immigration targets?

2. What are the main categories under which immigrants can enter Canada? The Liberal government in Ottawa has de-emphasized family unification as a criteria for immigration. Would you agree with that policy? What are the costs and benefits of such a change?

3. Some argue that immigrants, if they don't steal jobs, at least depress wages of native-born Canadians. Does this argument have any validity from a theoretical point of view?

4. The argument has been made that immigration can help fill certain labour market gaps in the economy more efficiently than if we trained our own workers. If that is the case, who wins and loses in such a system, keeping in mind the interests of the employers, consumers, and the workers themselves?

DISCUSSION QUESTIONS

1. It has been recommended that new immigrants not be allowed to use the country's social system until they've been in the country for a number of years. Would you agree with such a policy?

2. "The implications of Canada's immigration policy is more social than economic." Discuss.

NOTES

1. Canada's interest in immigration issues is also partly due to the debate on immigration problems in the United States, particularly California. With the passage of Proposition 187, California wants the federal government to limit illegal immigrants the benefits of health care, social assistance, and education. The United States has over 1 million illegal immigrants entering the country each year, a problem Canada has so far avoided.

2. Immigrants can enter Canada under three categories: through family unification, as independents, or as refugees. In the 1980s, 42 percent came into Canada by way of family-class immigration; 18 percent were refugees; and 40 percent came into the coun-

try as independents. About 70 percent of the refugees and family-class immigrants come from the Caribbean, Asia, Africa, and South and Central America, while 50 percent of the independents come from Hong Kong, Europe, and the United States.

3. The Economic Council of Canada, *Economic and Social Impacts of Immigration,* (Ottawa: Supply and Services, 1991).

4. Ather H. Akbari, "The Benefits of Immigration to Canada: Evidence on Tax and Public Services," *Canadian Public Policy* 15, no.4 (December 1989). Akbari has also calculated that the average foreign-born household will, over its lifetime, make a net contribution to the public purse as much as 45 percent higher than that of an average Canadian-born household "…so that the average immigrant-headed household transfers $210 annually to the Canadian-born household." (*Source: The Economist*, 24 July 1999.)

5. Ibid., Economic Council of Canada, p. 51.

6. Data for the United States shows that a 10 percent increase in immigration decreases native wages less than 1 percent. George Borjas, an immigration expert at Harvard University, cautions that the U.S. is attracting relatively unskilled immigrants which may have long-term economic impacts. See George J. Borjas, *Friends or Strangers: The Impacts of Immigrants on the U.S. Economy* (New York: Basic Books 1990).

7. Don J. DeVoretz, "Immigration and the Canadian Labour Market," *The Immigration Dilemma*, ed. Steven Globerman (Vancouver B.C.: The Fraser Institute, 1992) p. 173. Professor DeVoretz argues that the relatively poorer employment and income performance of immigrants after 1978 was due to an increased emphasis on family reunification class and a decline in the independent class.

8. Ibid., Herbert G. Grubel, "The Economic and Social Effects of Immigration," p. 99.

WEBLINKS

www.statcan.ca/Daily/English/980217/d980217.htm
1996 Census: ethnic origin, visible minorities.

international.metropolis.net/events/israel/papers/Siemiatycki.html
Immigration and urban politics in Toronto.

www.web.net/~ccr/biblio.htm
Myths and misconceptions about refugees and immigrants in Canada.

www.pcerii.metropolis.net/research-policy/research_content/4b_i.html
Visible minority immigrant professionals and evaluation of their credentials.

www.cpa.ca/cjbsnew/1996/ful_palmer.html
Determinants of Canadian attitudes toward immigration as highly correlated to the unemployment rate.

Myths About

the Role of

Government

GOVERNMENT SPENDING AND FUTURE SECURITY

 **MYTH** *"The government can't afford an aging population."*

A major concern among the younger generation is that they will be stuck with a large tax burden. Aging baby boomers will rely on social programs that are financed on a pay-as-you-go basis. Moreover, an aging population also means higher medical bills. Many believe that the financial demands on our nation's limited resources will be overwhelming. However, this pessimistic scenario may be exaggerated. Fewer workers means more capital and machinery which leads to higher productivity. As the labour force becomes smaller, higher wages will ease this decline by enticing older workers to stay in the work force longer. There's also room for higher female participation rates and immigration levels to increase the labour force. An older society does not mean a poorer one.

A common anxiety today is the notion that governments can't afford an aging population given the tremendous demands already put on the nation's limited resources. The scenario goes something like this: as the baby boom generation gets older and begins to retire, there will be fewer people contributing to the **tax base**. Not only will a greater proportion of the population be retiring than now, but also this group will live longer than past generations; and as everyone knows, the older we get the more medical attention we need. Eventually, the government will go bankrupt trying to pay out all health, retirement, and social insurance programs. Fewer workers will be supporting more retirees. By the time the baby boom generation leaves the labour market, there won't even be enough money around to cover the old-age pension. In short, "the government can't afford an aging population." To make things worse, there may be an **intergenerational conflict**, where the young resent having to support an older population given that a greater burden of social programs will fall on the shoulders of younger workers because these programs are paid for from current taxes.[1]

Before we examine this fallacy, let's be clear that governments do not go broke in the conventional sense, at least not the way companies or individuals do. There is the erroneous notion that if households have to live within their means, then so do governments. With individuals, if you spend more than you earn, your creditors can force the sale of your assets to pay off your debts. That's what we normally mean by going broke or becoming insolvent. Those who believe that governments must behave as individuals and balance their budgets are committing the **fallacy of composition**: what applies to the parts applies to the whole. But this is not so with governments because they have the power to change the law. If they need more money to pay their bills, all they have to do is borrow, raise taxes, or if they are really desperate, print more money. They also don't have a definite lifetime over which to balance their budgets. Governments only go broke in the sense that they cannot meet their obligations from current revenues. A helpful illustration of that point are the problems that occurred in Russia when that country defaulted on loan payments in the late 1990s. Foreign investment quickly dried up. They couldn't meet interest payments on loans from foreign lenders so the only real option left to the lenders was to refuse to extend further credit to delinquent nations. Often, however, the creditor nations lent more money to countries that couldn't make payments so that their capital markets wouldn't be thrown into disarray. No one can force a country, short of going to war, to liquidate assets to pay their bills. Therefore, countries don't go broke in the sense that an individual or corporation can. Countries that default on their loans, or run irresponsible spending policies, are either denied more lending or have to pay higher rates. In either case, standards of living fall.

It's true that more Canadians will be exiting the labour force over the next 20 years. A simple look at the demographics tells the story. Those between the ages of 45 and 64 accounted for 20 percent of the population in 1986, but they will account for 28 percent by 2011. Over the next 50 years, the proportion of the population aged 65 and over will double. Coupled with this "greying of Canada" will be a shrinking labour force. There will be only slightly more young people around in 2001 than there were in 1991. As baby boomers get older and begin to retire en masse, this aging population group will be collecting federal Canada pensions, old-age security benefits, and guaranteed income supplement payments. We can also expect greater demand for health care services. Under that scenario, many worry that the entire system will collapse as a growing number of Canadians get older and sicker with fewer workers to support them. Is this distressing scenario inevitable? It is unlikely for the following reasons: markets react to changes in demographics by substituting more capital for labour; the labour force won't necessarily continue to shrink indefinitely; and technology will most likely continue to advance as it always does.

CAPITAL TO THE RESCUE

It's true that the **labour force** will shrink as a share of the population, but that doesn't necessarily mean a smaller tax base from which governments draw their revenue. Economic wealth doesn't depend only on how many people are working, but also on how much physical and human capital exists. Physical capital includes machinery, buildings, equipment, dams, bridges, and so on. Human capital is made up of all accumulated knowledge and skills of a working population. These are what economists call inputs. As the labour force shrinks and the supply of labour decreases, wages tend to go up. When that happens, companies start substituting relatively cheaper capital to replace the more expensive labour. Workers now become more productive because they have more capital to work with. And it's productivity, or output per worker, that improves a country's standard of living. The more productive the economy, the larger the wealth base for the government to tax in order to meet growing expenditures. Sustaining a steady productivity growth level over a long period of time is the key to success. That's why Canadian GDP per worker has increased over time. The irony is that a shrinking labour force may actually make us better off by forcing the economy to become more capital intensive and more productive. This is what happened to Japan's economy in the late 1940s when its population experienced lower fertility rates. Japan began to run out of workers 20 years before the United States and Canada. Some economists have argued that it was this labour shortage that forced Japan to turn to machines to do their work, which led to Japan's phenomenal productivity growth rates that averaged over 10 percent a year for almost 20 years after 1945.

If our wealth and future well-being are actually measured by our productivity, how has Canada fared? We are one of the winners. Since 1950, we increased our real (taking inflation into account) income per capita from $6,000 to $22,000 by 1990. But we could have done better. During the 1960s and early 1970s our rate of productivity growth averaged close to 5 percent per year. If we had maintained that growth rate until 1995, we could have added another $200 billion to our gross domestic product thanks to the miracle of compound growth. Although our productivity levels have been disappointing, there are indications that the end of the low productivity rates of the 1970s and 1980s may be behind us.[2] (For a comparison of Canadian and U.S. productivity rates, check the Web site for the Centre for the Study of Living Standards: www.csls.ca.)

However, if we want to improve our standard of living, and increase capital investment, we have to save to get it. That means consuming less today, so we'll have more tomorrow. The more a country saves, the more funds available for investment and research and development. Canadians have traditionally been good savers, but that is changing even with the added incentives of **Retirement Savings Plans (RSPs)**. We are relying more on foreign savings to maintain our standard of living, a proposition that isn't sustainable in the long run. With less savings and less capital to work with, a large, aging population may very well mean a bleaker future.[3]

AN OLDER POPULATION DOES NOT MEAN A SMALLER WORK FORCE

The second assumption implied by this myth is that the labour force will shrink over time or become stagnant as the baby boom "bulge" ages. This is not necessarily the case. As we've already seen, a shrinking labour force means higher wages, which also implies that a greater number of older workers will want to keep working. Currently, those 65 years and over who are still working make up only about 15 percent of the Canadian labour force. Comparable figures in Germany are 22 percent, with 23 percent in the United Kingdom, 18 percent in the United States, and over 26 percent in Sweden. It won't take much to increase Canada's labour force as more people choose to remain in the work force longer in order to provide for their own old age. Simply increasing the mandatory retirement age from 65 to 67 could increase labour and take some pressure off Canada's Old Age security program. Older, more experienced workers, who remain in the labour market longer, are also more productive and valuable than younger workers.

If the past is any indication, women will continue to enter the labour force in greater numbers. Over the past decade, women have increased their participation rate to almost 60 percent, while that rate for men has remained roughly constant at 75 percent. Today more married women are part of the labour force to the point where single-earner couples are in the minority.

Another obvious way to increase the supply of workers is through immigration. The government can turn the immigration flow on and off as required. For example, in 1989 the number of immigrants was about 189,000 compared with only 85,000 in 1985. Canada's population has been increasing despite the fact that we are having fewer children. In 1960, Canadians had about 4 children per family. By the late 1990s, we had fewer than 1.5 children, which is below the 2.1 average per family needed to replace the population. If we assume current **fertility rates** and 200,000 immigrants a year, the Canadian population won't peak until the 2030s. In other words, Canada's low natural population growth rate doesn't necessarily mean a static or shrinking population or labour force.

TECHNOLOGY'S MANY SURPRISES

"The government can't afford an aging population" theme also makes the erroneous assumption that technology will somehow remain stagnant, or at best won't contribute to economic growth. No one can predict how technological advancements will improve productivity, but there are strong links between research and development, technology, productivity, and economic well-being. Who could have predicted the impact of microelectronics, genetic engineering, and materials (i.e., ceramics and plastics) research 30-odd years ago? Ignoring the dynamics of technological advances led to the faulty reasoning at the turn of the twentieth century about the massive shift of workers out of agriculture and into manufacturing. The contention then was that if workers left the fields for the factories, there would be no one to grow the food to feed everyone moving to the cities. What many didn't take into account were the giant strides occurring in agricultural technology, which transformed agriculture into one of the most productive sectors in the country.

Much of the optimism for future economic growth comes with growing applications of software technology. Paul Romer, an economist at Stanford University, and an economic growth theorist, says that the ability to continue to discover new and better software is at the heart of growth. He argues that software, unlike other factors of production, isn't subject to the law of diminishing returns. That makes the potential for economic growth limitless.[4] Many analysts predict an information revolution and strong growth without triggering an inflationary surge. That's exactly what is happening in North America at the end of the 1990s. Both the U.S. and Canada are experiencing sustained high levels of growth with low levels of inflation. In the United States, for example, a long-term modest productivity growth rate of 1.5 percent, can increase GDP per elderly person from $158,000 (U.S.) in 1993 to $207,600 in 2050. In short, technology and productivity are far more important to economic wealth than the age of the population.[5]

BUT DON'T THE OLD GET SICKER?

Perhaps one of the more compelling arguments against a bright future as a larger share of the population ages, are rising health costs. After all, the elderly consume a greater share of medical dollars compared to people in their twenties and thirties. Health care makes up Canada's biggest, single social program, consuming a third of provincial budgets in provinces such as Ontario. But unlike the United States, so far Canada has been able to contain health costs under a universal health program.

Canada spends about 9 percent of its GDP on health care compared with 12 percent in the United States.

But can we prevent a cost explosion in medical care as we get older? The evidence suggests we can. Serious thought has gone into this very question. After all, it is central to how governments spend limited resources (our tax dollars) on a product we all eventually need (medical care). One study found that even though we all need more medical attention as we age, the overall increase in health care expenditures is only 1 percent per capita per year.[6] Those who are worried about the impending doom and collapse of the health care system are usually projecting ahead by 30 to 40 years. Given that time line, the accumulated health costs can look overwhelming. But an economy can generate substantial increases in wealth to more than cover the added strain of health expenditures. However, the days of unrestrained medical costs are behind us; provincial and federal governments are under increasing pressure to hold the line on health spending. This will probably result in less high-cost hospital care and more out-patient facilities. We'll be spending smarter, not more. As we get older, we'll have to make tough choices about how to spend our health care dollars, but there's no evidence this will be any more of a burden to future generations.

That's not to suggest that we will be able to afford all the rich social programs we've come to expect over the last few decades. If we don't increase our savings rate, if technology stagnates, or productivity remains stubbornly low for whatever reason, then an aging population will threaten our standard of living. If that happens, we may have an intergenerational conflict on our hands as the young come to resent the generous pension and social entitlement programs of their elders. That doesn't have to be the case. Policies that encourage savings and investment, along with immigration limits, should help us avoid the burdens of an aging population.

KEY TERMS

Tax base	Labour force	Fertility rates
Intergenerational conflict	Retirement Savings Plan	
Fallacy of composition	(RSP)	

REVIEW QUESTIONS

1. Why are the young worried that they will be stuck with a larger tax bill in the future given an aging population? Is this scenario inevitable?

2. How does an economy react to a shortage of labour? Does a smaller work force always indicate a poorer economy? (Keep in mind the role of productivity and capital/labour substitution.)

3. Given that fewer young people are entering the labour force over the next decade, what are some government policies that could counter the trend of a shrinking labour force?

4. Labour is much like any other commodity, the less there is, the higher its price. Using supply and demand diagrams, how does this fact almost guarantee that labour force shortage may not be as great as anticipated?

DISCUSSION QUESTIONS

1. What are some of the more important scientific and technological discoveries in the past two decades that have had an impact on productivity and economic growth?

2. Do workers become less or more productive the older they get?

3. Many people of the so-called Generation X blame the baby boomers for a lack of jobs in the economy. Are they justified in their criticism of the older generation?

4. What could happen if the young shoulder a bigger burden of social programs in the event that the economy doesn't create enough wealth?

NOTES

1. "Generation Xers" have some basis to be resentful of baby boomers. Canada's generational accounts show that those aged 25 in 1991 can expect to pay net payments of $219,000 each to the government over the remainder of their lifetimes. Those aged 50 in 1991 can expect to make net payments to the government of only $28,000 over the rest of their lives. Source: Christopher Good, "The Generational Accounts of Canada," *Fraser Forum* (August 1995).

2. During the 1980s, investment in capital increased over 100 percent to $47 billion, but we had to wait until the 1990s to see any impact on productivity. It seems that all that investment in computer technology is paying off with higher worker productivity.

3. Professor Laurence Kotlikoff, an economist at the University of Boston, worries that unless baby boomers (including "Generation X") save more, they will end up with a much poorer future. Compared with their parents, baby boomers can expect to retire earlier, live longer, rely on less inheritance, receive less help from their children, and pay higher taxes. Source: *The Fortune Encyclopedia of Economics,* ed. David R. Henderson (New York: Warner Books, 1993), p. 235.

4. For a fascinating discussion of growth and software, read "Economic Growth and Investment in Children," *Daedelus,* Vol. 123, No. 4 (1994).

5. "The Economics of Aging: Why the Growing Number of Elderly Won't Bankrupt America," *Newsweek,* 12 September 1994.

6. Jac-Andre Boulet and Gilles Grenier, *Health Expenditures in Canada and the Impact of Demographic Changes on Future Government Health Insurance Program Expenditures,* Discussion Paper 123, Economic Council of Canada, Ottawa 1978. In another study, Canada's chief statistician arrived at roughly the same conclusion. In his study, "Can We Afford an Aging Population?" Ivan D. Fellegri said that, "... should long-term economic growth continue as it has in the past and unit costs evolve as assumed, then public spending in health, education and pensions would represent 50 years from now about the same claim on the economy as present in spite of the aging of the population." See Ivan D. Fellegri, "Can We Afford an Aging Population?" *Canadian Economic Observer* (October 1988).

WEBLINKS

www.hrdc-drhc.gc.ca/isp/
Old Age Security and the Canada Pension Plan.

www.statcan.ca/Daily/English/970729/d970729.htm
Statistics Canada: The working-age population is greying.

www.informetrica.com/prodserv/mer/mer1409a.htm
Canada's rank on the United Nations' Human Development Index.

www.uottawa.ca/academic/med/epid/pub.htm
The Canadian Study of Health and Aging.

EXAMINING THE GST

13

"The GST is a bad tax."

No one likes paying taxes and the GST is no exception. Despite its unpopularity, the GST is better than the Manufacturers' Sales Tax (MST) it replaced. The MST put an unfair burden on Canada's manufacturing sector. The GST applies to a wider range of products and follows more closely the two basic principles of taxation: equity and efficiency. What the designers of the GST did not anticipate was how unpopular the new tax would be, and how expensive it would be to implement.

Nobody likes taxes, but, perhaps the most universally despised and misunderstood is the **Goods and Services Tax (GST)**. It has been described as a tax only an economist could love. Consumers now pay taxes on services (as well as goods), something they never had to do before 1991.

Critics of the GST have argued that the tax would fuel inflation, tax the poor more than the rich, cost the government millions to administer, and slow economic growth, to say nothing of the pain and anguish it would cause everyone while adjusting to it. Even an increase in cross-border shopping in the mid-1990s was blamed on the GST. Despite the arguments and evidence to the contrary to most of these claims, the conventional wisdom persists that the GST was a bad idea and that we would have been better off leaving things the way they were. What many forget is that things were not that good with the earlier federal sales tax, or **Manufacturers' Sales Tax (MST)**, which the GST replaced. The GST is a 7 percent sales tax that applies to a wider range of products, replacing a tax that carried a higher rate but covered a narrower range of products. There are some exceptions. The GST does not apply to some groceries, agricultural and fish products, prescription drugs and medical devices, track betting, day-care services, financial and educational services, and long-term rents. (In the fiscal year 1998/99, 50.3 percent of all federal revenues came from personal income taxes, while employment insurance premiums and the GST both brought in about 14 percent of all federal revenues.)

The one advantage of the old tax was that we didn't see it because it was buried in the prices of the goods we purchased. And because we didn't see it, we assumed someone else paid for it. But everyone who bought manufactured goods paid the MST, even in Alberta, the only province that doesn't have a sales tax other than the GST. The truth is that the old MST was doing serious damage to the economy.

GOOD AND BAD TAXES

The first thing to understand is what constitutes a good tax. To most people, a "good tax" is an oxymoron. Nonetheless, governments have to raise money somehow. The question is, what's the best and fairest way to do so? On this question governments should follow two principles when considering raising taxes: the **equity principle** and the **efficiency principle**. The first has to do with making sure that the tax burden falls mainly on those who can afford to pay more, while the second simply means that the tax should not disturb the existing condition of the economy. In other words, a tax should not distort our buying patterns, or change our incentives in order to favour one good or service over another. This is known as tax neutrality. For example, if the rate of tax is higher for clothing than for movies, consumers will tend to buy fewer clothes and see more movies, thus giving an artificial incentive toward investing in services and away from goods production. For the economy to work efficiently, the decision about how society allocates its resources should be left to the consumer and not be distorted by the tax system. It should be appreciated that the principles of equity and efficiency are often in conflict. More equity often means more inefficiency, while an efficient tax may be inequitable. The challenge for policy advisors is to find the right balance. In any event, tax experts had been calling for the replacement of the MST for years because it was a bad tax on both counts.

Just because the MST applied to manufactured goods does not mean that manufacturers paid for it. Like most taxes, they were passed along to the consumer without regard to questions of fairness, thus violating the equity principle. In the language of economics, the federal sales tax was a **regressive tax**, which means that the poor pay a higher proportion of their income than the rich.

The federal sales tax also distorted consumption preferences, thereby violating the efficiency principle. The MST rate of 13.5 percent was applied to a narrow range of manufactured goods while services generally avoided any sales tax. In effect it changed relative prices between goods and services, making manufactured goods more expensive in relation to services. It's not surprising that consumers tended to buy more services at the expense of manufactured products. But was that enough of a reason for the Conservative government under Prime Minister Brian Mulroney to introduce a tax consumers were bound to hate? According to many tax experts, the answer was yes.

THE BURDEN OF TAXES AND THE BENEFITS OF THE GST

Taxes are a burden on the economy in two ways: First is the direct cost of compliance, which means the amount of time and money businesses spend on filing, keeping books, and accounting procedures. The second burden is the indirect cost known as the **dead-weight loss** to the economy caused by making the economy less efficient. In the latter case, as prices increase because of taxes, manufacturers produce below optimum output levels. Under the old MST, the government knew it was too expensive in terms of lost jobs and higher costs (see Figure 13.1). In other words, any tax discourages output by causing a fall in production. In some cases, the cost of compliance was as high as 26 percent of total taxes paid by small firms.[1] It's hard to estimate how many jobs were lost because of sales taxes on manufacturing, but it's safe to say they were in the tens of thousands. For example, in 1995 the Bank of Canada came out with a study estimating that Canada lost over 130,000 jobs in the early 1990s because of higher payroll taxes alone. Under the new GST, all goods and services are subjected to a 7 percent tax, with some exceptions as stated above.

One might wonder whether the gain in efficiency from lowering taxes on goods is not cancelled out by the dead-weight loss from the new tax on services. The simple answer is no. The reason for this is that the deadweight loss arising from a tax increases more quickly in proportion to the scale of the tax itself. A broader, but lower tax rate is better than a higher, but narrower tax rate because the former encourages more production than the latter. Most economists assumed that the GST would have a smaller dead-weight loss per dollar of revenue raised because its rate of taxation is lower than the MST.[2]

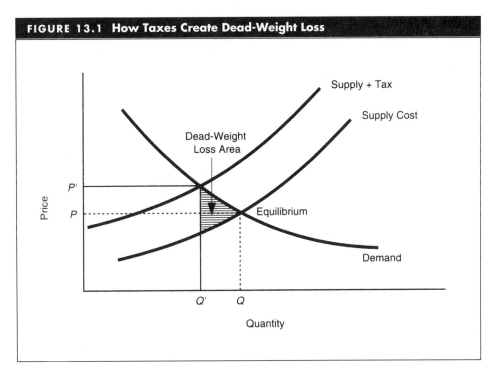

FIGURE 13.1 How Taxes Create Dead-Weight Loss

Note: A tax causes a leftward shift in the supply curve and a new price–quantity equilibrium from *PQ* to *P′ Q″*. At the new equilibrium, consumers pay a higher price with less output. But there is also a "dead-weight loss" represented by the triangle made up of a loss in **'consumer'** (upper part of the triangle) and **'producer' surplus**.

These are not the only benefits of introducing the GST. One of the major challenges facing governments is to encourage more investment in order to improve productivity, competitiveness, and employment. Instead of helping matters, the manufacturers' sales tax was discouraging investment for manufactured goods. The manufacturing sector was actually shrinking, in part because of the distortions caused by the former tax. Our antiquated tax system was unwittingly making Canada less competitive by taxing investment.[3] To make matters worse, the federal sales tax also tended to favour imports, taxed exports, and was costly and complicated to administer.

This was nothing new. Since 1940, numerous tax studies had recommended that we get rid of the MST. We had to wait over 50 years for something to be done. It was estimated that by replacing the MST with the GST, the economy would add as much as $10 billion to annual output. By lowering the tax on manufactured goods, the government has reduced the dead-weight loss on the taxation of goods production.

Politicians persisted with the old tax mainly because it was politically expedient. By 1991, the MST was bringing in over $18 billion a year. To compensate for the high taxes in manufacturing, the federal government implemented numerous tax write-offs and exemptions for businesses. By the end, the MST applied to only 75,000 firms, with over 22,000 special rules and exemptions. The real winners during the era of the manufacturers' sales tax were the army of tax lawyers and accountants hired to find tax loopholes for corporations.

The tax was eventually changed in an attempt by Ottawa to find a way to make our industries more internationally competitive. Other countries had already implemented or were moving towards a **value-added tax**, such as the GST, that taxed consumption rather than production. (The United States is the only major country that does not have some form of value-added tax.) After NAFTA was signed, it was time to reduce the tax burden on the goods-producing sector of the economy.

WHY WE HATE THE GST

Although the reasons why the GST was introduced are valid, they still didn't impress the average Canadian. Questions were asked such as, "Won't the GST be inflationary?", "What's to keep the retailer from keeping prices the way they were and pocketing the differences?", and "Won't the tax affect the poor more than the rich?" The answer in each case is no.

The first, and biggest, fear about the new tax was that it would be inflationary. There was an increase in prices when the tax was introduced in January 1991, but that was a one-time increase. The consumer price index went up 2.4 percent for January. At that rate, inflation would have gone up about 30 percent for the year if it had continued, but it didn't. Inflation for the year was 5.6 percent and only half of that was due to the GST. For inflation to exist, the rate of price increases has to rise over an extended period of time. By 1999, the rate of change in the consumer price index was the lowest level in 30 years. Clearly, the GST wasn't inflationary. What did change, of course, were relative prices. With the removal of the MST, the price of services went up and those of goods tended to go down.

The second major concern was that the supplier or retailer would not pass on the savings from the elimination of the MST to the consumer. But consider the following: many retailers selling appliances, for example, have two objectives, making money and keeping or increasing market share. If they had their costs reduced by 13.5 percent because of the removal of the MST, and then added a 7 percent GST, their prices should have dropped by 6.5 percent. If they did not pass on those savings to the consumer, it would not have taken long for competitors to get more business by lowering prices. In theory, competition would guarantee that cost reductions would be passed along to the consumer. Because of the recession, when the GST was introduced, many retailers absorbed the new tax outright. Even though the GST is essentially a tax on consumption, who pays the tax depends on the bargaining power between buyer and seller.[4] Besides, if consumers are truly price insensitive, businesses do not have to wait around for tax reductions to raise prices if they want to make more money. Sellers always have the option to increase their prices if the market will bear it.

The third concern was that the poor would be affected more than the rich with a tax no one can avoid. In other words, the GST is a regressive tax, breaking the principle of equity. The federal government tries to mitigate this, however, by giving a rebate of up to $76 four times a year to low income earners. This compensates for the regressive nature of the tax.

One criticism of the GST is valid: it is more complex and expensive to implement than first realized. In fact, Canada's GST may be the most complex value-added tax in the world according to some Canadian tax experts.[5] The main reason was that many provisions were built in to help alleviate the cost to small businesses, nonprofit organizations, charities, the "MUSH" (municipality-university-school-hospital) sector, real estate, and financial institutions, along with exemptions to basic groceries. The more exemptions to the tax, the more complex it became. When this system was introduced to over two million firms, many facing retail sales taxes for the first time, complying with the new tax became a burden. In time, however, these costs have come down as firms adapted to the complexities.[6]

The Department of Finance has estimated that the start-up costs and administration of the tax were about $700 million for 1990. This probably underestimates the cost of getting the program off the ground as thousands of businesses spent time and money learning the new system. However, as we've already seen, the manufacturers' sales tax was also expensive to administer.

HAS THE GST DONE ITS JOB?

Now that we have some experience with the new value-added tax, we can ask if it has performed the way it was intended and it seems, so far, that it has. Consumer prices did jump when the tax was introduced, but continued to rise only moderately throughout 1991. On the other hand, prices for machinery, equipment, and other investment goods went down. The bad news is, however, that spending in services and the retail sector has gone down as the cost of services went up in relation to manufactured goods. Both of these developments were anticipated with the new tax. On the negative side the federal government made the tax too complicated, which resulted in massive foul-ups and errors by first-time filers. In hindsight the government should have avoided exemptions to the tax, which were made in response to lobbying by special interest groups. It would have been better to reduce the overall rate, allowing fewer exemptions or none at all. Another glaring error was the refusal of the provinces to blend their sales taxes into the GST when it was first introduced, thereby making tax collection more difficult than it need be.

However, by 1997, Quebec had managed a partially blended tax, while Nova Scotia, New Brunswick, and Newfoundland have all blended their sales taxes with the GST. Other provinces should follow suit in the coming years.[7] And although the GST is considered one of the most complex and expensive taxes to administer, these costs are also declining. But despite all the adjustment costs and its unpopularity, the GST is better than the tax it replaced—and because it brings in $20 billion annually, it's sure to stay around a while.[8]

KEY TERMS

Goods and Services Tax (GST)	Equity principle	Regressive tax
	Efficiency principle	Value-added tax
Manufacturers' Sales Tax (MST)	Dead-weight loss	

REVIEW QUESTIONS

1. Governments try to follow the principles of equity and efficiency when imposing taxes. What are the objectives of each of these principles?

2. Define the dead-weight loss of a tax on society and explain how it changes depending on the elasticity of the demand curve. Why do governments tend not to tax commodities that have elastic demand curves?

3. One of the major worries about the GST and the elimination of the MST, was that businesses wouldn't pass the savings of a lower tax on to the consumers, and would pocket the difference themselves. Why is this unlikely to happen?

4. How was the old federal sales tax damaging to Canada's manufacturing sector? How did this tax unwittingly discourage investment and encourage imports?

5. The GST is often called a regressive tax. What does this mean? What can be done to make the tax fairer?

DISCUSSION QUESTIONS

1. "People don't mind paying taxes as long as they don't see them." Is that true? If so, what does it say about the design of taxation policy in Canada?

2. Do you believe the GST has led to a larger underground economy? What are ways people avoid paying this tax? What should governments do about it?

3. What are the benefits and disadvantages of blending the GST with provincial sales taxes?

NOTES

1. Richard Bird, David Perry, and Thomas Wilson, *Tax Reform in Canada: A Decade of Change and Future Prospects,* Discussion Paper No. 1, International Centre for Tax Studies, University of Toronto, November 1994.

2. The extent of the dead-weight loss depends on the elasticity of demand of the goods that are being taxed. The more elastic the demand curve, the higher the dead-weight loss. That's one reason governments tend to tax products with inelastic demand curves, such as tobacco and alcohol, rather than those with elastic demand curves, such as fruit juice and toys.

3. In 1989, the Economic Council estimated that despite tax credits to offset taxes on manufactured goods, the average tax on investment was still about 4 percent. See William Watson and Andrew Coyne, "Special Report: The GST," *The Financial Post,* 19 December 1989.

4. Even a monopolist would lower prices with a tax cut if it wanted to maximize profits. A lower tax means a lower marginal cost, and profits are maximized where marginal cost equals marginal revenue (MC = MR).

5. Ibid., Bird, Perry, and Wilson, p. 28.

6. Some have claimed that the GST has created a bigger underground economy. There is some validity to this claim, but little work has been done to estimate the taxes lost to the GST. However, the GST may also have brought some underground activity into the open. Firms can only get a refund on the GST if they file for one. Once a firm files, they cannot claim for credits on their purchases while avoiding taxes on their sales.

7. There is a debate about whether blending the GST with provincial sales tax is a good idea. Some argue that blending the taxes may be more efficient, but it also makes it easier for governments to raise taxes without consumers noticing.

8. In the federal election of 1997, the federal Liberals promised to scrap both the GST and NAFTA agreements. Since then, Prime Minister Jean Chrétien has become a strong supporter of both.

WEBLINKS

www.ccra-adrc.gc.ca/menu/EmenuHDA.html
Canada Customs and Revenue Agency: GST.

www.fin.gc.ca/gstove/gstov5e.html
Finance Canada: Towards Replacing the Goods the Services Tax.

www.dtonline.com/taxref/trcontax.htm
Introduction of a VAT in the U.S.

www.fin.gc.ca/toce/1996/HSTTOC-E.html
Department of Finance: Harmonized Sales Tax.

TAXES AND THE QUALITY OF LIFE

C h a p t e r

14

 **MYTH** *"Higher taxes mean less work (and vice versa)."*

High taxes have always been recognized as a disincentive to work harder. The higher the marginal tax rate on income, the less effort is made to earn an extra dollar of income. On the basis of that logic, the Reagan administration in the United States lowered taxes to increase work effort, believing it would lead to more economic growth and ultimately more government revenue. The experiment failed largely because the incentives to work harder and earn more were not well understood. What looks good in theory doesn't always work in practice. That's why it is difficult to design taxes for low income Canadians that encourage more work effort rather than less.

In 1981, the Reagan administration in the United States conducted one of the biggest social and economic experiments in modern times. Their Roth–Kemp tax bill, which cut taxes by 25 percent, was based on the simple notion that people hate taxes, and that if taxes were cut, people would work harder because they could keep more of what they earned. If people earn more, they in turn will save more, invest more, and start more businesses to the advantage of the entire economy. This **supply side economics** came to be popularly known as **Reaganomics**. The logic of the theory was impeccable. Supply siders maintained that the higher the marginal tax rate, the lower the amount of effort put out by workers. Why work harder if the government takes proportionally more of each dollar earned? The result was, therefore, obvious: if the government wanted people to work harder, all it had to do was lower taxes.

From there it is a short step to conclude that if people work harder, governments will benefit with higher revenues. Everyone wins: the taxpayer with lower taxes, governments with richer coffers, and the economy, in general, with a fiscal shot in the arm. The Reagan advisers predicted that with lower taxes, the government would be able to balance its budget by 1983 and still spend billions to build up its military. What could be more sensible and straightforward? There was only one problem. It didn't work.

Government revenues didn't increase, while the U.S. national debt doubled. What happened? How could such logic and common sense have failed so miserably? The Reagan government discovered what most theoreticians have known for a long time. What looks good on paper does not always work in practice. Workers when offered higher wages, might work harder but not always and not under all conditions.

INCOME VERSUS SUBSTITUTION EFFECT

To understand why Reaganomics didn't work, we have to look at the choices or trade-offs between labour and leisure. Think of leisure as any other good in that it produces what economists call *positive utility.* Given that each day has a fixed number of hours, we can only increase our leisure time by working fewer hours. To get more leisure, we give up more work. There's an implicit trade-off between work and play. When we have a trade-off between these two goods, the opportunity cost of leisure time is measured in lost income. Put another way, the opportunity cost of leisure is the sacrificed goods and services that extra income can buy. If a net wage is $15 an hour, an extra hour of leisure will cost $15, or the things $15 can buy. Taxes decrease the opportunity cost of leisure. The higher the tax, the less expensive it becomes to substitute leisure for work. This is known as the **substitution effect**.

A proportional tax rate reduces the opportunity cost of labour by an equal amount. For example, if a worker earns $15 an hour, a 33 percent tax rate will reduce labour income to $10. A progressive tax rate takes a bigger and bigger bite out of labour income, which reduces the opportunity cost of leisure time even more. Both proportional and progressive taxes reduce the opportunity cost of leisure but by different amounts depending on the hours worked. In the final analysis, the higher the tax, the cheaper leisure becomes. The less expensive commodities are, including leisure, the higher the demand.

The implications for tax policy seem straightforward. When taxes go up, people will work less because leisure time becomes less expensive. If that is true, it should also hold that a reduction in taxes, whether proportional or progressive, will encourage more work as people substitute work for leisure. This is because the opportunity cost of leisure goes up. Economist Arthur Laffer, one of Reagan's advisers, concluded that tax cuts would actually increase government revenues as more workers chose to work and earn more. The relationship between government revenues and taxes was captured in what came to be known as the **Laffer curve** (see Figure 14.1). However, Laffer overlooked another effect going on at the same time: the **income effect**.

It is true that as wages go up, or taxes fall, more labour is offered, but there is a limit, and that is when the income effect starts to occur. As people earn more income, they feel richer and their demand for *all* goods and services goes up, including the demand for more leisure time. Just because someone receives more money does not mean that they will put in more hours of work. There comes a point when the income effect overrides the substitution effect and less labour is supplied as income increases. In this case, if marginal tax rates are decreased more and more, it will eventually cause workers to put in fewer hours rather than more, contrary to what supply side theory tells us. American companies found this out when they started large-scale developments in Algeria after that country's independence from France was gained in 1962.[1] Algerian wages then were only about one-tenth those in the United States. To encourage more work, the U.S. companies paid Algerian workers one-third of the U.S. wage rates or three to four times the average wage in Algeria. Supply side economics would have predicted that higher wages would encourage more work; however, the opposite happened because workers could now afford to buy larger amounts of leisure time. (It is actually possible that people will work *more* in cases where taxes are raised as people try to maintain their previous standard of living.) These results are not unique to Third World countries. It has been shown that people do not respond to changes in after-tax pay rates. There is actually a tendency for work effort to decline slightly. Many people have an optimum level of income, and higher after-tax pay reduces the number of hours needed to earn that income.

It is not enough to know what people might or might not do under certain conditions. We need to know "how much less" or "more" they will work. The question is essentially quantitative and not subject to theory alone. If taxes are cut by 25 percent, tax revenues will go down by the same amount if nobody works any harder. It has been estimated for the United States, that if taxes were cut for those in the lower tax rate category, the poor would have to increase their work effort by two and one-half times the percentage increase in after-tax wage rates for the government to collect the same amount of tax. In other words, for governments to replenish tax

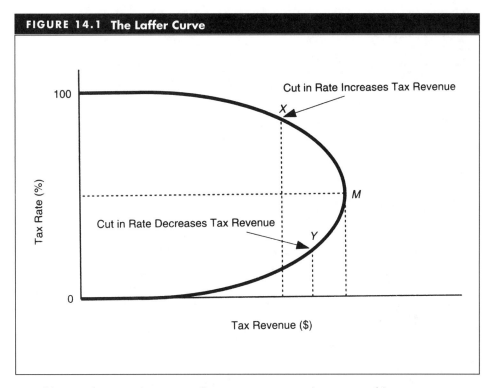

FIGURE 14.1 The Laffer Curve

Note: If the tax rate is at *X*, reducing taxes will increase tax revenues to the point at *M*. If the tax rate is at *Y*, a tax increase will bring in more revenues. The optimal tax rate is at *M*.

revenues from a tax cut, it takes an extraordinary amount of work effort.[2] After all, if people are already working an eight-hour day, how much more will they work if tax rates decrease? Supply side advocates underestimated exactly how much work that would be. Besides, how people change their work effort in response to changes in wages depends on their occupation, age, sex, and a whole range of other factors that are difficult to measure.

However, Professor Martin Feldstein of Harvard University has estimated that, if income taxes were raised by 10 percent across the board for all income earners, government revenues would only go up by $21 billion (U.S.)—a far cry from the $65 billion (U.S.) if no one changed their work behaviour. In other words, the dead-weight loss of such a tax increase would be $44 billion (U.S.). (See Chapter 13 for dead-weight loss.) Conversely, Feldstein estimates that a 10 percent tax cut would generate benefits that far exceed the shortfall in government revenue. And the higher or more progressive the income tax structure, the larger the dead-weight loss of taxes. It seems that President Reagan's tax cuts weren't wrong, they were just too extreme.[3]

POVERTY AND LESSONS FROM SUPPLY SIDE ECONOMICS

What does this mean for Canada? We can apply some of the lessons learned from the supply side economics experiment to the idea of introducing a **negative income tax,** or a **guaranteed annual income (GAI)** in order to eliminate poverty and bring efficiency and equity to the tax structure without, at the same time, destroying the incentive to work. At one point or another, all of the three major political parties in Canada have endorsed overhauling the way we help the poor by supporting some system of negative income tax. The Macdonald Commission in 1985 proposed revamping the social security system in favour of a Universal Income Security Program. A plan for a guaranteed annual income, based on a negative income tax, has been around for years.

The negative income tax plan is structured on the idea that instead of having an inefficient system of welfare and income support programs to help the poor, we should reform the existing tax system by giving the poor a minimum income and, therefore, make a substantial effort to eradicate poverty. A negative income tax works as follows: If a family earns no income, they would get a "negative income tax" or annual payment of, say, $10,000. If that same family earns $1,000 in income, this family would get a negative income tax of $9,500. If they were not allowed to keep more of their income, there would be no incentive to work for that extra income. A family earning $10,000 would receive $5,000 from the government, bringing their total income to $15,000. In other words, people below some break-even point (for example, $20,000) would be allowed to keep half of what they earn. After $20,000, workers would pay "positive taxes" on their income. Simply giving low-income families, or individuals, a lump sum to bring them up to the poverty line would wipe out any incentive to work. If everyone is guaranteed $20,000 off the bat without any incentive to work, why would anyone bother to earn anything below that amount? The working poor would be better off quitting their jobs and going on social assistance.[4]

The purpose behind the negative tax scheme is to eradicate poverty without destroying the incentive to work. That is the theory, but how does it work in practice? As with most economic and social questions, the answers are not so clear or obvious. The results of studies in the United States are disappointing. Negative income tax ended up making people work less. In some cases, the disincentive to work increased almost 60 percent.[5]

In Canada in the mid-1970s, the federal government paid $17 million to over 1,000 families in Manitoba to test the idea of a negative income tax and its effects on work incentives. The program was called The **Manitoba Basic Annual Income Experiment**, or **Mincome** for short, and took about 20 years to complete. The findings from Mincome are not as discouraging as those in the United States. There is still a tendency for people to choose more leisure than earn more income, but its impact is small.[6] Negative income taxes do not discourage work as much as some might imagine, but they do not seem to encourage much work effort either; however, there are advantages. A negative income tax is less costly to administer and is certainly fairer than the system we now have to transfer income to the poor.[7] The current way we transfer money to the poor is so inefficient that we spend $9 to move $1 between classes. Canadian governments spend $300 billion a year on social programs, but only $13 billion is sufficient to bring up to the poverty line all Canadians who are currently below it.[8] The real beneficiaries of Canada's income distribution programs are the middle class. Those earning between $60,000 to $70,000 get about $12,200 in government benefits compared to $9,700 for those earning less than $20,000.[9]

APPENDIX: IS A SINGLE OR FLAT TAX THE ANSWER?

We have made the argument that we never know how taxes will affect the incentives to work. However, over the last few years there's been a growing interest in replacing our current income tax system, based on progressive taxes, with a **flat** or **proportional tax**. Economists have argued that our system of collecting taxes is complicated, unfair, and expensive. Our tax system is so riddled with loopholes, exemptions, and inconsistencies, that increasing marginal tax rates doesn't mean a bigger tax base. A flat tax may actually be a better tax if it discourages tax evasion and avoidance. In the process, it may actually help get the incentives pointed in the right direction.

That's the hard lesson of the last two decades as countries confronted the limits of tax increases. From 1980 to 1998, over 55 nations had reduced their top marginal tax rates, not as a benefit to the rich, but because they were doing serious damage to their economies. By early 2000, the federal government and almost all the provincial governments have moved in the direction of lower taxes—the first time taxes have been cut in over a generation. In Ontario, the government of Mike Harris cut Ontario income tax over 30 percent in the late 1990s, while managing to eliminate the deficit in 1999. The federal government, under finance minister Paul Martin, also announced tax cuts for individuals and businesses in his year 2000 budget.

Rather than cut income taxes or business taxes on an ad hoc basis, some have suggested that Canada adopt a flat tax. This has already become the policy position of the Canadian Alliance party as it proposes a 17 percent flat rate for all income earners. Even some members of Parliament, such as Liberal member Dennis Mills, have advocated a flat tax. The flat tax has considerable support and momentum in the United States.

The main argument for a flat tax is that the current system is too expensive in terms of compliance costs and slowing of economic growth. Canadians conservatively spend about $10 billion a year simply filing their tax returns. Revenue Canada spends another $2.2 billion keeping 26,000 workers busy administering and enforcing the Income Tax Act. A flat tax should save us at least half that much. And few would mourn the loss of a tax industry that now thrives on a complex tax system. Then there are the dead-weight losses to the economy as people and businesses change their consumption and investment patterns to accommodate higher taxes. Raising a dollar of revenue through taxes decreases the size of the economy by more than a dollar because taxes distort the incentives of businesses and households to work, save, and invest.

It is estimated that the total U.S. tax bill (including compliance and dead-weight losses), is an astounding $593 billion (U.S.) each year. That's twice what the Americans spend on defence. A reasonable estimate for Canada would be that taxes could be costing our economy around $60 billion (U.S.). Even more if you consider that Canada's top marginal rates are higher than those in the United States. Lawrence Kotlikoff of Boston University estimates that switching to a consumption or flat tax in the U.S. would increase real wages by 7 percent and GDP by 8 percent. For Canada, that could mean an economy that's $50 to $60 billion bigger.

A major criticism of a flat tax is that it taxes everyone at the same rate. A progressive tax has always been considered fairer because it taxes the rich at a higher rate than the poor. An extra dollar of income to a rich person was assumed to be of less value to a richer person than to a poorer person. Redistributing income, through the tax system, was therefore seen as justifiable.

However, fairness is a slippery concept. Logic and compassion tells us the rich should pay more than the poor. The question is: how much? To most people, fairness simply means that the rich can't completely avoid paying some taxes. There's little comfort knowing that, in theory, the rich pay high marginal rates. And that's the problem with higher marginal rates, the rich can avoid paying taxes by hiring tax lawyers and accountants to find ways of avoiding taxes. Proportional taxes with no loopholes or exemptions would encourage greater tax compliance by the wealthy. For fixed income workers, knowing that businesses can't write off their box seats at the Sky Dome would help restore some faith in our tax laws.

But how do you protect low income workers through a flat tax? Mainly through generous personal and child exemptions. The Canadian Alliance party in Canada recommends giving everyone a $15,000 personal exemption along with $5,000 for each child. This way a family of four would have to earn $40,000 before paying any income tax. Such a plan would exempt about 62 percent of tax filers. Any income above that level would be taxed at one rate.

A flat tax would also make compliance easier. Most people require professional help to do their taxes. Under a flat tax with few exemptions, individual tax forms would be no longer than a page.

The transition costs to a flat tax won't be cheap. But the key obstacle may be that Ottawa doesn't have the stomach for major tax reform after so much political capital was expended introducing the GST. Another problem is the unavoidable reality of higher taxes for the middle class. Higher tax exemptions for the poor and lower taxes on investment income means more revenue has to come from the middle. It'll be hard explaining to the middle class that they'll have to pay more for the abstractions of a healthier economy. But if the U.S. decides that a flat tax is the way to go, Canada will have little option but to follow if we hope to remain competitive. Canada is already losing thousands of jobs because businesses won't locate here because of our high taxes.

KEY TERMS

Supply side economics
Reaganomics
Substitution effect
Laffer curve

Income effect
Negative income tax
Guaranteed annual
    income (GAI)

Manitoba Basic Annual
    Income Experiment
    (Mincome)
Flat or proportional tax

REVIEW QUESTIONS

1. Define income and substitution effects and describe how they can frustrate the intention of policy makers to increase tax revenues. (Hint: make reference to the Laffer curve.)

2. Do people necessarily work harder when taxes are cut? Even if people wanted to worker harder, what prevents them from doing so?

3. What are flat taxes? What are the main arguments in their favour? What are the problems of introducing a flat tax for Canada?

4. Why are progressive taxes considered fairer than proportional or flat taxes?

DISCUSSION QUESTION

1. Reaganomics or supply side economics was based on the assumption that a tax cut would increase the incentive to work harder. Does this mean that if the Canadian government wanted to increase revenues it should lower the average marginal tax rate?

NOTES

1. Roger LeRoy Miller, Daniel K. Benjamin, and Douglas C. North, *The Economics of Public Issues,* 8th ed. (New York: Harper Collins, 1990), p. 129.

2. Most people with jobs had very little opportunity to increase their hours of work even if they had wished to do so. The problem of encouraging more work effort from an aging

population may be even harder as older workers and those approaching retirement begin to value their leisure time more. See Benjamin Friedman, *Day of Reckoning* (New York: Vintage Books, 1989), p. 242.

3. Martin Feldstein, "Tax Avoidance and the Dead-Weight Loss of the Income Tax," *The Review of Economics and Statistics*, November 1999.

4. That's what happened in Ontario when welfare rates went up 29 percent, in real terms, from 1980 to 1994. Over that time, welfare case loads more than tripled. "High Rates Mere Lure to Welfare, Court Told," *The Globe and Mail,* 15 November 1995.

5. These results come from studies done in Seattle and Denver by Michael Keely and Philip Robbins, discussed in their article "Labour Supply Effects and Costs of Alternative Negative Income Tax Programs," *Journal of Human Resources* (Winter 1978).

6. Derek Hum and Wayne Simpson for the Economic Council of Canada, *Income Maintenance, Work Effort, and the Canadian Mincome Experiment* (Ottawa: Supply and Services 1991), p. XVI.

7. A number of provinces, such as New Brunswick, Ontario, and Alberta are experimenting with "workfare" policies that require welfare recipients to do either community service or be in a training program before collecting social assistance.

8. William Watson, John Richards, and David M. Brown, *The Case for Change: Reinventing the Welfare State* (Toronto: C.D. Howe Institute, 1994).

9. According to the Fraser Institute, 47 percent of the electorate are net beneficiaries of the current tax system. Many of the benefits of government spending go to families in the top earning brackets. Patrick Luciani, "Welfare Works, Pigs Can Fly and All We Need Is a Little R&D," *The Financial Post,* May 1994.

WEBLINKS

equity.stern.nyu.edu/~nroubini/SUPPLY.HTM
Supply Side Economics: Do Tax Rate Cuts Increase Growth and Revenues and Reduce Budget Deficits?

www.gmu.edu/jbc/fest/files/Monissen.htm
Explorations of the Laffer Curve.

www.pangea.ca/~cane/gai.html
Guaranteed Annual Income; Mincome.

members.home.net/gilseg/flattax.htm
The Flat Tax: Canadian Social Research Links.

NATIONAL DEBT AND THE FUTURE

MYTH — *"The national debt will bankrupt the country."*

Perhaps the most crucial issue facing the federal government over the 1990s was control of the national debt. The debt had grown so rapidly that Canada had one of the highest debts, as a share of GDP, of any nation in the world. Just paying the interest on that debt had become a serious burden to the country.

Nevertheless, many misunderstand the true implications of a growing debt and deficit believing that the country will soon go bankrupt unless we bring it under control. The real consequence of a bigger national debt isn't bankruptcy but a gradual lower standard of living for everyone.

In 1993, when Paul Martin became the Minister of Finance, he made fighting the growing **national debt** his number one priority. According to the numbers, he had every reason to be worried about Canada's rising financial problems. Many believed Canada was "hitting the wall" with a growing debt crisis. Canada was carrying one of the highest per capita debt loads in the world. In 1981, the per capita debt was $4,500. By 1994, the national debt was over $500 billion, or the equivalent of $18,000 for every man, woman, and child in the country.

And things weren't getting much better. In the early 1990s, the **deficit**, the annual shortfall between tax revenues and expenditures, was growing by over $30 billion a year. The interest on the debt was around $40 billion in 1994–95, which consumed more than one-third of total federal spending. The interest on the debt was more than Ottawa spent on transfers to the provinces, the military, and employment insurance combined. In the early part of the last decade, international investors saw Canada as a risky place to invest. To improve things, the government felt it had to do something drastic to get the debt problem under control. That's why in February of 1995, Martin brought down one of the toughest budgets in Canadian history. And he was determined to do it, not by tax increases, but by slashing government spending.

Conventional wisdom says that unless we buckle down and pay off the debt and deficit, they will remain as millstones around the neck of future generations who will curse us to our graves for accumulating such monstrous debts. But of more immediate concern is that the country would be bankrupt if we continued to spend more than we take in from taxes. Will Canada go bankrupt? Will the national debt be a true burden on our grandchildren? Was the Finance Minister right to crack down on the debt? All these problems are critical. But the reasons why governments must act to control spending aren't as straightforward as many people think. To understand why, let's examine how the debt came to be so big, how to think about it, and what are the real consequences of a growing debt.

THE NATIONAL DEBT: "MY, HOW YOU'VE GROWN!"

There are two main reasons why the debt increased so much over the past three decades: first, increased government spending and second, lower economic growth. Let's start with runaway spending. In the mid-1970s, the federal government reformed unemployment insurance, welfare, and pension plans by indexing them to the level of inflation. As inflation went up, spending on these programs rose automatically (practically guaranteeing future inflation); and as these programs grew, so did government spending. The same decade also saw world oil prices rise dramatically. The government, in order to protect the provinces from increased energy costs, cut energy taxes and increased subsidies to the more energy-deficient provinces through the National Energy Program. The higher energy costs, along with imported inflation from the United States, led to higher prices pushing the inflation rates into the low teens. The government decided to fight higher prices by "cooling off" the economy with high interest rates.

The good times were over, and the suffering began. The higher interest rates created lower demand for goods and services. Personal and business bankruptcies soared and the unemployment rate was over 13 percent by 1983. Interest rates were over 20 percent. The recession, which was caused by fighting inflation, was the most severe since the depression of the 1930s. As the recession set in, government transfer payments to provinces (mainly unemployment insurance) escalated uncomfortably. Since, of course, recessions also mean that less is collected in taxes the government had to borrow money to meet the higher transfer payments by selling bonds. The stage was set for a growing debt crisis. As the recession dragged on, the fastest growing part of government spending was interest payments on the growing debt.

As the economy began to recover after 1983, government revenues began to improve. Instead of showing some restraint, the federal government spent every cent it got and more. The real problem with growing debts was that Ottawa assumed it could go on spending. The government hoped that the economy would keep on growing, providing a bigger tax base. That didn't happen. Taxes as a share of GDP went from 31.5 percent in 1980 to 37.5 percent by 1993. Government finances have been in deficit every year since 1975. By 1994, Ottawa was paying one-third of its budget spending on interest payments. Compare that to 11 percent in the mid-1970s. Every time the interest rate goes up 1 percent, the national debt rises about $4 billion annually. The last time the federal government ran a surplus on its national accounts was in the late 1960s.

One of the themes in this book is the mystery of declining productivity rates since the early 1970s and its implications for our standard of living. We simply weren't creating enough wealth as we once used to and no one knew why. Now we had the worst of both worlds, higher taxes and spending, and an economy that wasn't growing fast enough. Now trapped in a vicious circle, in trying to solve the problem of high prices with high interest rates, the government had saddled the country with a new and more intractable problem. A growing debt that won't go away anytime soon.

Aside from its size, why do so many economists and politicians worry about the debt? First, because Canadians don't save enough, we have to go abroad to finance current consumption. As a portion of GDP, Canada's net foreign debt was almost 50 percent in 1994. Of all **G7** countries, we were first in foreign debt standings. Once, Canadians were capable of borrowing from our own citizens to finance government spending, but now we had to borrow heavily on international markets.[1] The more dependent we are on foreign capital, the more vulnerable we are to rising interest rates. If other countries no longer trust our currency, they may be less willing to finance our debt. New Zealand found itself in that situation in the early 1980s when for a time it could not find a buyer for its government bonds. The second problem is that higher debts mean higher taxes down the road. As the debt goes up so do taxes. In the mid- to late 1990s, things looked pretty bleak regarding the national debt. Economists, the public, and the business community were calling for drastic action to get the debt under control before it bankrupted the country.

HOW TO THINK ABOUT THE DEBT AND DEFICIT

Now that we have a rough outline of what caused the problem, and why some people are worried by it, let's look at how big the debt and deficits really are. It's important to understand the dimensions of the problem before scrambling off to try to solve it. To begin with, most people are overwhelmed by the sheer dimensions of the debt.

However, if we look at the **budget deficit** from another point of view we can more accurately examine its real dimensions. To begin, the deficit is only one year's shortfall between what the government spends and what it takes in from taxes. You could say that the total Canadian debt is the accumulated deficits since Confederation. The nominal deficit is the actual deficit unadjusted for inflation. If we want to know the real deficit, we have to remove the effects of inflation. For example, if prices go up 10 percent this year, and the deficit goes up 9 percent, then the *real* value of the deficit actually drops by 1 percent. In 1989, the nominal deficit was more than 3 percent of GDP, but the *real* deficit was less than 2 percent. In 1981, the federal government actually ran a small surplus, even though the nominal deficit was positive.

Economists also look at the relative size of the debt compared to the GDP. In 1995, the federal debt was around 81 percent of national income. That was a substantial increase from 1975, when it was substantially lower as a share of GDP. By 1999–2000, the debt as a percent of GDP was down to 61 percent. It's anticipated that by 2005 it will be well below 50 percent of GDP. That number will continue to drop as we run surplus year over year and as the size of the GDP goes up.[2] But we've had a heavier debt load in the past. Canada was carrying a debt of over 100 percent after the Second World War (see Figure 15.1). It's not so much the actual size of the debt in terms of dollars that's important, but its size in relation to the whole economy for any given year. It's the same as putting a mortgage on a house. A $400,000 mortgage is large when the value of the house is $500,000, but it looks more manageable when the house appreciates to $1 million. As the value of the nation's assets grows, the relative size of the national debt shrinks. It is the *relative size* of the debt that counts, not the actual size. But even this analogy doesn't take into consideration Canada's true assets. The debt is a measure of liabilities without considering the nation's assets. Who can put a value on the mines, resources, factories, and land, along with the skills and knowledge of the entire population? Whatever that value is, it would certainly dwarf the size of the national debt many times over.

But there are other consequences from the debt that worry economists, such as forcing up interest rates and pushing up inflation. Some argue that deficits put pressure on interest rates. The argument is that there's only so much public and private savings out there, and if governments run high deficits they compete with the private sector for these funds. The higher the demand, the higher the interest rates to attract the needed funding. Economists call this the **crowding out effect**. Looked at another way, the more the government uses up of total national savings, the less there is available for the private sector to invest in plants, technology, and equipment. It sounds plausible in theory, but there's not much evidence to back it up. Another theory holds that it doesn't matter whether the government pays for the deficit through current taxes or borrows by selling bonds. Debt financing or paying for government spending with taxes are equivalent. This theory assumes that people don't make spending decisions based on any one year's income, but on income earned over a lifetime. This **life-cycle hypothesis** assumes people are forward-looking consumers. They know that higher deficits mean higher taxes which means more taxes down the road, so they consume less today in order to pay higher taxes tomorrow. The implication is that the size of the deficit doesn't really matter! Although there's some evidence that this theory may be right, the idea is still controversial and held by a small group of economists.[3]

There are those who argue that inflation is a consequence of high deficits, but that depends on how the government finances the deficit. Here, it has three options: raising taxes, selling bonds to the Bank of Canada (i.e., printing money), or borrowing from the public by selling bonds. The Canadian government traditionally uses this last option mainly because the other two options carry more consequences for the economy. If the government paid the debt with higher taxes, there would

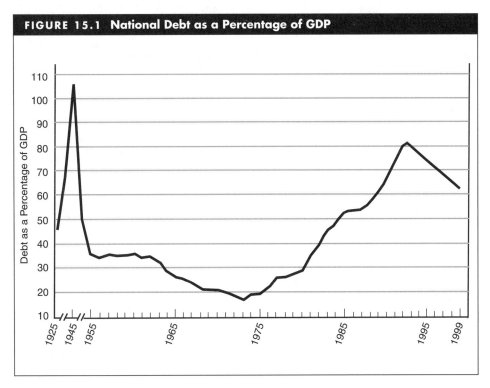

FIGURE 15.1 National Debt as a Percentage of GDP

Source: Department of Finance Budget Papers February 1995; February 2000.

probably be more unemployment because of lower overall demand for goods and services. If it printed more money to pay its debts, the increase in the supply of money would probably result in more inflation. The government borrows to pay its debts because in the short run it doesn't destroy jobs or increase prices.[4]

The next question, of course, is whether we can afford to service the debt or keep up the interest payments. It's important to understand that the actual burden of the public debt is the share of income it takes to carry it; in other words, what percentage of national income goes to paying the interest on the debt. In 1980 it was about 3 percent, by 1994 it was closer to 6 percent. By 2000, this figure was down to about 4 percent. Can we afford to carry the debt? The answer is yes, especially with the growing economy and where spending is controlled. That's the real problem with the growing debt and deficit. With a slow growing economy, more of our national income has to go to servicing the added debt. It becomes easier with a faster growing economy.

Then there is the question of Canada going broke or bankrupt if we don't manage to pay it off. We discussed in Chapter 12 that countries don't go bankrupt like individuals or businesses. If a country defaults on an international loan, as Mexico and other developing countries have done, no one confiscates its roads and factories. These countries find it harder to raise money in the future, creating severe domestic problems. When that happens the **International Monetary Fund (IMF)** extends financial relief, but only under strict conditions that restrict monetary and fiscal policy. In the case of Mexico when it defaulted on its loans in the early 1980s, creditors got together to restructure Mexico's loans and divert more financial problems. A country that defaults on its loans is bad news for both the debtor and creditor.

What about the next generation? Won't they be left to pay off the national debt if we don't get it under control? It's true that debts incurred to help the present generation of taxpayers will have to be paid by taxing future generations. Generation X is already resentful of the baby boomers for running up the debt. But our financial future is not completely bleak. If the government decides to enrich the nation's social security fund with deficit financing, those not yet born will pay higher taxes throughout their income earning years but eventually they will benefit in their retirement years (when their incomes decline) because of the very programs their taxes have supported. When Reagan cut taxes in the early 1980s, it was estimated that a 30-year-old taxpayer would save $12,000 (U.S.) over his or her lifetime. Yet that individual would receive from $10,000 to $15,000 less in today's dollars because retirement benefits were decreased partially to pay for the tax decrease. What seemed like the lifting of a huge burden created a small effect overall.[5] Our children may not be as badly affected as many think. They will inherit the vast richness of this country, including the accumulated knowledge and technology, and fixed capital of past generations—the very things needed to increase future incomes in their lifetimes. Many of those assets are the results of debts incurred by the government today.

However, an uncontrolled and growing national debt can do the economy harm. The main problem with our growing debt is that the discretionary part of the budget is growing slower than the nondiscretionary part. This means that the government is allocating a larger share of tax revenues in areas it has little or no control over such as servicing the debt. This has put at risk some of our social programs such as health, education, social services, and equalization programs. Nondiscretionary funds could have been used to build the nation's capital stock and infrastructure as a foundation on which to increase future per capita income. The more we spend in areas where governments have little control, the less is available for highways, water and sewage systems, and government research and development. Private investment will be discouraged if governments can't increase their spending on **fixed capital formation**. This is the real cost to future generations: we'll have a smaller capital base and a less-developed infrastructure on which to increase our overall standard of living. Most of government borrowing will support current consumption.

Now that we have a better understanding of the problem, how should governments go about handling the debt and deficit? Raising taxes isn't a good idea because it won't eliminate one of the causes of the debt in the first place—unrestrained spending. If the last two decades are any indication, higher taxes simply mean more spending. We also know, from previous chapters, that higher taxes slow economic growth by lowering investment, and that means less wealth and a lower tax base. More borrowing is also a poor option because that simply delays the inevitable. The only real option is to reduce government spending. That doesn't mean getting the debt to zero. That's both economically unnecessary and politically difficult. It also doesn't mean balancing the budget over any given year. The real challenge is to reduce the growth of the debt below the rate of growth of the economy, thereby shrinking the relative size of the debt over time. That's already happening as we enter the new millennium. Governments at all levels are controlling spending while reducing taxes. In the 2000 budget by Finance Minister Paul Martin, tax cuts were announced for both businesses and individuals. This turn of events was thought unimaginable only a few years earlier.

There's no question the debt and deficits are serious, but not because they will bankrupt the country or leave future generations with ever-increasing taxes. The real challenge for governments is to reduce spending on programs that simply sustain high levels of consumption. The real burden of uncontrolled spending is higher taxes and eventually a lower standard of living for everyone.

KEY TERMS

National debt	Budget deficit	International Monetary
Deficits	Crowding out effect	Fund (IMF)
G7	Life-cycle hypothesis	Fixed capital formation

REVIEW QUESTIONS

1. a) What are the main reasons for the growth in the national debt?

    b) What are the major dangers of uncontrolled spending?

2. Explain how future generations both benefit and lose by larger debts?

3. a) "Countries can't go bankrupt like individuals and businesses."

    b) "Higher debts today mean a lower standard of living tomorrow." Explain both comments.

4. What are the pitfalls of financing a growing debt with foreign borrowing?

DISCUSSION QUESTIONS

1. a) In your opinion, what is the best way to get the deficit and debt under control?

    b) How far should the government go in getting the debt under control?

2. In the 1970s and 80s, why was it so hard for the federal government to control spending?

3. The government could easily wipe out the deficit tomorrow if it slashed expenditures by $30 to $40 billion. As Finance Minister, would you take this course of action?

4. For individuals, borrowing to sustain current consumption is a bad idea. Is it a bad idea for governments as well?

5. By the year 2000, governments were for the first time in modern memory running budget surpluses. What happened in the economy in the late 1990s to cause such a change in economic fortune?

NOTES

1. In the 1970s, the Canadian government was able to finance 80 percent of the deficit by borrowing from domestic savings by selling bonds. Because of high Canadian savings, the deficit wasn't as serious a problem because we "owed the debt to ourselves." Both liabilities and assets were owned by Canadians. All that has changed as we come to depend more on foreign savings.

2. Canada's debt to GDP ratio was declining rapidly in an environment of strong economic growth. But much of the credit also has to go to Canada's high income tax rates and growing surpluses in employment insurance. (See Federal Budget 2000 at: www.fin.gc.ca)

3. This view, called **Ricardian equivalence**, is named after the famous nineteenth-century economist David Ricardo, because he first noted the theoretical argument.

4. Some economists argue that even if the government borrows, the results are inflationary. They reason that as the deficit increases, the political temptation to solve the problem by printing money will be too great. The government is simply putting off inevitable inflation by borrowing in the present. So far, there's little to support that case. Even the Nobel economist Robert E. Lucas Jr., at the University of Chicago, no longer believes deficits are inflationary. See Michael Parkin and Robin Bade, *Economics: Canada in the Global Environment,* 2nd ed. (Don Mills: Addison-Wesley, 1994), p. 799.

5. Lawrence Kotlikoff, "Deficit Financing," *The Sciences* (May–June 1989).

WEBLINKS

**www.camagazine.com/cica/camagazine.nsf/publicprint/
Economicoutlook_2000_JunEnglish**
Canada in the recession of the 1980s.

echerchepolitique.rescol.ca/keydocs/oct96rep/05_fiscal-e.htm#key
Key factors in national debt buildup.

recherchepolitique.rescol.ca/keydocs/oct96rep/05_fiscal-e.htm#target
Knowledge a Debt Target?

www.tdbank.ca/tdeconomics/market_analysis/current/ml1223.htm
Better Prospects for Canada's Economy in the Next Decade.

IV

Myths About

Growth and the

Environment

Chapter

ENVIRONMENTAL PROTECTION AND THE LAW

 **MYTH** *"We have a right to a clean environment regardless of cost."*

Environmentalists generally advocate that governments use tougher laws and more regulations to secure a cleaner environment. They argue that because the air and water are free, businesses have no incentives to stop polluting unless governments force them to do so. A more efficient solution to cleaning up the environment is to treat the air and water as any other factor of production. Only then will industry have the proper incentives to economize on their use and reduce pollution in the bargain. In any event, to live is to pollute. The question society has to answer is, how much pollution is it willing to live with and at what cost?

Everyone is talking about cleaning up the environment. Not only are they talking about it, they all want action. This is a far cry from the early 1980s when environmental issues took a back seat to other social and economic priorities. Even corporations are jumping on the "green" bandwagon to help sell their products. There's almost unanimous agreement about the need to reduce waste, cut back noxious gas and chemical emissions, prevent the further erosion of the ozone layer, and clean up lakes and rivers. But are more regulations and tougher laws the answer? Are there other ways to protect the environment at a lower cost to society?

WHY POLLUTION EXISTS

Before answering those questions, it is important to examine why there is a problem in the first place. Conventional thought believes that unregulated markets cannot protect the environment. The theory goes something like this: air and water are "public" or "free" goods—that is, industries and individuals can use up as much as they want because they don't have to pay for them. Polluters don't consider the costs to society (known as **externalities**) resulting from the damage to the environment, just the direct costs of inputs in their production processes.[1] An electricity-producing company worries only about how much it pays in wages, rent, interest, and taxes. It does not worry about how much it costs to clean up sulphur dioxide from burning coal. Why should it? As far as many of these firms are concerned, there's no incentive to do so. The atmosphere isn't like other factors of production. If the price of labour increases, there's a clear incentive for firms to economize by hiring fewer workers and buying more machines. Because the atmosphere is, in a sense, a free good, the total price of producing energy in this case doesn't reflect the cost of a damaged environment. In the long run, society ends up paying the full cost with polluted air and water, greater health problems, and a depletion of wildlife and vegetation. Without government intervention, the argument goes, unregulated free markets are incapable of protecting the environment.

There are a number of possible solutions to the problem. One is for governments to pass laws that restrict certain pollutants. Possibly governments will set a maximum level of allowable pollution, and leave it up to individual companies to develop and pay for the necessary technology to meet these standards. We'll call this approach **command and control.** Industries are commanded by laws and controlled through careful monitoring. Most environmentalists approve of more regulations, along with stringent laws and stiffer penalties, to force industries to cut back on pollution.

Another method, favoured by most economists, is to use market forces to encourage less pollution by putting a price on polluting the environment.[2] The idea, in other words, is to sell industry the **right to pollute**. This is where environmentalists and economists part ways. Environmentalists hold that the market can't be trusted to do the job; economists see the problem as a flaw in the market that can be corrected.

Regardless of which method is used to reduce pollution, we can't get rid of *all* pollution. A pollution-free society is impossible to achieve as long as industrial processes involve the use of raw materials. Legislation and government programs can't change the laws of physics. Economic theory suggests that the more pollution is reduced, the more expensive it is to eliminate. In other words, the **marginal cost** goes up the more pollution we eliminate.[3]

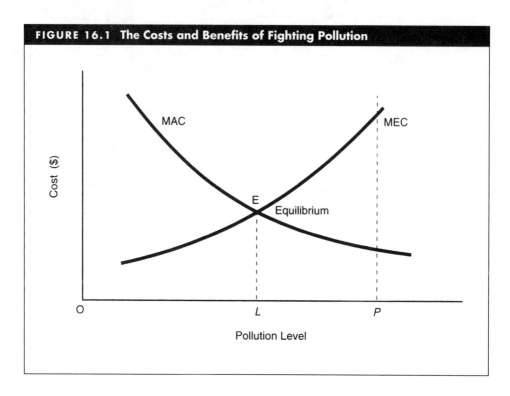

FIGURE 16.1 The Costs and Benefits of Fighting Pollution

Note: The graph above shows the cost of fighting pollution with abatement equipment and the external cost of pollution to our health and environment. The *Marginal Abatement Cost* (MAC) rises the closer we get to zero level of pollution (right to left). The more pollution society produces, the higher the *Marginal External Cost* (MEC) — left to right. At a level of pollution *OP,* pollution is worth fighting because the benefits outweigh the costs. But not for pollution levels less than *OL* where costs are greater than the benefits to society. Where MAC and MEC cross at (E) is known as the *Efficient Level of Pollution.*

Some argue that we should pay any price to get rid of all pollution and to move as close to a zero level of pollution as possible (see Figure 16.1). But what if it costs 50 percent of the GNP to eliminate 90 percent of all air pollution? Is it really worth the price? We might have cleaner air, but less health care, education, or public housing. Suddenly, *"any* price" seems less appealing. We may deserve a cleaner environment, but the extent of it must be based on what we are willing to pay, not on a right to a cleaner environment regardless of cost. The question then becomes, how much pollution are we willing to tolerate and at what price?

WHY ENACTING MORE REGULATIONS DOES NOT ALWAYS WORK

Many environmental activists argue that people have a right to clean air and water regardless of cost. Suppose we take the environmentalist's approach and impose on industry the highest standards regarding water pollution and enforce these standards with tough fines and penalties. Laws may be implemented that threaten executives with jail if their companies pollute, which has been done in the past. But the existence of law is one thing; gaining compliance to it is quite another. For example, more than 25 years after amendments to the Fisheries Act in 1971, only a few pulp and paper mills discharge effluents that are *not* lethal to fish—a direct violation of the intent of the act. Experience shows that if industry believes laws are unfair or too costly, they will fight them in court and their chances of winning are pretty good. Under the Canadian Environment Protection Act (CEPA), which was introduced in 1988, thousands of pollution violations were laid. However, only a few ever resulted in convictions. The CEPA was eventually amended in early 2000 having to admit that its command-and-control approach had failed.

There are many reasons the command-and-control approach is ineffective. Complicated statutes have to be set in place. These could take years to implement. Regulatory agencies have to define precise standards and the best available technology to be used. Governments then have to hire an army of scientists to monitor the regulations and officials to enforce the laws. When cases eventually go to court, government regulators find themselves understaffed and overworked, going up against high paid lawyers representing wealthy corporations. Even when violators are proven guilty, the fines are usually small compared with the damage done to the environment.[4] In short, the process of command and control is unnecessarily adversarial and inefficient, to say nothing of costly. CEPA alone costs the taxpayer about $75 million a year to operate.[5]

SELLING THE RIGHT TO POLLUTE

From an economic viewpoint, the problem can be treated completely differently. Instead of threatening the polluter with penalties, the market can be used to reduce the level of pollution. The market system works in such a way that the government could sell a fixed number of permits to companies that would allow them to discharge a given level of pollutants. A company could pollute up to, but not exceeding, limits specified by the number of permits it is allowed, or is financially able, to buy. Unused permits could then be sold on the secondary market. For example, if the marginal cost (the cost of eliminating an extra unit of pollution) for company A is $500 because it has the latest abatement equipment and $3,000 for company B which doesn't, the first company can make or save money by selling its pollution rights to company B. If the price of the permit is $2,000, company A gains $1,500 ($2,000 - $500) while company B saves $1,000. Total savings to the economy is $2,500 ($1,500 + $1,000). However, if the price is above $3,000, it's less expensive for company B to invest in pollution-abatement equipment, than to buy a permit on the open market.

This system has three basic virtues. First, selling permits encourages firms to save money by reducing their emissions. If a company holds 10 permits but needs only eight, it can sell its remaining permits to a less efficient firm. Second, the system rewards those firms that use the best pollution abatement technology and penalizes those that don't, thereby saving society's resources. Third, if government wants to curtail pollution by 50 percent in a given year, it simply issues half the number of permits the next year.[6] By doing so, it makes unused permits even more valuable, thereby encouraging more companies to install better pollution abatement equipment.[7] Under the existing process of strict government regulation, there's no incentive for firms to clean up more than the law requires. If the law states that a firm can emit 10 tonnes of goo into the river each year, there's no reason for that company to spend a dime to decrease the amount of emissions. This is not so with market incentives.

What happens to less efficient firms with outdated pollution controls? If they're allowed only 10 permits but need 11, for example, they'll have to buy the extra one from a firm that doesn't need it. The price for that extra permit will be determined by the market and the value of the permit will depend on how many were issued in a given period. The less efficient polluter will keep buying permits as long as it's less expensive than to acquire new equipment. Pollution permits, as a result, reward firms that have modern pollution abatement equipment and penalize those that use old technology.

In both the command-and-control approach and the market approach, the objectives are the same: to reduce overall pollution emissions. Under the command-and-control approach, if everyone is required to reduce emissions by 50 percent, it's harder for a firm using the most modern technology to do so than for one with outdated methods because the former's marginal costs are higher than those of a less efficient firm. Regulations tend to reward inefficiency while penalizing pollution-conscious companies. In other words, it provides the wrong incentives. With government controls there are no incentives to clean up more, whereas with permits freely traded on the market, it's in the interest of polluters to become more efficient. With this system, the chances of success are greater. Society wins in two ways: less pollution and added tax revenues from the sale of the permits.[8]

Some environmentalists don't like the economist's solution because it smacks of a right to pollute. They argue that a rich company would simply buy permits to pollute. It could do this if its marginal cost of pollution abatement exceeded the price of the permit. Otherwise, the firm would be acting irrationally. Others believe that free markets don't work, or that firms aren't interested in saving money. There are centuries of experience and evidence to disprove the first criticism, and simple logic to counter the second.

Objections to the market approach will not go away. Some argue that a price tag on air and water cheapens society's view of the environment. Moreover, objectors say, that a clean environment should be considered a right and not simply a way of saving money. To an economist, these lines of reasoning make little sense. What's important are the results. Should society care how the environment is protected as long as we have cleaner air and water.[9] [10]

USING TAXES TO DECREASE POLLUTION

Taxes can have the same results as permits. Some economists make the case that if taxes for each product are set at a level that just covers the social and private costs of production, then you have what is called **allocative efficiency**. In other words, the taxes raised would be spent to clean up the damage done to the environment. With permits, you know exactly how much pollution will result because governments control how many permits are issued. Taxes are a hit-and-miss proposition. If the objective is to reduce chemical emissions by three and one-half tonnes, taxes have to be estimated and firms monitored to gauge how they react to the tax. Taxes are then adjusted accordingly. In theory, the results are similar to permits, but the process is costly and time-consuming.

If issuing permits is such a great idea, why aren't governments moving in that direction? In fact they are. Years of regulatory failure have prompted some governments to change their ways. The U.S. government is using the free market approach by issuing permits to reduce air pollution under their Clean Air Act. The program has been endorsed not only by economists, but by a number of environmental groups as well. The U.S. experience teaches that tradeable permits work. A company that closes down or installs improved pollution-abatement equipment receives **emission credits** that it can sell. Illinois, California, and Wisconsin have set up computer systems to keep track of credits nationwide. More of these central marketplaces will spring up as more states allow companies to pollute only if they have permits. Companies are being allowed to bank these emission permits for sale or use in the future. This gives firms even more economic incentives to reduce pollution levels below what the law requires. Even in the fight to protect the ozone layer under an international agreement called the Montreal Protocol, transferring rights to producers and users of chlorofluorocarbons (CFCs) and halons was the least expensive and most effective way to reduce these emissions. Both Environment Canada and the U.S. Environmental Protection Agency support this approach.[11]

Unfortunately, the Canadian government decided to take a different tack with its 1990 Green Plan. Here it was to spend $3 billion over five years to eliminate 44 toxins and reduce waste by 50 percent by the year 2000 using more regulation and no market incentives. However, by 1995 some of these objectives were modified because of budget constraints. Ontario's Environmental Protection Act has raised the maximum fine for companies that pollute up to $50,000 a day and up to $250,000 a day for hazardous waste. The new act also calls for sending officials to jail if found guilty of willful pollution.[12] Will the plan work? One can only hope so, for the sake of the environment and the taxpayer. If past experience is any indicator, we'll end up with a dirtier environment and a less efficient economy.

APPENDIX: THE ROLE OF PRIVATE PROPERTY

Even though many believe that governments are more far-sighted in protecting the environment than the private sector, that fact hasn't been confirmed in either theory or fact. Many economists now believe that when private property rights are clearly established, the private sector's market-oriented decisions will tend to allocate resources to their highest valued uses across time, while the political and administrative decisions made in the public sector will tend to allocate resources to uses for which current political supporters exert the strongest immediate pressures. That's what we tend to see happening. Private property owners of natural resources often have a stronger interest in preserving those resources than governments do. Politicians behave differently. Because they have to be elected every four years or so, they must satisfy voters at the next election. They are accountable to current voters only, and therefore have a strong incentive to concentrate on the current benefits of their constituents. That's one reason why the cod fisheries have disappeared on the Canadian east coast forcing the federal government to ban all fishing on the Grand Banks. There's no clear ownership of those resources. To get elected, governments allowed fishermen to continue fishing even though they knew of the future dangers of overfishing. Political expediency, in effect, took precedent over conservation. In British Columbia, for example, governments are in a conflict of interest as owners of the forests. They must satisfy the demands of conservationists and loggers simultaneously. This conflict often leads to a **tragedy of the commons**, where a resource is allowed to be overharvested because there are no clear property rights.

KEY TERMS

Externalities	Marginal cost	Emission credits
Command and control	Allocative efficiency	Tragedy of the commons
Right to pollute		

REVIEW QUESTIONS

1. "A clean environment is like any other commodity, the more we want, the more we have to pay for it." Explain that statement.

2. Why isn't it possible to have a completely pollution-free environment?

3. Explain the major differences between the traditional command-and-control approach to protecting the environment compared to more market-oriented solutions. Why are more regulations and laws not always effective in protecting the environment?

4. What are the strengths and weaknesses of using taxes to help decrease pollution emissions?

DISCUSSION QUESTIONS

1. How clean should the environment be? Who decides? How much is it worth?

2. Why are governments not always the best custodians of the environment? Think of examples where governments have been the problem rather than the solution.

3. Even if governments decide to "sell the right to pollute," does that mean the end of public involvement in environmental issues? Under what circumstances does the right to pollute break down?

4. "The collapse of the cod fisheries in Atlantic Canada is a classic case of 'tragedy of the commons'." Comment.

NOTES

1. Economists refer to damage to the environment as externalities, or an added cost to a third party or society. These costs usually arise when there's no private ownership of property; in this case air and water. If there was clear title to the property, the owner could sue for damages. When there's no clear ownership, as with the environment, governments use other means to cope with externalities.

2. Professor Alan S. Blinder in his book, *Hard Heads, Soft Hearts* (Reading, Mass.: Addison-Wesley, 1987), gives a lucid account of the economist's approach to the environment.

3. A U.S. study by the Environmental Protection Agency (EPA) found that it would cost $60 billion (U.S.) to reduce effluent emissions by 85 to 90 percent, and an additional $200 billion (U.S.) to eliminate the remaining 10 to 15 percent. In other words, the "marginal cost" of fighting pollution keeps rising. That's why "zero tolerance," or getting rid of that *"last"* ounce of pollution is neither feasible nor economical.

4. In 1985, Dow Chemical Company of Sarnia was fined a total of $16,000 for four violations for dumping tar into the St. Clair River. This fine was hardly a burden to Dow. Ford Canada was fined $5,000 on three counts of spilling oil into the Detroit River under the Ontario Water Resources Act in 1988.

5. In all fairness, there have been some successes using this approach in Canada. Sulphur dioxide emissions were down substantially over the 1980s and 1990s, but at a cost of $1.5 billion to the taxpayer and industry. Ontario Hydro estimated that it can comply with rigid provincial pollution abatement measures by the year 2000 at a cost of $2.5 billion. The question now arises, can society achieve similar or better results at a lower cost?

6. Who gets to buy the permits can be determined by a number of criteria, including share of output in an industry. The permit system will also be policed, but when a firm is found polluting beyond its limit, it will be fined according to set penalties, with no court action.

7. The market system would not work with highly dangerous toxins. In such cases the only acceptable means of control is a complete ban.

8. It is estimated by the EPA that the United States spends over $70 billion a year on reducing pollution. Studies show that using the market approach could save up to $50 billion without increasing the level of pollution.

9. Odd as it may seem, some industries prefer regulations to free markets when it comes to pollution control. They know their costs under regulations, but not under the pollution permit system. One argument is that they cannot know the value of their permits when it comes time to sell.

10. As a matter of record, it was a Canadian economist, John Dales, who originated the idea of tradeable emission permits in his now famous book *Pollution, Property and Prices*, published in 1968 by University of Toronto Press.

11. Douglas A. Smith, "The Implementation of Canadian Policies to Protect the Ozone Layer," in ed., G. Bruce Doern, *Getting It Green* (Toronto: C.D. Howe Institute, 1990), p. 111.

12. The C.D. Howe Institute has given the Green Plan high marks on intent but low marks on process because it fails to use "market approaches as a complement to traditional regulation." See G. Bruce Doern, *Shade of Green: Gauging Canada's Green Plan* (Toronto: C.D. Howe Institute, 1990), p. 10.

WEBLINKS

www.pollutionprobe.org/
Home page of Pollution Probe.

www.web.net/cela/
Home page of Canadian Environmental Law Association (CEPA).

www.essaydepot.com/sociali/green.html
Green permits.

www.fin.gov.bc.ca/tbs/Green%20Discussion%20Paper.htm
Environmental tax shift.

www.osler.com/publications/dbic/dbcenv.html
Environmental law.

NONRENEWABLE RESOURCES

 **MYTH**   *"We are running out of nonrenewable resources.*

There is a universal anxiety that because the world population is increasing, one day we will run out of nonrenewable resources. It seems obvious that the more the population grows and consumes, the less oil, coal, copper, and other resources there will be for future generations. Therefore, many have predicted dire consequences if we continue to consume at current rates. Surprisingly, that bleak scenario hasn't emerged. Not only are we not running out of nonrenewable resources, but evidence also shows that the known quantity of many nonrenewable resources is actually increasing.

No one can argue with the fact that the world has limited resources. After all, earth's resources are fixed by nature. We therefore live in a finite world. On this point there is no dispute. Yet many people make the false assumption that because we have a limited oil and minerals supply and limited agricultural growing capacity that some day, if we keep consuming as we are today, we'll find we have run out of some vital resource. It only stands to reason that with the world's per capita consumption continuing to rise, especially in the West, and with a growing global population, the well will eventually run dry. Although the first premise of finite resources is true, it is a myth to conclude that the world will run out of any resources whether they are **renewable resources**, such as agriculture produce or **nonrenewable resources**, such as oil and minerals. What will save the earth's resources from being exhausted? The answer lies partly in the working of the **price system**. We will examine why the myth of limited resources is so predominant in our thinking about resources, and then we will discuss how a free market system works to ensure that the earth's resources won't disappear.

IT ALL BEGAN WITH REVEREND MALTHUS

The belief that the world was on a collision course with nature began in the late eighteenth century when Reverend Thomas Robert Malthus predicted that the world's population growth would eventually increase beyond the capabilities of agriculture to feed it, resulting in widespread famine and death. Although his dreaded forecasts did not materialize, that did not stop modern-day Cassandras from following in his footsteps, not the least of which were those who forecast the dire projections of the **Club of Rome** report in 1972. This neo-Malthusian group, made up of European and American academics, used computer models to forecast how exponential economic growth would exhaust the world's resources in the next couple of decades if the rate of consumption remained the same as it was when their report, *The Limits to Growth,* was published. The Club of Rome's report received a lot of publicity and created substantial controversy. Although the forecasts were discredited, the report's notoriety remained. Ironically, the study made the same errors Malthus made. First, it ignored the advance of technology; once this crucial oversight is taken into account, the dire predictions disappear. Second, it failed to take into account the fact that people, industry, and governments change their behaviour when prices rise.

Just prior to this, other pessimists also issued dire warnings. In 1968, Paul Ehrlich, a famous ecologist and professor at Stanford University, wrote in his book, *The Population Boom,* that population growth was outstripping the world's supply of food, fresh water, and minerals. He used the ecological concept of carrying capacity to argue that the earth could support only so much population growth. Again the idea is the same one advocated by the Malthusians. Ehrlich painted a bleak future for the human race if it did not change its ways. He went on to say in his later book, *The End of Affluence,* that due to a combination of ignorance, greed, and callousness, a situation had been created that could lead a billion or more people to starve. He predicted that before the year 1985, mankind would enter a genuine age of scarcity in which "the accessible supply of many key resources will be nearing depletion."[1] He also predicted rising food prices as food production bumps up against the limits of a world with diminishing capacity for more agricultural output. However, the only place where the world has experienced real famine and food shortages is in Africa where these tragedies were caused by political conflicts and government mismanagement. Even India, a country with 1 billion people, hasn't experienced a famine in over 50 years.

Ehrlich remained so sure that the world was using up all its resources that in 1980 he predicted that by 1990 the price of most minerals would rise. In a well-publicized bet with the economist Julian Simon, who predicted the opposite would happen, Ehrlich chose five minerals: nickel, copper, tin, chrome, and tungsten that he felt would rise in price. By the end of 1990, the price of each mineral had fallen in real dollar terms. Simon won the bet.[2]

But we don't have to go back 20 years for dire predictions of natural resource exhaustion. The U.S. Worldwatch Institute, a well-known environmental group, is continually warning of the damages of diminishing resources.

THE PRICE SYSTEM TO THE RESCUE

Why is it that a growing population, an increase in incomes and GDP, and the highest level of consumption ever experienced in history do not come even near to depleting the word's resources? Some argue, as Erhlich does, that we just don't know how much oil, copper, and minerals are in the ground but that prices will rise as we get closer to the limit. A more fundamental explanation, however, originates from the workings of free markets and the price system. Whenever a shortage of a resource is created by an increase in demand, or a decrease in supply, the price of that product goes up. It's a simple matter of supply and demand. That part is straightforward. The interesting thing is how markets react to rising prices. Forecasters who project dire consequences assume we go on consuming regardless of the cost, until the resources disappear. But when prices rise, three things tend to happen in varying degrees to the scarce resource: we consume less, we look for less expensive alternatives, and we search for more. The prediction of the Club of Rome's report wasn't lost on the **Organization of Petroleum Exporting Countries (OPEC)** cartel when they quadrupled the price of oil in the early 1970s from $2 a barrel. In 1979, the price of oil was six times the 1973 level, and energy analysts predicted prices of over $100 (U.S.) a barrel by the end of the decade. What followed should be a lesson to anyone who doubts the working of the price system.

In the short term, little could be done about rising oil prices except to pay the higher bill. In time, oil-dependent nations in the West responded as any rational consumer would by using relatively less expensive, alternative energy forms, such as hydro, natural gas, and nuclear power. As a result, more marginal energy sources (e.g., solar, wind, and methane gas) also came into their own and their relative costs compared to petroleum began to drop. Consumers began demanding smaller, more fuel-efficient cars, became involved in energy conservation, and generally weaned themselves from expensive Middle East petroleum. Industry began adopting more energy-efficient technologies and shutting down wasteful energy manufacturing.[3] Even though GDP consumption per capita rose 21 percent from 1973 to 1986 in OECD countries, energy per capita dropped by 6 percent over the same period. The developed countries were adjusting to higher oil prices. All these actions had the desired effect. By 1986, the real price of oil (after inflation) was at the pre-1973 oil shock level. This stunning turn of events sent OPEC reeling as the **cartel** members broke rank and began undercutting each other hoping to hold on to diminishing markets.

As prices rose during the 1970s, the profit motive kicked in as billions were invested in searching for new oil. In 1970, the known reserves of oil stood at 34.8 years. By 1990, oil reserves increased further to 43.4 years. Natural gas reserves, which are a by-product of oil exploration, also increased from 44.6 years to 58.2 years over the same 20 years.[4] It is estimated that recoverable reserves of all forms of fossil fuels may be 650 times current annual consumption worldwide.[5] Because of these massive reserves, new energy forms, and conservation, the International Energy Agency does not expect the price of oil to go beyond $40 (U.S.) a barrel during the first quarter of the next century. The supply of energy has proven to be much more responsive to price changes than many believed. In the language of economics, the **elasticity of supply** for oil is higher in the long run. The higher the price, the more oil comes on stream, and that means prices cannot stay high for long. In fact, oil is so abundant that gasoline prices in 1998 were substantially lower after adjusting for inflation than at any other time since the late 1940s. Short-term prices will fluctuate, given shifts in supply and demand, but the long-term trend in energy prices is down.

For other resources, the U.S. Geological Survey estimates the known resource bases of gold will last 31 years; mercury, 80 years; tin, 60 years; zinc, 55 years; lead, 41 years; and natural gas, 65 years.

If the price should rise higher, there is still plenty of scope for conservation that will keep the price of energy in check. This is one area where there are substantial gains to be made. One Canadian study found that conservation had big payback for businesses. Companies could save the equivalent of $22 (U.S.) a barrel by investing $13 in energy conservation. Dow Chemical, for example, found that it pays to conserve. In 1988, the company invested around $22 million in over 95 energy-saving projects. That investment earned them a return of 190 percent.

The trend to lower resource prices is such that for at least one hundred years, virtually every natural resource has experienced declining prices. And a drop in prices is a market signal of less, not more, scarcity. Other important facts are that natural resources today are about half as expensive relative to wages as they were in 1980; they are on average three times less expensive today than they were 50 years ago; and eight times less costly than they were 100 years ago.

THE ROLE OF TECHNOLOGY

Aside from the powerful role of price in conserving natural resources, technology is another important factor in making sure we'll never run out of nonrenewable resources. Technology has already reduced the amount of iron ore lost during the mining and smelting process. Likewise, new techniques have also made it economical to force more oil out of previously abandoned wells. The evidence of trends in the prices of natural resources suggests that technology has provided continuing increases in the effective stocks of finite resources.

One can also argue that the billions invested over the years in alternative energy forms, such as nuclear fusion, led to the scientific breakthrough that could one day see a new kind of energy that is inexpensive, clean, and virtually inexhaustible.[6] Because the major fusion fuel, deuterium (an isotope of hydrogen) can be easily extracted from water in endless quantities, fusion could produce far more energy from the "top two inches of Lake Erie than exists in all the earth's known oil reserves."[7] With that promise, we may see the end of the world energy problem within 100 years.[8] Technological advances are also preserving other nonrenewable resources. Where copper once was used to transmit electronic information over great distances, today fibre optics have greater capacity to carry voice and digital information at lower cost. The raw material for fibre optics and semiconductors is common sand, a resource in endless supply. In this sense, there are no finite natural resources.

The main lesson for governments in preserving resources, or encouraging their development, is that prices should be allowed to move freely so that the balance between supply and demand can be maintained. Governments should not intervene in markets under the misguided impression that by keeping the price of a resource below market price it is improving the welfare of its citizens. Consider the cases of Eastern Europe and the former Soviet Union. In their effort to catch up to the West, they kept the price of fossil fuels below the cost of exploration, refining, and distribution. This led to a monumental waste of oil and coal because there was no incentive to economize. In China, the situation is even worse. China uses four times as much energy to produce one unit of GDP as Japan.[9] When nonrenewable resources are kept below world prices through government policy, it leads to waste and inefficiency.

Many people believe that the burst in productivity and increase in our standard of living since the industrial revolution occurred because we have exploited and depleted our natural resources at the expense of future generations. But as we have seen, rising productivity may, in a real and lasting sense, actually augment humanity's stock of natural resource capital.[10] And given that information and knowledge is becoming the most important "natural resource," the capacity for the world to improve its standard of living is almost limitless. Ironically, the price of labour has steadily increased indicating a shortage of people rather than an over abundance. This isn't to suggest the world won't experience periods of resource crises. In the short run, we will always encounter problems where there will be shortages of one resource or another. The long run is a different story. In 1995, Professor Paul Erhlich again challenged Julian Simon to another bet, claiming that population growth will still one day outstrip the earth of its resources and that their prices will inevitably go up. Erhlich believes it is only a question of time. If markets are allowed to function freely, and history is any indication of what will happen, Julian Simon would win the bet again.

KEY TERMS

Renewable resources

Nonrenewable resources

Price system

Club of Rome

Organization of

Petroleum Exporting

Countries (OPEC)

Cartel

Elasticity of supply

REVIEW QUESTIONS

1. When the prices of resources increase, what are the key factors that will ensure we preserve our nonrenewable resources when markets are allowed to work unimpeded? What is the special role of technology?

2. "Only if governments encourage the consumption of resources below market prices will there be a danger that we'll run out of resources." Explain this statement. In your answer refer to the situation in former communist countries.

3. What does it mean for a commodity, such as oil, to be price inelastic in the short run, but price elastic in the long run?

4. How did consumers and businesses in the West adjust and adapt to rising oil prices during the energy crisis of the 1970s? What policy lessons can be drawn from that experience?

DISCUSSION QUESTIONS

1. The dire predictions of Thomas Malthus and Paul Ehrlich of mass starvation have never materialized (except in African nations where starvation is caused by political conflicts rather than world food shortages). Why not?

2. "The only resource that will always be in short supply is intelligence and imagination." Discuss.

NOTES

1. As quoted by John Tierney in "Betting the Planet," *New York Times Magazine* (2 December 1990), p. 76.

2. Ehrlich still thinks that the price of these minerals will increase, but 10 years was not enough time for shortages to make themselves apparent. Simon was still willing to take Erhlich's bet. See John Tierney, "Betting the Planet," *The New York Times Magazine* (2 December 1990), p. 52.

3. Countries that have a higher standard of living tend to encourage those industries that are more energy efficient. For example, an aluminum smelter spends $1.20 on energy for every dollar allocated to wages and capital, while a producer of inorganic chemicals (oxygen or chlorine) spends $0.25 on energy. A computer manufacturer spends only 1.5 cents. OECD countries moved away from energy-intensive industries to more energy-

efficient ones. See "Energy and the Environment," *The Economist* (31 August 1991), p. 130.

4. To put these figures in historical perspective, the world's known oil reserves stood at 100 billion barrels in 1950; by 1970 they had risen to 550 billion barrels, and by 1990, to over 1 trillion barrels. See "Energy and the Environment," *The Economist.* In fact, from 1950 to 1990, we have more known resources of almost all minerals, including iron, tungsten, lead, zinc, tin, bauxite, phosphates, and chromite.

5. The CATO Institute in Washington D.C. predicted in their publication, "Earth Report 2000," that total petroleum reserves at current rates of consumption range from 231 years of conventional production to 800 years of unconventional production. (*Source:* Ronald Bailey, *Earth Report 2000* (New York: McGraw-Hill, 2000).

6. "Breakthrough in Nuclear Fusion Offers Hope for Power of Future," *The New York Times,* 11 November 1991, section 1, p. 1. The article goes on to say that nuclear fusion could be commercially feasible within 50 years.

7. Ibid.

8. Another promising area of a limitless energy source is the sun. It's estimated that the production of chemical fuels generated from the sun can easily deliver upward of 450 exajoules a year (one exajoule being equivalent to the energy released by 22 million tons of oil). The process requires converting sunlight to a chemical that can be stored and shipped. The problem is that this promising solar technology is underfunded. In IEA countries, 60 percent of R&D for energy goes to nuclear power, and only 4 percent to solar and biomass. See Israel Dostrovsky, "Chemical Fuels from the Sun," *Scientific American,* (December 1991). See also "Energy and the Environment," *The Economist.*

9. "Energy and the Environment," *The Economist.*

10. Geographers at Cornell University have found that the greatest consumers of land in New York state since World War 2 have not been landfills, subdivisions, roads, or airports, as many assumed. In fact, forest growth is the culprit. New York state has more forest cover today than 50 years ago because less land is needed for agriculture due to productivity increases in farming. See David Johnston "Environmental Groups Misinform the Public," *The Chronicle of Philanthropy,* (May 1995).

WEBLINKS

www.pbs.org/kqed/population_bomb/
Paul Ehrlich and the population bomb.

www.opec.org/193.81.181.14/Default.htm
Home page of OPEC.

www.discoveryplace.com/
Petroleum Place Inc., the Energy Industry Exchange.

www.nrcan.gc.ca/
Home page of Natural Resources Canada.

THE COST OF RECYCLING

18

 **"Recycling always makes good business sense."**

Many people believed that compelling others to recycle their paper and bottles through municipal curbside collection was a solution to some of our environmental problems. But recycling alone has proven to be an expensive burden for many municipalities. Although it is an important component to reducing waste, just as important are proper incentives for consumers and businesses to produce less waste. Landfills, incineration, and user-pay programs are also important in the arsenal of waste reduction. Which method we use should be based on cost, efficiency, and source reduction, and not simply on the notion that recycling is the best of all possible worlds.

Few programs have caught the public's willingness to preserve the environment as much as recycling. The program seems so logical: if we could recover, sort, and recycle the millions of tonnes of material we were putting into landfill, we would put less pressure on the environment. The whole system would eventually be self-financing because the waste could be sold as inputs into the production of goods. It was such an appealing idea that thousands of communities started curbside collection programs of bottles, cans, plastics, and old newspapers. The idea seemed too good to be true.

Unfortunately, recycling has two major shortcomings: first, the costs of collecting, sorting, and shipping recycled waste are often greater than what business is willing to pay for the waste, which makes it a bad business proposition; and second, the environmental benefits are not what had been anticipated. What is supposed to be a win-win proposition appears to be a lose-lose situation instead. What's wrong? Critics of **Blue Box programs** have claimed that the curbside recycling is on a collision course with economic reality, and that it was never realistic to assume that recycling would pay for itself.

However, it wasn't economics that was the impediment, but rather ill-considered programs that misused economic principles. Before getting into the details of what went wrong and what to do about it, it is important to examine insights that economics may provide about the recycling process.

GOOD INTENTIONS AND BAD ECONOMICS

The economic system produces waste at each stage of the production process: at the time when resources are extracted from the earth; at the production stage; and finally, when products are used up and eventually discarded as litter, sewage, or garbage. In nature, however, since everything is eventually recycled there is no such built-in tendency to waste in the production process. Traditionally, the science of economics has said nothing about waste because it carried a zero price. In other words, the effective cost of polluting the environment was too low to bother about. But as the damage to the environment became more obvious, we began attaching real value to the environment, not only aesthetically, but also as an assimilator or repository for waste. When discarded rubbish washes back to shore, or toxic waste leaches through the ground, real harm is being done to the earth, and its capacity to absorb the waste is shrinking. This is not the fault of economics or economists, as some environmental critics claim, but of ignorance of the true cost of production.

Recycling was seen as a panacea to the problems of waste in modern society. If we could only recover everything we throw out, we could save the environment and keep the world's resources intact. However, there are two fundamental reasons why this rationale won't work. The first reason has to do with **entropy**.[1] This means that not everything can be recycled or reused. Of the millions of commodities and products used in the economy, the majority dissipate throughout the economic system. For example, think of the impossibility of recapturing lead in pencils after they have been used. Even if we could recapture the carbon dioxide from burning fossil fuel, we cannot make another form of energy from it. Junked cars have little to give up in terms of recyclable materials: the lead in car batteries is generally recycled, but the wood and plastics are almost impossible to extract without spending large, unfeasible amounts of money. Entropy puts a physical limit on creating a closed economic system. We have to live with the reality that not all the waste at each stage of production can be reused or recycled.

The second reason has to do with cost. Untold millions of tonnes of materials are thrown out because they're just too expensive to recover given the current market conditions and demands. In economic terms, the **marginal costs** surpass the **marginal revenue** of recycled material recovery. This second factor goes to the heart of the recycling crisis: it is simply not worth the cost, unless policies are in place to encourage the purchase and use of recycled material in the production process. Furthermore, it makes no sense to collect, sort, and sell recycled material at less than the cost of collecting it. For example, it costs between $200 to $300 per tonne to collect recycled materials compared to $50 for regular garbage. The net cost to taxpayers is $193 per tonne (cost of collection minus the value of the materials collected).[2] Some claim that these costs are worth paying to protect the environment, but others are willing to pay only for programs that are effective. The way it stands now, municipalities find themselves warehousing mountains of newsprint, cans, bottles, and plastics with no markets in which to sell them. Municipalities cannot go on subsidizing curbside collection indefinitely. It is not only the public sector that is losing money. Private companies that went into the recycling business hoping to profit from the need and public demand to recycle are losing, too. Some municipalities are seriously considering abandoning curbside collection of bottles and paper because of the cost.

One problem is that the price of recycled materials is highly unstable, making the whole process more expensive to the taxpayer. Baled aluminum was worth less than $800 a tonne in 1993 and more than $2,000 in 1995. By 1997, aluminum prices fell drastically. In 1991, glass brought $60 a tonne and by 1993 it was about $40. In the early 1990s, Metro Toronto got only $16 a tonne for its newsprint, which went down from $30 a few years before. Recycled steel brings in only $77 a tonne, which is $115 less than the cost of collecting it from households. The lower the price governments get for recycled material, the higher the cost to the taxpayer. By 1995, the price of newsprint went up considerably because of the higher demand in the United States and shortage of newsprint productive capacity. The price of newsprint was so high that "paper thieves" were raiding households for their garbage. The problem, however, is that municipalities cannot rely on a high price for paper or cardboard in the long run.[3] These costs do not take into consideration the time spent by consumers cleaning and sorting bottles, plastics, and paper.[4]

The absurdity is that when prices are low much of this material, for one reason or another, ends up in landfill anyway. Glass companies are very picky about the colour of glass they want, while the rest is dumped. Some municipalities have already cut back their Blue Box programs because of cost problems. As a result, much of the material is dumped.

Banning products outright is not always the solution either. In the case of plastics, it may end up doing more harm than good. For example, McDonald's bowed to public pressure to eliminate its polystyrene containers, but the paper wrappings they are now using may do the environment even more harm.[5] The same anomaly arose with diapers. It's assumed, by some, that cloth diapers are better than disposables because they can be used over and over. But in a study done by Arthur D. Little, a Boston consulting firm, it was found that cloth diapers actually cost the environment more in water and energy consumption, than do disposables.[6] Given our limited resources, there have to be less expensive and more effective ways to cut down on waste to the benefit of taxpayers *and* nature.[7]

THE LIMITS OF RECYCLING

If we all agree that because of the laws of physics not everything can be recycled, and the laws of economics dictate that not everything *should* be recycled if cheaper ways can be found to solve the waste problem, can we still save the environment? The answer is yes. The following discussion presents some solutions.

User-Pay Programs

The first goal of any waste reduction program is to discover the root causes of the problem, and that offer means making polluters (businesses as well as households) pay the true costs of waste disposal. Programs that simply collect bottles and cans, regardless of how much is tossed out, have no incentive to cut down on waste disposal. If taxes are fixed, consumers assume that garbage collection is free, and act accordingly. They may feel better about recycling, but the real costs are just passed along elsewhere. However, if consumers are forced to pay for the paper or materials they now throw out, they will demand less of it from manufacturers.

Some American cities have experimented with charging people according to the amount of garbage they throw out. Although there are some problems with this approach (such as tossing garbage over the neighbour's fence or along a roadside at night), the results in places like Tacoma and Seattle, Washington, look promising. People are throwing out less garbage. If consumers are not held to account, they have no reason to demand less packaging or returnable packaging from businesses. The way we now pursue waste reduction, everyone loses—governments, consumers, corporations, communities, and the environment.

The question of who owns the waste goes to the heart of the matter. Some environmentalists make the claim that corporations should be responsible for disposing of the products they sell after they have been used. This is actually the premise for a law in Germany that compels retailers to take back packaging from consumers, and manufacturers to then retrieve it from retailers, and so on down the line until 80 percent of it is recycled. The problem is that the program is horrendously expensive and the only one that will end up paying is the consumer as companies pass along the costs.

Market Forces and Waste Reduction

As environmentalists have often stressed, recycling is just one way to cut down on waste disposal. A far more effective means is to discourage waste in the first place. The free market already has built-in incentives to cut down on waste by producing lighter packages that reduce material and shipping costs. The U.S. National Center for Policy Analysis found that plastic milk jugs weighing 95 grams in the early 1970s today weigh only 60 grams. Competitive markets have also cut back the weight of 12 ounce steel cans by 65 percent, and aluminum cans by 35 percent over the past three decades. In order to encourage more reduction and less waste, it's important that corporations are not subsidized in the use of virgin raw materials. Recycling cannot hope to compete in these cases. Policies that make virgin materials less expensive to use range from provisions for writing off the costs of finding minerals and fuels to favourable capital gains treatment for an industry such as logging. One industry in which recycling has actually made a business more competitive is cardboard-box manufacturing. By using recycled content, Canada's cardboard-box producers save on virgin wood fibre and chemicals, and can lower costs to compete with low-cost U.S. cardboard-box producers.[8]

One way governments can encourage the market to produce less waste is to use their procurement programs to buy only from firms that have achieved certain waste-reduction standards, or, that have purchased products with a set amount of recycled material. Another way would be to create a program that would encourage newspapers to use more recycled fibre by setting a national target, and then allowing papers that exceed that standard to sell their spare share to others that failed to meet it. In the final analysis, the most effective policy is for governments to set goals and limits for waste reduction and let the market determine the most efficient means of reaching those goals. This is one area where the judicious use of government regulation may do more good than harm. But perhaps a more effective measure is to design fiscal policies that give plastic and bottle companies greater incentives to reduce the material content of their products. The Canadian packaging industry, for example, has been very effective in reducing the raw materials that go into their products, but they are given little credit for reducing waste that would eventually end up in landfills. The Canadian soft drink industry reduced the material content of its products by over 51 percent through source reduction. This was done through market forces and competition, not through government mandated programs. The Ontario domestic beer industry was able to achieve a 94.3 percent waste reduction rate for its cans. In other words, less materials were needed to produce 1,000 hectolitres of beer in 1972 than in 1993. About 75 percent of this waste reduction was from "hidden diversion gains" and only 25 percent from recycling.[9] As far as sustainable resource use is concerned, cans consume only 1 percent of steel production and bottles only 7 percent of plastic output. Even the most stringent waste-management policies will have little impact on the stewardship of these resources. Economic incentives to help them use the best technology is a far more effective way of reducing waste than arbitrary regulations that mandate waste reduction levels.

Landfills and Incinerators

One of the least appreciated solutions to the waste problem is the use of landfills. The perception is that garbage dumps are stinking heaps of toxic waste. Actually, they are generally benign.[10] Filling them with glass and other nonbiodegradable material is not a threat to the environment. Philosophically, it would be hard to differentiate between putting a bottle or a rock into the ground. Any real distinction would be based on nothing other than sentiment.

Regardless of how much we recycle and reuse, there will always be a growing need for landfills that have to be relatively close to population centres. One way to get over the fear of them is to have municipalities see them (and promote them to their citizens) as sources of income. This is an effective way to get over the **not-in-my-backyard syndrome (NIMBY)**. In 1991, the Ontario government refused to allow the City of Toronto to sell its garbage to Kirkland Lake, where it would be dumped in a safe, open-pit mine. The argument to disallow the sale was based on the dubious logic that waste should stay where it's made as a matter of principle. By 1999, the Ontario government lifted that ban, allowing Toronto to ship its waste to Northern Ontario. This would be advantageous to both Toronto, which needs more landfill, and Kirkland Lake, which could use more money now that some of its uranium mines are closed. The only impediments are environmental assessment studies related to the transportation of waste via railway.

However, we are not running out of safe places to put landfills. It is estimated that all of America's garbage for the next 1,000 years would fit into a single landfill space only 120 feet deep and 44 miles square. The problem isn't one of space, but of acceptance. No one wants to live next to a landfill unless they are compensated for it. Instead of governments dictating where landfills will be and forcing people to live next to them, they could select a few environmentally safe sites and offer to pay communities. Many people would offer to live next to landfills, instead of opposing them, if they could be paid to do so.

Incinerating our waste has long been opposed by environmentalists for the valid reason that toxic pollutants are no better for humans than they are for the environment. But incineration technology that turns waste into energy has improved, making it environmentally safer when materials are burned at extremely high temperatures. In Sweden, where this is done, plastics are known as "white coal." In the 1980s, the critics of incineration made the case that the energy produced from burning garbage wasn't worth the cost. Today the technology exists to produce energy from incineration, and it is competitive with other forms of energy. The problem arises out of the need to guarantee adequate supplies of garbage to keep the incinerators in operation.

In the final analysis, recycling is only one method that can be used to cut down on waste, and often it is not the most cost-effective. Policies that assume everything can be recycled, regardless of the cost and without incentive programs to encourage guaranteed supply and use of recycled material, are doomed to fail. Today everyone recognizes the value of cutting back on waste for the benefit of the environment. It would be a shame to dissipate that cooperative spirit with misguided government programs.

Finally, who should pay for recycling? The consumer who initially buys the goods or the producer who makes them in the first place? The answer is, both. For recycling to work, incentives have to be used to encourage consumers to cut consumption of recyclable material; and incentives have to be set up to make it economically viable for corporations to reduce material inputs. Simply collecting cans, bottles, and newspapers without a well-considered scheme of what to do with them only leads to waste and higher municipal taxes.

KEY TERMS

Blue Box programs	Marginal cost	Not-in-my-backyard
Entropy	Marginal revenue	syndrome (NIMBY)

REVIEW QUESTIONS

1. What are the attributes of recycling. Why does it enjoy such universal appeal?

2. Without programs that guarantee that there will be adequate demand for recycled products such as glass, cans, and newsprint, any recycling program will most likely fail. Comment.

3. If the observation in Question 2 is true, what can governments do to see that there's enough demand for recycled products?

4. Physics says that not everything can be recycled, while economics says not everything should be recycled. What is meant by both of these viewpoints?

5. Many environmentalists want manufacturers to be responsible for the disposal of the goods they sell after they have been used by the consumer. Will this guarantee that there will be less waste in the system?

DISCUSSION QUESTIONS

1. In hindsight, was McDonald's decision to ban polystyrene containers a wise environmental move? Would you advocate the banning of products such as plastics to help the environment and reduce waste?

2. Do you believe that if people were paid, they would be more willing to live next to landfill sites? Should governments use such a policy, not only for landfills, but to encourage people to live next to undesirable locations such as drug rehabilitation centres, nuclear plants, and airports?

NOTES

1. Entropy is also known as the Second Law of Thermodynamics. See David W. Pearce and R. Kerry Turner, *Economics of Natural Resources and the Environment* (Baltimore: Johns Hopkins University Press, 1990), p. 38.

2. These numbers are according to the Metropolitan Toronto Department of Works. See *The Globe and Mail,* 5 March 1992, p. A15. By 1995, because of a shortage of newsprint, the price of paper and cardboard increased substantially, making recycling a feasible proposition. However, because of the instability of prices, recycling, in many cases, is still a dubious proposition.

3. Kruger Inc. of Montreal, which actually gets its old newspapers for free from the city of Albany N.Y., gets only $7 a tonne for it on the market which doesn't even cover the cost of bailing. See *The Globe and Mail,* 23 December 1991, p. B3.

4. One study in New York City estimated that the total cost of recycling one tonne of glass, plastic, and paper was $3,000 (U.S.) when all costs are taken into account. (*Source:* "Recycling is Garbage," by John Tierney, *New York Times Magazine,* June 1996.)

5. Perhaps the most celebrated incident of public pressure to recycle is the case of McDonald's restaurants. The company came under extreme pressure to ban its polystyrene hamburger clamshells even though it was planning to undergo a massive recycling program for the polystyrene. But the public would have none of it, and McDonald's finally relented and switched to paper wrappings. (The company could only take so many letters to "Ronald McToxic" from school children. The kids may have felt they were helping the environment, but that's not what happened.) It's true that McDonald's waste going to landfills dropped by 70 percent with the use of paper, but plastics make up only 16 percent of all landfill material and are relatively benign because they don't degrade or leach into the ground. McDonald's switch to paper killed an initiative to find ways to recycle the plastics from the thousands of restaurants throughout North America. Without a steady supply of plastics, companies are reluctant to invest in recycling programs. More important, paper wrappings are far less efficient as a thermal insulator, which means greater food spoilage, and eventually more landfill

needs. See George C. Lodge and Jeffrey F. Rayport, "Knee-Deep and Rising: America's Recycling Crisis," *Harvard Business Review* (September–October 1991).

6. Michael Fumento, "Recycling's Dubious Economics," *Investor's Business Daily,* 29 November 1991, p. 2.

7. In 1992, Metro Toronto land-filled about $1 million worth of newspapers because of a strike at a paper plant in southern Ontario. The Province of Ontario also subsidized the shipping of newsprint to South Korea and Nigeria, at considerable expense to the taxpayer, during the strike. See *Financial Times of Canada,* 3 February 1992, p. 4.

8. Kimberly Noble, "Box Industry Stands Up to Heavy Odds," *The Globe and Mail,* 7 September 1992, p. B1.

9. *Source:* Donald Dewes and Michael Hare, *Reducing, Reusing and Recycling: Packaging Waste Policy in Canada* (Toronto: University of Toronto Press, 1999).

10. Landfills are composed mainly of paper (40 percent). Plastics only account for 16 percent and another 20 percent comes from building materials, which are almost impossible to recycle. See William Rathje and Cullen Murphy, "The Truth about Trash," *Smithsonian* (July 1992), p. 119.

WEBLINKS

www.nextcity.com/main/town/9blue.htm
The Blue Box Conspiracy.

www.metrotor.on.ca/works/what/waste/swm/approach.htm
Metro Toronto's approach to waste management.

www.glassworks.org/glassworks/summer96/userpay.html
User Pay: Is Your Municipality Ready?

www.enviroweb.org/issues/landfills/
The basics of landfills.

www.grievousangels.com/highgrader/articles/adamsreview.html
The Adams Mine Landfill Proposal: A Community Perspective.

ZERO-GROWTH AND THE ENVIRONMENT

 **"No-growth policies will save the environment."**

Some people believe that rapid population growth and unrestrained economic growth are the chief factors destroying the earth's environment. Without economic growth, we would not have toxic dumps, global warming, holes in the ozone, polluted lakes, and a myriad of other environmental disasters. But slowing or stopping economic growth is not the answer to a cleaner environment. Economic growth is, in many ways, the answer to a healthier environment.

Few would dispute the claim that modern life has had devastating effects on the environment. Without economic growth, there would not be global warming, an ozone problem, toxic dumps, rain forests slowly burning away, lead poisoning in schoolyards, ever-expanding landfill sites, acid rain, dead lakes, oil spills, and Chernobyl. None of these environmental tragedies would be possible without our craving for greater economic growth and higher standards of living. With growing world population levels, the only solution it seems is to stop economic growth. It is easy to understand where the notion that slowing the growth rate of the population and the economy would save the planet. If growth is the problem, then no growth is the answer, but is stopping industrial growth the best solution? Will the world be a cleaner, safer place if we put the brakes on economic development? The short answer is, no. The no-growth solution would actually make things worse.

WANTS VERSUS NEEDS

The basic premise of the zero-growth school of thought is that economic growth cannot be sustained indefinitely in view of the natural limits of the ecosystem. Economic growth, and an improvement in the standard of living, are incompatible with a healthy environment. Those who advocate that we turn off the lights, shut the taps, and pull the plug on modern society argue that since growth is based on corporations selling us products we really do not need in order to maximize their own profits, the destruction of the environment is unnecessary at best and unconscionable at worst. Besides, given that GDP increases cannot be sustained indefinitely because resources are limited, we should stop now because of the damage being done to the ecosystem. Environmentalists, such as Dr. David Suzuki, go as far as to blame economics itself for instilling in us the false values of profits, consumerism, and greed. They argue that free markets are incapable of delivering products people demand, and that it is a myth to believe that consumers, through their spending power, get the products they need.[1]

The zero-growth school also asks that even if we could produce all the goods we wanted, what could we possibly do with them all? Dr. Suzuki believes that "the human intellect cannot endlessly find new resources or create alternatives because the Earth is finite."[2] There's a notion that the world's resources are somehow limited. What Dr. Suzuki fails to realize is that even if resources are in short supply, the creativity and imagination to use them are not. Technology transforms our lives in ways no one can predict with certainty. Who could have imagined that today's humble and ubiquitous home computer would be faster and more efficient than the largest computer used in the Pentagon after the Second World War? One day our great-grandchildren may look back in amazement that we used fossil fuels for energy, or that we did not have the knowledge to cure cancer, heart disease, or AIDS.

Those who want to stop growth have a nostalgic view of the past as being a simpler, better time, without the stresses and strains of modern life, when people were more in harmony with their environment. Nothing is further from the truth. It was common for people to die of common food poisoning before chemical additives brought safe food to the reach of millions. Those who justifiably want to cut down on needless packaging forget that it greatly reduces food spoilage and waste. The average Mexican household throws away three times more food than do North American households. They throw away more than half the amount of food required to provide an adult with a nutritionally balanced diet, all because of a lack of proper storage and packaging. Many blame the internal-combustion engine for high levels of pollution, but few remember that it also helped reduce the amount of disease-carrying manure pollution long before the engine led to a quantum increase in the volume of traffic. In time, new technologies will replace fossil fuels as a way to move traffic and people. Just as products and corporations have their life cycles, technologies also go through the stages of birth, growth, and, eventually, death.[3]

The advocates of zero-growth have little or no faith in the economic concept of **consumer sovereignty**, or, in other words, the ability of the consumer to dictate to the producer, through the market, what should be produced. Farmers and food producers, for example, are joining the environmental thrust largely because consumers want environmentally safe products, less packaging, and more natural foods. Consumers, not corporations, are demanding these things; and corporations are listening, adapting, and anticipating. Anyone who hasn't noticed this trend simply isn't paying attention. Environmental consciousness will only get stronger as the next generation demands even more changes to how we consume and dispose of our waste.

THE COST AND CONSEQUENCES OF ZERO-GROWTH

Even if growth could be stopped, there is no guarantee that people or the environment would be better off. If the Victorians had taken the same attitude and stopped growth, future generations would have been deprived of a tenfold increase in the standard of living, and the advances in dentistry, open-heart surgery, antibiotics, birth control, central heating, personal computers, the Internet, jet travel, and a thousand other things we take for granted in a modern world. Moreover, we have gained social advances through growth. It is hard to image women's liberation without the advances in technology that made many of the tasks associated with parenting and housekeeping so much faster and easier.[4] It's odd how we can marvel at the advances we have made over the last century but have little faith that we can continue to make advances in the future. Part of the problem is that we see future goods as being static, or more of the same, rather than products satisfying new needs. Freezing growth impedes the creation of wealth on which research depends to advance science and technology, and in turn impedes increases in productivity. One cannot assume that without a growing economy, technical progress will continue without interruption.

By slowing the economy we would be hampering the necessary scientific advances needed to solve environmental problems. Despite all the bad news about the environment, there have been significant success stories, and most of them are due to scientific breakthroughs. In OECD countries since 1970, urban levels of sulphur dioxide have fallen by 30 to 75 percent, airborne dust and grit by 40 to 50 percent, and lead concentrations by 85 percent in North American cities. In Canada, water and air quality has improved over the last two decades (see Figure 19.1). Some 30-odd years ago Lake Erie was a horror story; today it has been brought back to life and is the largest commercial fishery in the Great Lakes. Lakes once thought dead because of acid rain can be brought back to life. It is estimated that sulphur dioxide emissions in Canada have dropped from a high of almost 6 million tonnes in 1970 to under 2.5 tonnes by the mid-1990s. Programs to clean up the environment cost industry and the taxpayer billions that would not be available if the economy was not creating the necessary wealth. Much of the environmental damage, such as toxic dumps, the unsafe disposal of PCBs, and the removal of asbestos and lead contamination are mistakes of the past that will take billions to rectify. Where will the money for these clean-up jobs come from if not from a growing economy? Technology isn't cheap. It'll take years of research and billions of dollars to switch from fossil fuels to solar power or safer forms of nuclear power. In the end, everyone will benefit, including the environment.[5]

Ironically, many of the proponents of less economic growth also advocate that the West pay for the billions needed to reduce the emission of carbon dioxide that is supposed to lead to the greenhouse effect and the overheating of the earth. Advocates of this theory have been successful in getting their message into the general consciousness of the population although a considerable amount of scientific information is emerging that refutes the dire consequences of the greenhouse effect. Even if the greenhouse problems are as great as many believe, is spending scarce resources on eliminating the carbon gases the best way to save lives? The answer is, probably no. First, because we don't know enough about the impacts or causes of the greenhouse scenario, and second, because those resources could be used more wisely, eliminating the death and suffering of millions of people around the globe today. It isn't ozone depletion, radon gas, Alar, pesticides, or nuclear waste that kills people. According to the World Health Organization, more than 4 million Third World children under the age of 5 die each year from simple respiratory diseases caused by burning cow dung and wood for cooking fuel in poorly ventilated huts.[6] UNICEF estimates that a further 3.8 million children in developing countries die each year from easily and cheaply treatable diarrhoeal diseases caused by impure drinking water. The problem is that sewage problems are at the bottom of the environmental agenda attracting little attention in the media. No one has yet died from global warming or eating genetically modified food stocks, still these issues receive most of the media attention.[7] Relatively small amounts of money wisely spent on improving the world's water quality would go a long way in saving millions of lives.

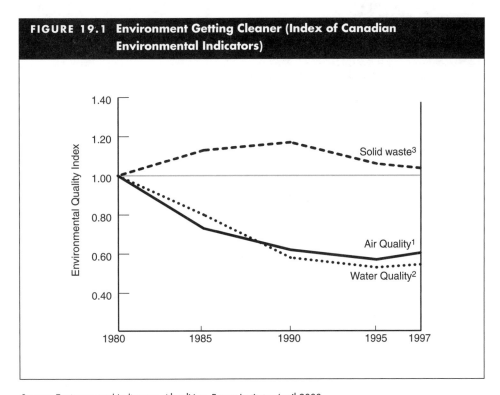

FIGURE 19.1 Environment Getting Cleaner (Index of Canadian Environmental Indicators)

Source: Environmental Indicators, 4th edition, Fraser Institute, April 2000.

Another dangerous trend in Third World countries is the overuse of coal as an energy fuel. It will come as no surprise if these countries resist any international treaty that calls for a slowdown in their energy consumption while they are trying to catch up with the developed world.[8] Unfortunately, two of the world's most populated countries, China and India, will look to coal for their energy since they have so much of it.

Coal still generates over half the world's electricity, more than any other fuel. Not only are developing countries more dependent on coal than the West, but they use it less efficiently. Because the Third World and former socialist countries do not know how to properly price fuel, such as electricity, the World Bank estimates that they use 10 to 20 percent more than they need. State-of-the-art technology exists to remove 95 percent of the sulphur dioxide from coal-fired stations, 99 percent of the ash, and 90 percent of the nitrogen oxides. The main drawback is money. The question, then, is how to get the Third World to use less energy, save the environment and still improve their standard of living. There are no easy answers, but two possible options are to transfer to the Third World the latest Western technology, or literally to pay developing countries not to pollute. Asking them to adhere voluntarily to some international pollution quota is a nonstarter and sure to fail. In short, economic growth will be needed to, first, create the wealth to clean up past environmental and pollution hazards; second, encourage more R & D in alternative energy sources; and third, raise the standard of living in the Third World without destroying the world's environment.

OTHER REASONS GROWTH IS NEEDED

People's interest in protecting nature and the environment is also related to their standard of living. Those with higher incomes are more interested in environmental issues. The "slash and burn" practices currently destroying the rain forests of the Amazon jungle are the result of poverty and ignorance. That is why the UN-sponsored **Brundtland Report** recommended that the concept of **sustainable development**, the idea that growth and protecting the environment were not diametrically opposed, was the only viable option available. To meet the needs of the world's poor, a five to tenfold increase in economic activity would be necessary.[9] One cannot expect nations that can hardly feed themselves to be concerned with how they might mistreat the earth's ecosystem. The real threat to developing countries today is not foreseeable environmental distress, but poverty, which according to the World Bank kills 34 million people a year, more than the population of Canada. Slowing economic growth will not improve their chances of living. By some estimates, once a country's per capita income rises above $4,000 (U.S.), it produces less pollutants per capita because it can afford technology such as catalytic converters and sewage treatment facilities. Countries, like Mexico, are at the $4,000 threshold now. With a rising standard of living, it becomes possible to increase the amount of education available to Third World countries. There is a close relationship between more education and family size: women with a high school education in developing counties have an average of three children, while those without average seven.

Those who argue for growth for its own sake would be just as wrong as those who want no growth. We are not talking about a mindless increase in GDP without regard for the kind of growth that is generated. Unfortunately, growth is too often seen as a meaningless drive to build more shopping malls and factories that churn out products ad infinitum that no one needs or wants. But there is no reason to fear growth that uses technology to produce products and services that improve the quality of life. Growth and productivity shouldn't be feared as the enemy of the environment, but rather as a way to increase wealth and the means to enhance our standard of living, and that also means a healthy and sustainable environment. It is a distorted morality that trades away helping the poor today so we can help unknown generations in the future by keeping resources in the ground and by stopping economic growth.

KEY TERMS

Consumer sovereignty   Bruntland Report   Sustainable development

REVIEW QUESTIONS

1. Economists, such as John Kenneth Galbraith, often claim that consumers have little control over what is produced. In the case of environmental products, do you believe that it is still true that corporations do not provide products demanded by the consumer?

2. Many of those who advocate zero-growth base part of their argument on the fact that much of our economic growth today is based, not on real "needs," but on artificial "wants." Define the difference between needs and wants, and argue whether this line of reasoning holds up under close scrutiny.

3. What are some of the consequences of a zero-growth policy for Third World nations and the environment?

4. Do you think that the market system is capable of delivering sustainable development, that is, development that meets the needs of this generation and future ones as well? What should governments do to encourage the objective of sustainable development?

DISCUSSION QUESTIONS

1. "If our ancestors had followed a zero-growth policy, we and our environment would be better off today." Discuss this statement.

2. Even if it were possible to maintain zero growth in the economy, it would soon become politically intolerable. Discuss.

3. Those who advocate zero growth make the implicit assumption that providing for future generations is more important than providing for those living today. What are your thoughts about such an assumption on economic and moral grounds?

4. Should we hold developing countries to the same high environmental standards of countries in the West?

NOTES

1. The notion of a difference between "wants" and "needs" was popularized by the economist John Kenneth Galbraith in his book *The Affluent Society*. We need goods like food, shelter, clothing, and education, but we want Big Macs, Giorgio Armani suits, rap music, cellular phones, and vacations in Tuscany. Needs are genuine and come from within, and wants come from without. On closer inspection the difference between needs and wants is in the eye of the beholder and does not stand up to much scrutiny. In Galbraith's world, even culture would be trivial. (But try telling children that they really

don't need a PlayStation.) In a world where we're mesmerized by advertisers and marketers, "zero-growthers" see rampant consumerism, more useless gadgets, built-in product obsolescence, and more pollution.

2. "Why Conventional Economics Spells Doom," *Toronto Star,* 2 March 1991, p. D6.

3. The coal-burning locomotives that evoke strong nostalgia today were once considered by many to be "soot-belching contraptions" that were a blight on the landscape. Each generation has its own detestable technology.

4. Richard Lipsey, *Economic Growth: Science and Technology and Institutional Change in a Global Economy,* Publication No.4 (Toronto: Canadian Institute for Advanced Research, June 1991), p. 30.

5. Anyone interested in understanding that the environment is not deteriorating should read the excellent book by Gregg Easterbrook entitled, *A Moment on the Earth*, published by Penguin, 1995.

6. Greg Easterbrook, "Forget PCB's. Radon. Alar," *New York Times Magazine,* 11 September 1994.

7. Much research is now coming to light that global warming may have a positive side. The earth has gone through long phases of hot and cold spells. An increase in temperatures means less harsh winters and longer growing seasons. Nevertheless, as Professor Thomas Schelling at Harvard states, "I conclude that in the U.S. and probably Japan, Western Europe, and other developed countries, the impact on economic output (of global warming) will be negligible and unlikely to be noticed." See Thomas Gale Moore, *Global Warming: A Boon to Humans and Other Animals* (Stanford University: Hoover Institution, 1995), p. 5.

8. In global terms, Canada is a minor polluter. We produce only 2 percent of the world's CO^2, 2 percent of nitrous oxides, 2 percent of CFCs, and only 1 percent of sub methane gas. This means we can't go it alone. We need the cooperation of all countries to reduce the gases that contribute to the earth's warming. See *Canada's Green Plan.*

9. Dr. Suzuki was highly critical of the Brundtland Report. He argued that the only solution to protecting the environment was no growth and massive income distribution from developed to underdeveloped countries. If this were done, per capita income would be around $2,750 (U.S.) in 1985 dollars. A family of four would be below the poverty line in the United States and Canada. No one would accept such a utopian proposal. The environment won't be better protected by making everyone poor.

WEBLINKS

www.geocities.com/Athens/Parthenon/5173/greenhouse_effect.html
The greenhouse effect.

www.fraserinstitute.ca/
Home page of the Fraser Institute.

www.williams.edu/CES/faculty/mlevy/brundtland.html
The Brundtland Commission Report 10 Years On.

iisd.ca/
Home page of the International Institute for Sustainable Development.

Part

V

Other Economic

Myths

Chapter

20

SMALL

BUSINESS

 **"Small businesses drive the economy."**

The media, governments, and small business associations give the impression that small businesses are the main driving force behind the economy and, therefore, should be given government assistance. The reality is that the performance of small businesses is misunderstood and exaggerated, while that of large firms is underestimated. Much of the growth of small businesses can be explained by the restructuring of large companies as they contract out more of their work. When given a choice, people prefer working for large companies because wages, pensions, and job security are better than in small firms.

In early January 1995, 25,000 workers lined up in freezing weather for the privilege of filling out an application to work at a GM plant in Pickering, Ontario. Many of them had camped out all night. Anyone watching the story on TV or seeing the photos on the front pages of newspapers would have assumed all these workers were unemployed. The truth is that most of the workers lining up for work had jobs.[1] The problem wasn't a weak economy, but the lack of performance of small businesses.

Most small businesses have failed to produce jobs that pay a decent wage and provide adequate employment stability. If General Motors decides to offer $22 an hour for a job that requires no more than a grade 10 education, a lot of people will be enticed to try their luck. To anyone familiar with introductory economics, it's a simple question of supply and demand: the higher the wage, the more workers are willing to offer their labour.

The poor performance of small business wasn't supposed to happen. Anyone following the media in the past few years would have sworn that big businesses were taking it on the chin while the future belonged to small, more flexible and adaptable companies that would make us more competitive. Did we underestimate the performance of large companies and overestimate that of small ones? In a word, yes. We know now that small businesses aren't the job producers we once thought, and large ones aren't as inflexible as we were led to believe.

FULFILLING THE POLITICAL AGENDA OF THE RIGHT AND LEFT

Why didn't we notice that small businesses were underperforming? Part of the reason is that many people, including the media, governments, and small business associations, repeated the myth that "small was beautiful" so often that it became the conventional wisdom. Any criticism of small businesses was tantamount to heresy in public policy circles. The reality is that small firms haven't performed all that brilliantly, while large companies are doing surprisingly well.[2]

Perpetuating the myth of small business as saviour also fulfilled the philosophical agenda of both the Right and the Left. Conservatives see the emergence of small business as the return of the independent entrepreneur willing to take risks and reap the rewards of hard work, ingenuity, and perseverance. On the other hand, social democrats were convinced that the growth of small businesses was a sign that society was weaning itself away from the grasp of big business, oligopolies, and monopolies. Governments were more than willing to go along encouraging the establishment of small businesses mainly because it was an inexpensive **industrial strategy**; besides, governments could be seen as encouraging a natural trend in the economy.

THE DECLINE OF THE SMALL

Part of the perception that small firms were the way of the future was perpetuated by a growth in academic studies that glowingly reported on the potential of small businesses to revitalize industries and communities, such as the "Third Italy" movement in Northern Italy. But in countries such as Germany, Japan, and the United States, large businesses have been the big net job producers while small firms are characterized by low wages, poor benefits, and high worker turnover. What happened to the dream that small firms were the wave of the future? Weren't the big companies, like IBM, General Motors, and retail giants such as Sears, suffering financially? Weren't smarter, more flexible, and efficient, smaller firms supposed to take their place?[3]

As with most things economic, the perception didn't quite fit the reality. Despite all the hoopla about the performance of small business, the fact is that we don't know much about the changing structure of the economy. For example, we don't know the relationship between small and large firms. But there's a tendency for many large companies to out-source many of the services they once performed in-house, which gives the impression that small firms drive the economy. Dupont Canada in Kingston, Ontario, a firm of about 1700 workers, now contracts out everything from janitorial services to printing, gardening, painting, carpentry, and even machine-shop work, all jobs once done in-house. Why do your own photo-copying when you can use the local Kinko, who pays minimum wages? Because most small companies concentrate on delivering services, they have natural links with the performance of large companies, especially in manufacturing, resource industries, and financial services. This gives the impression that small businesses are flour-ishing when in fact jobs are being reshuffled and are dependent on the performance and restructuring of large companies.

Small business advocates still make the claim that smaller firms are responsible for a majority of new jobs. This claim is valid in Canada, but the numbers have to be looked at carefully. New evidence shows that small firms both create and destroy jobs at about the same rate as large corporations, and that small manufacturing firms have higher gross rates of job creation, but not higher net rates. In other words, there's a lot of churning going on as small firms appear and disappear on the market.[4]

Economists at Statistics Canada concluded that small firms employing less than 20 workers did indeed create more net jobs than large firms. In fact, the larger the firm, the fewer jobs created. Several methods were used to count jobs and the results held true for each. These findings seem to be bucking an international trend. But that was for new start-ups; when comparing the performance of *existing* small and large firms, large ones tended to create jobs at the same rate as small ones.[5] What is often overlooked is that firms employing over 500 workers still account for almost 40 percent of the total jobs in the commercial economy. If you include firms who em-ploy over 100 workers, that figure goes to 56 percent.[6]

Nevertheless, it's the job creation of small firms that so excites public policy in encouraging more small businesses. But job creation is only half the story. No one understands the underlying patterns that drive the formation of small firms and how they interact with large ones. What we do know from other studies is that job quantity and job quality are different. For one thing, smaller firms pay less. In the 1970s, small firms paid about 72 percent of the average wage in large firms. Twenty years later, that share was down even further.[7] This wage differential exists even when one takes into account education, age, or occupation of workers in small and large firms. One reason given for the proliferation of small firms is the payment of low wages, especially for newer firms. Another reason for the wage differential is that large firms are more likely to be unionized. Less than 10 percent of workers in small firms belong to some union compared to over 44 percent in firms of over 500 employees.

The disadvantages of smaller firms don't end there. The smaller the firm, the poorer the pension plan coverage. An hour worked in a large firm is five times more likely to be covered by a pension plan than in a small firm, according to Statistics Canada. Just as with wages, pension plans are directly correlated with the level of unionization, and that's related to firm size. Workers employed in larger firms are less likely to be laid off; when they are, they tend to return to work more quickly. The average stint for a worker in a small firm is 18 months compared to 47 months with a large firm. That's why most job seekers look first to large firms for work: they pay more, have better fringe benefits, and there's less chance of being laid off.

Aside from the raw facts of the comparisons between firms by size, there's also a social dimension as to why most workers prefer working with larger companies. People are social beings who need to belong to organizations that provide stability and predictability in their lives. Larger companies provide a social dimension that small firms sometimes can't. As people get older with kids to raise and educate, that stability becomes more important. There's little question that the workers lining up for work at General Motors were seeking not only a better paying job, but also one that could provide for their futures as well. The harsh realities of the last recession in the early 1990s brought home the hard truth that few people have the inclination, drive, or taste for risk to be successful entrepreneurs. The potential rewards may be high, but most prefer the comfort of a steady paycheque if they can get it. As anyone who's worked in a marginal small business knows, the hours can be long, the work taxing, and the potential for advancement nil.

THE RETURN OF THE BIG

Along with the lacklustre performance of small firms, big companies are far from dead. To start with, it appears that big companies are better suited to a changing economic environment than small ones. In a world where small firms should be flourishing, for the first time since the 1970s the number of small firms is starting to shrink in the United States. Even though there's a growing pool of **venture capital**, less of it is making its way to small economically viable ventures despite the flurry of interest by investors in dot-com firms at the beginning of this decade. Part of the reason is that only big firms can carry the needed risk in order to succeed in a global economy. Consider two household commodities: TVs and cars. Both industries are dominated by big companies that are getting bigger rather than smaller. In the case of television, the costs of developing the next generation of high definition screens are enormous, and once standards are set by the U.S. Federal Communications Commission, the companies with the winning design will have access to a guaranteed market. To go after this market, Zenith joined forces with AT&T, the French company Thompson collaborated with Phillips and NBC, while Warner joined forces with AOL. This is a classic case of big business working with big governments in order to minimize risk and economic failure. To be a player, companies must have the financial resources to stay in for the long haul.[8]

Even on the much publicized **information highway**, which is supposed to be a boon to small and fledgling enterprises, the industries bringing the technology to market are a complex blend of cable, telephone, satellite, computer, and software companies—all big and well financed. Even many of the small dot-com companies, that made their founders unimaginably rich as technology stocks soared, came crashing to earth as reality returned to the stock market a few months later.

As for cars, companies such as Honda, Toyota, and Ford now have global production systems. Cars assembled in one plant are being shipped worldwide, and not just to local markets. Honda and Toyota are assembling cars in the United States and then shipping them back to Japan. That way they can avoid currency fluctuations and take advantage of large-scale production. This phenomenon isn't restricted to these commodities. IKEA, the Swedish mass producer of low-cost furniture, is one of the world's most efficient distributors and retailers of innovative products. One can go down the list of large, imaginative, and flexible manufacturers from British raincoats to French wines, Italian clothes, and Swiss watches, all produced and distributed worldwide. Companies such as Sony and Toshiba can produce an array of products geared specifically for individual markets worldwide. Large companies can not only achieve economies of scale, but they also have the capacity to deliver **economies of scope**. This isn't to suggest that smaller firms don't make a contribution, but in most cases not as leaders, but as followers. Even in the area of high technology, the real job-creators are large firms. In the United States, although 85 percent of all individual enterprises employ less than 100 workers, 91 percent of all workers were employed by only 5 percent of the firms. The same goes for Canada; of the 365,000 workers in the communications industry, 85 percent work in plants that employ more than 500 workers.[9]

Mega-companies, ranging from Nortel to Wal-Mart, are showing their ability to achieve record sales and profits, headlines once reserved for "fleet-footed" entrepreneurs. They are doing things common to any successful endeavour such as adapting to change, decentralizing authority, hiring carefully, and controlling costs, but at a faster rate than many predicted—a phenomenon known as concentration without centralization. Along with the greater use of information and computer technology, this makes for a deadly combination for success. Smaller firms are trying to fight back, but big firms have greater know-how when it comes to getting their products to market.

WHAT SHOULD GOVERNMENTS DO?

Despite the return of big business and the emerging studies showing that small isn't always better, it would be wrong to underplay the importance of small businesses. After all, companies such as Apple and IBM started out as small companies. They've provided thousands of people with the opportunity to get experience in a tight labour market. But it would be equally wrong to exaggerate the role of small businesses where their emergence is more a question of necessity rather than choice. If we know anything about small businesses, we know that for the most part small ventures bring large risks. After all, only one in five start-ups are left standing after five years.

That brings up the issue of public policy. Because of the misguided perception that small businesses drive the economy and are seen as job-creation machines, there is growing political pressure to make it easier for small firms to flourish by providing them with preferential tax and regulatory treatment, subsidies, and government guaranteed loans. Banks are also being pressured by governments to increase lending to small businesses. But there's a fundamental flaw in this reasoning from those advocating further help for small businesses. If they are the engine of economic growth, and resources are flocking to invest in these businesses, one would expect that higher potential profits would be the main motivation for investors. In that case, taxpayers shouldn't be asked to subsidize ventures in which potential returns are attractive. If the returns to investment in small businesses are below market averages, again taxpayers would be wasting money supporting marginal ventures. After all, how many people would want their retirement savings invested in companies that the banks regard as too risky?

Any programs that encourage commercial development that doesn't impede the workings of a market economy should be encouraged. Lower corporate taxes are a good policy whether the firm is small or large. But encouraging the expansion of small firms would simply distort the allocation of society's resources and leave taxpayers and consumers worse off. That's why the government **set-aside programs** to help small businesses are a bad idea. They haven't worked in the United States, and they won't work here. In the end, such programs increase the cost of government purchasing and decrease overall economic efficiency. Designing industrial policy based on firm size rather than encouraging competition and efficiency is self-defeating.

KEY TERMS

Industrial strategy   Information highway   Set-aside programs
Venture capital   Economies of scope

REVIEW QUESTIONS

1. Describe how large companies outperform small ones. (Give at least three examples.)
2. Using supply and demand curves, explain why thousands of people would line up for work at General Motors in the dead of winter.
3. Explain why the performance of large companies was so underestimated in the past decade and how they have been able to recover in a world where the ability to react to changing consumer demand is so important.

DISCUSSION QUESTIONS

1. Banks are often criticized for discriminating against small firms. Should small firms be treated differently from large firms when applying for loans?
2. Should governments give small businesses a break by setting aside a certain portion of government contracts for small businesses? Who are the winners and losers with set-aside programs?
3. "Small businesses are no different from other special interest groups." Comment.
4. Would you rather work in a large or small firm? Justify your answer.

NOTES

1. At Pebra, an auto parts plant in nearby Peterborough, Ontario, 25 workers called in sick to line up for a chance at a job with General Motors. A few others flew in from as far away as Alberta. *The Globe and Mail,* 10 January 1995.
2. Small firms are usually classified as those employing 99 workers or less; medium-sized firms between 100 and 499 workers; and large firms above 500.
3. Much of this thinking about the resurgence of big business and decline in small firms can be found in Bennett Harrison's book *Lean and Mean: The Changing Landscape of Corporate Power in the Age of Flexibility* (New York: Basic Books, 1994).
4. One prominent study in this area is *Small Business and Job Creation: Dissecting the Myth and Reassessing the Facts,* by Steven J. Davis, John Haliwanger, and Scott Schuh, Working paper no. 4492 (Cambridge, Mass: National Bureau of Economic Research, October 1993).

5. *Have Small Firms Created a Disproportionate Share of New Jobs in Canada? A* Reassessment of the Facts, by G. Picot, J. Baldwin, and R. Dupuy. No. 71, Analytical Studies Branch, Statistics Canada, (November 1994).

6. Ibid., p. 21.

7. Ted Wannell, "Firm Size and Employment: Recent Canadian Trends," *Canadian Economic Observer* (March 1992).

8. It should be added that bigness is no guarantee of success. The Japanese and European business-government alliances will most likely fail, leaving the Americans winners in HDTV. IBM also ran into trouble because it thought it was big enough to ignore its competition and what the consumer wanted.

9. For Canada, over 90 percent of all exports come from companies employing over 500 workers. Although firms don't have to export to create economic wealth, large firms tend to have a bigger capacity to lead the economy into economic recovery.

WEBLINKS

strategis.ic.gc.ca/SSG/mi07237e.html
Small Business Quarterly Report: Spring 2000-08-29.

www.sbcmag.com/Additional/cibc3.html
Small Business Fuel Canada's Economy as Bankruptcies Decline, Say CIBC Economists.

www.ilo.org/public/english/employment/ent/sed/publ/wp4.htm
Job quality and small enterprise development.

www.statcan.ca/english/IPS/Data/11F0019MIE98128.htm
Recent Canadian evidence on job quality by firm size.

GOVERNMENT
STATISTICS

 **"Government statistics never lie."**

The accuracy of government data is something many of us take for granted. Businesses rely on government information in order to make investment decisions; labour unions need good data for collective bargaining; policy analysts need good statistics to advise governments; and the rest of us need accurate information to make decisions about employment opportunities. But how accurate is this information? It may come as a surprise that data gathering and analysis are more art than science. Although Statistics Canada is one of the world's leading processors of information, the accuracy of its output shouldn't be taken for granted.

If you want to know who won last night's game, what do you do? Check the morning paper. Is it going to rain tomorrow? Tune in to the weather channel. But what if you want to know how the economy's been doing? No problem; just wait for the necessary information from Statistics Canada. What could be more reliable than a CBC announcer telling us that Canada ran a trade surplus with the United States this month? Or that inflation is up 3 percent, and unemployment is down to 9 percent? After all, it's government data, right?

Unfortunately, the reality is not as simple. Regardless of the efforts governments make to acquire the best information they can, statistics are often more a matter of art than science. There is often a trade-off between accuracy and the resources needed to collect and analyze data. The problem is that much of what the government publishes, as well as information from the private sector, is at best an approximation of what's happening in the economy. The implications are serious for the simple reason that government policies and programs are driven primarily by accurate information about how the economy is performing. Sound economic policies can't be built on the shifting sands of poor economic information. What this chapter will show is that government economic statistics should come with the sticker: Buyer Beware.

INFLATION: LOWER THAN WE THINK

Let's start with perhaps the most misunderstood and least accurate data that Statistics Canada releases—the rate of inflation as reported by the **Consumer Price Index (CPI)**, the most commonly reported measure of changing prices.[1] The number is an index because the CPI is based on measuring the change in prices of a bundle of goods and services that a typical consumer buys over two time periods. This index of goods keeps track of changes in the cost of products such as groceries, health care, transportation, fuel, insurance, housing, even bank loans—everything the typical consumer buys. In total, there are about 500 goods and services that make up the CPI. But there are flaws in the CPI that tend to overestimate price increases: substitution effects, the introduction of new goods, and changes in the quality of goods.

The first mismeasurement of prices has to do with the **substitution effect**. As prices change, consumers adjust their consumption patterns accordingly. If the price of apples goes up this week, I buy more bananas; if the price of movies rises, I stay home more often and watch TV. In other words, consumers adjust quickly to changes in relative prices. But these behavioural changes aren't captured in the inflation index quickly enough, leading to an upward bias in prices.[2] In a perfect world, these relative price changes would be picked up instantaneously. To be fair, Statistics Canada makes a pretty good effort in keeping up with our changing preferences, but the changes aren't as instantaneous as our reactions to changing prices.[2] To compensate, the Government of Canada releases a number of inflation measurements used by economists, each with their own strengths and weaknesses.[3] The media focus on the CPI because it applies to a range of goods that consumers buy.

The second distortion in measuring price changes has to do with the introduction of new goods. Statistics Canada is pretty slow at getting around to revising its basket of goods, at least a lot slower than consumers are at changing their buying habits.

When it does finally get around to including new products, it usually does so at the mature stage of a product's life cycle, which means the really big drop in prices has been missed. In other words, products go into Statistics Canada's basket of goods after they've been on the market a few years, but by then prices have usually come down substantially. That was certainly the case when satellite dishes first came on the market. Over a four-year period, prices dropped by 95 percent. After that, price changes were considerably more modest. At the same time, there's no price index for software. For some firms, software makes up the most important nonlabour component in their company. It's estimated that leaving out the introduction of new goods alone leads to an upward bias in the CPI of almost 1 percent annually.[4]

The third weakness of the CPI is that it doesn't take into consideration the changes in the quality of goods produced. Even though today we can buy electronic equipment that's much more powerful than it was yesterday, inflation measurements only take into account the price of a commodity, not the quality improvements. Although the price of new personal computers from one generation to the next doesn't change much, consumers are getting a lot more computer power per dollar spent, measured in millions of instructions per second (MIPS).[5] The same goes for producer price indexes. In the case of pharmaceuticals, the inability to properly measure prices for generic and new drugs means that the rate of inflation for drugs is overstated by as much as 50 percent.

What are the ramifications of an upwardly biased inflation index? To start with, the cost of what governments buy, i.e., what the taxpayer buys, goes up more than it should because most government purchases are directly tied to an inflation index. If the government ties pension plans to the cost of living, the government can overspend if the CPI exaggerates inflation. In the United States, the Bureau of Labor Statistics estimates the government could save $150 billion over five years with a better measure of inflation. We don't know what the saving would be for Canada, but perhaps hundreds of millions of dollars could be saved with a more accurate measure of inflation. And because the CPI is used also in the private sector for labour wage settlements, the savings to the entire economy could be significant. That's why it matters if the rate of consumer inflation is 3, 4, or 5 percent. It can also be argued that the Bank of Canada's determination to control inflation compounds the problem because it adds an additional burden to the economy with higher than necessary interest rates to keep price increases in check.

THE NATION'S OUTPUT: LARGER THAN WE THINK

Whenever economists want to know how the economy is performing at its most basic level, they turn to the **Gross Domestic Product (GDP)**. In very general terms, the GDP is a rough measure of overall economic activity, and not an indication of national well-being. It should be made clear that no one indicator can tell us how well-off we are. To do that we would have to examine a whole array of indicators, such as health and education. The GDP indicates, however, how many things we have this year compared to last year. If *real* GDP goes up, after adjusting *actual* GDP for inflation, we may not be any happier as a society, but materially we're better off. Simply, GDP is the sum of the money values of all final goods and services produced in Canada within a year. The important point here is that the goods are *final*, not intermediate or primary goods such as inputs into further production, i.e., machinery or iron ore. In the end, it consists of everything from jeans to cars to haircuts to vacations. The market prices of all goods are added up to give us the GDP for any given year.[6] Goods produced the previous year don't count.

Just like the rate of inflation, the GDP is only an approximation of what is produced in any given year because it doesn't measure all economic activity. Whereas the CPI overestimates increase in prices, the GDP underestimates the size of the economy. For one thing, in order to be counted, a good or service has to be in the organized or above-ground economy. Things that are illegal, such as smuggled cigarettes or prostitution, aren't counted. By leaving out such activities, the size of Canada's GDP is automatically undermeasured. In some countries, such as the Netherlands, where prostitution is legal and taxes are paid, the sex trade is included in official government statistics. There aren't any good statistics that estimate the size of the underground economy, but Statistics Canada estimates it's around 10 percent of GDP. It's probably even bigger since the introduction of the GST as more people try to avoid higher taxes, particularly where cash transactions are the norm.

Another criticism, which comes from women's groups and feminists, is that the GDP undervalues the work of volunteers and women who do most of the domestic labour. These are omissions that society would have to pay for if they weren't done for free. A further oddity of GDP is that it doesn't account for leisure time.

Another misuse of the national output figures occurs when the per capita GDP of one country is compared with that of another. We often hear that Canada's income is 20 times that of Poland; what's left out is the fact that many Poles grow their own food and make their own clothes—activities that are not reflected in the official statistics. We're still a lot richer, but not by as much as the GDP figures tell us.

Just as these factors tend to underestimate the total goods and services produced, the official numbers also overestimate the GDP by including a number of 'bads'—everything from a vandal breaking a window to natural disasters. Occasionally one hears that after a disaster, such as a hurricane, the re-building that follows stimulates jobs and economic activity. Such reasoning, however, is flawed. When the Ocean Ranger oil-drill sank off the coast of Newfoundland in 1982, the resources that were devoted to rescue, relief, investigations, and finally compensation to the families technically all added to the national product, but none of them left society better off because those resources could have been used to increase Canada's standard of living in other ways. Environmentalists have long argued that the GDP overestimates the country's well-being because it doesn't account for the damage to the ecosystem by higher levels of economic activity. They often point to the Exxon Valdez oil spill off the coast of Alaska in 1988, which ironically increased, rather than decreased, the GDP of the United States. Wars represent an extreme example of factors that falsely push up GDP and end up giving us a flawed sense of economic well-being.

UNEMPLOYMENT: WORSE THAN WHAT THEY TELL US, OR IS IT?

One would think that it would be a relatively easy matter to get an accurate picture of how many people don't have jobs. When it comes to measurement, nothing is easy. Counting the number of unemployed at any given time has always been a source of contention, especially to those without jobs who swear that things are worse than the official numbers indicate. Unemployment statistics measure not only the number of workers without jobs, but also the average length of time they've been out of work. This data is collected by surveying those who are unemployed on any given day. This technique automatically gives an upward bias to unemployment figures, because the odds are higher that those surveyed will have been out of work longer when the survey is conducted. In other words, those unemployed for short periods are unlikely to be home when the pollster calls.[7]

But the biggest complaint about unemployment figures is that they underestimate the true number of unemployed workers because they overlook discouraged workers who have dropped out of the labour market. Anyone not looking for work over a four-week period is not counted by the Labour Force Survey. This is a particularly bad problem in areas of high chronic job shortages, such as the Atlantic Provinces, where the unemployment rates are almost double the national levels. When discouraged workers are taken into account, the real level of unemployment for a province is usually one-third higher than the official data reported by Statistics Canada. However, some economists have argued that unemployment rates are skewed upwards in the Atlantic Provinces due to the 10–40 syndrome (working 10 weeks and collecting 40 weeks of EI). It's been argued that Canada's unemployment rates are partly higher than those in the United States because of the more generous unemployment provisions in Canada, which encourage nonparticipants to register as unemployed, even though they aren't really participating in the labour market.

Another problem is that unemployment data can't deal with the vast amount of **underemployment** in the economy—that is, people working at jobs they are overqualified to do. In other words, Ph.D.s and M.A.s driving cabs or waiting tables. At the same time, there are hundreds of thousands of part-time workers who are willing and able to work full time. As far as Statistics Canada is concerned, a job is a job is a job and consequently it makes no provision for the vast amount of underemployment or part-time workers. Of course, we also have the situation where a large number of workers who work full time would prefer part-time work. But information tells us that the number of part-time workers who want full-time jobs is increasing, and that means the unemployment rate isn't giving us an accurate picture of what's going on in the labour market.

It should be kept in mind that just as GDP is an imperfect indicator of economic well-being, higher rates of unemployment aren't always a sign of bad times. For some people more leisure time (unemployment) can be a positive rather than a negative. After all, an indicator of good times is that people can afford to 'buy' more leisure time. It's important to keep in mind that there's nothing in economics that says the choice to work 80 hours a week is preferable to working only 10 hours. Unemployment, or low levels of employment, can be a rational choice, and often not a bad one. This last point may seem a non-sequitur given the arguments made previously about how unemployment is actually mismeasured. This point also has implications for measuring GDP. How do you measure the satisfaction one gets from early retirement, longer holidays, or a shorter work week? It's important to keep in mind that when it comes to gauging economic well-being, things aren't always what they appear, making the problem of measurement all the more difficult.

OTHER MEASURES OF ECONOMIC PROSPERITY: CAPACITY UTILIZATION AND PRODUCTIVITY

So far we've discussed the flaws in measuring GDP, price changes, and unemployment. In one form or another, they are all measurements of how we're doing as an economy. Two other indicators of economic performance and prosperity are **capacity utilization** and **productivity**. Capacity utilization is the difference between the actual and potential output of a firm or an entire economy. This indicator is important because it shows whether industries or the economy are close to full capacity. It is widely used by policy analysts to advise governments whether to stimulate or slow down economic growth. In the past, government statisticians could easily keep track of an economy's potential output by counting the number of machines and buildings in the economy. That's not so simple today. Firms can now add to capacity by reorganizing production with smarter uses of technology and improved management skill. Firms are adding massive amounts of productive capacity without the knowledge of Statistics Canada, making government policy all the more difficult. It's estimated that Texas Instruments in the United States has added an 'invisible factory' worth $400 million by reducing time and improving manufacturing yields. Such innovations are happening right across the corporate economy.[8]

When it comes to productivity, things get even worse. Productivity numbers are supposed to show how fast worker output is growing. It's the most important indicator of economic well-being, because we can't increase our standard of living without improvements in productivity. Canada's productivity had been growing at rates of 3 percent up to the mid-1970s, but fell off sharply after that—a fact that has puzzled economists ever since. Could it be a measurement problem? As the economy moves more to a service economy, the government has little understanding of how to measure productivity for a whole range of industries such as banking, software, legal services, wholesale trade, and communications. When Canadians were engaged mainly in farming and manufacturing, it was easy to measure how many logs per worker were cut, or bushels of wheat were harvested. It becomes more difficult to measure the productivity of a corporate lawyer or software engineer.[9] When services make up 70 percent of the economy, one gets a clearer understanding of the dimensions of the problem. The problem is further compounded by the fact that productivity is measured by dividing real GDP (GDP adjusted for inflation) by the number of workers in the economy. Having already determined that all three of these factors are less than perfectly measured (prices, output, and labour), it's not surprising that productivity measurements are off as well.[10]

CONCLUSION

Despite all the criticisms of the data put out by organizations such as Statistics Canada, data today are a lot better than they used to be; and according to the World Bank, Canada's data are perhaps the best in the world. That means we don't go through as many data revisions as does the United States. If U.S. data were as accurate as Canada's, George Bush may have won the election against Bill Clinton in 1992 because the preliminary growth figures were revised upwards after the election.[11]

It's been said that the objective in the 19th century was to draw accurate maps of a country; today it's to get a good set of economic statistics. Only with good data and information can economists get a better understanding of how the economy functions and recommend policies that work. As Sherlock Holmes said, "Data, data, data; I can't make bricks without clay!" How strong the structure will be depends on the quality of the raw materials.

KEY TERMS

Consumer Price Index (CPI)

Substitution effect

Gross Domestic Product (GDP)

Underemployment

Capacity utilization

Productivity

REVIEW QUESTIONS

1. Explain how the Consumer Price Index tends to overstate inflation. Use practical examples to illustrate your answer.

2. Explain why the GDP may underestimate a country's productive activity and why it may not be an accurate indicator of economic well-being. Provide examples.

3. How does Statistics Canada underestimate the rate of unemployment? Some economists have argued that the United States has lower levels of unemployment than Canada because we have more generous employment insurance schemes. How can more generous EI lead to higher levels of official unemployment rates?

4. What are the ramifications of an upwardly biased CPI for fiscal and monetary policy?

DISCUSSION QUESTIONS

1. Some environmentalists have argued that GDP overstates our well-being because it doesn't account for the damage done to the environment with greater economic activity. If the environment were factored into the GDP, would it necessarily be a better indicator of economic well-being?

2. "Hurricanes and other natural disasters are good for the economy because they create jobs and increase the demand for goods and services." Do you agree with this line of reasoning? Justify your answer.

NOTES

1. The CPI is known as a Laspeyres index because it uses a base period or past bundle of goods as the weighting "yardstick." If you were to use a current bundle of goods as the weights and work back in time, you'd have a Paasche index. A weight simply means the share of income one spends on any good. If you spend 15 percent of your income on rock concerts, that's the weight assigned to that commodity.

2. You've probably realized that because the CPI is based on a weighted index over time of an *average* bundle of goods, we all experience potentially different inflation rates; the CPI captures just the average price increases based on a typical bundle of goods. It is also known that inflation is different across regions, towns, and provinces and even among different demographic groups.

3. A common inflation measurement is the GDP deflator which measures the change in all prices in the economy, both producer and consumer goods. It is an overall measure of inflation that is lower than the CPI. For more information about how inflation indexes are constructed, see Michael Parkin and Robin Bade's book *Economics: Canada in the Global Environment* 2nd ed. (Don Mills: Addison-Wesley, 1994).

4. This estimate comes from the work of Professor Erwin Diewert at the University of British Columbia. In 1980, the average price in the U.S. of a backyard satellite dish was about $40,000; by 1984 it was down to $2,000. Neglecting the introduction of new household electronic products led to an upward bias in this category alone of 10 percent over 5 years.

5. Economist William Nordhaus found that statisticians vastly overestimate the price of goods through history. For example, he found that the price of light when measured by conventional methods has gone up 180 percent in nominal terms since 1800 when, in fact, the price then was actually 1000 times higher than it is today! Professor Nordhaus argues that big inventions and improvements have been ignored in a range of goods including cars, radios, photocopiers, and even zippers. Source: "The Price of Light," *The Economist* (22 October 1994), p. 84.

6. The old measure one sometimes hears of is the *Gross National Product* or GNP. The difference is that the GDP consists of all goods and services produced in Canada by domestic or foreign companies, while GNP consists of goods produced by Canadian firms whether in Canada or abroad. The GDP is considered the more accurate picture of what's happening in the economy.

7. I picked up this nifty piece of information from Steven Landsburg's delightful book, *The Armchair Economist,* published by Free Press. He makes the same point that there are always plenty of people around to observe a crowd, but there's no one around to observe a vacuum. That's why the doctor's waiting room always seems crowded, because the chances are higher that you'll be there when most patients are waiting.

8. The tendency for firms to move around the world looking for cheaper inputs and bigger markets also undermines the credibility of capacity utilization numbers. When a firm experiences tighter capacity at home, it can now add needed capacity by shipping production abroad. Ibid., *Business Week,* p. 113.

9. Professor Diewert estimates that productivity growth for the economy is understated by almost 1 percent a year. To highlight what that means, an economy with a productivity growth rate of 1 percent needs 72 years to double its standard of living; one that grows at 2 percent only needs 36 years.

10. This point was brought to my attention by Professor Harvey King at the University of Regina.

11. As Professor Ferguson at the University of Guelph notes, all data released come with bands of uncertainty, which means the media often read too much into new statistics.

WEBLINKS

www.bankofcanada.ca/en/backgrounders/bg-i4.htm
The Consumer Price Index.

www.cs.cmu.edu/Web/Unofficial/Canadiana/README.html
Canadiana: The Canadian Resource Page.

www.oecd.org/std/gdp.htm
OCED statistics on GDP for 29 countries.

www.statcan.ca/english/Subjects/Labour/LFS/lfs-en.htm
Labour force survey, July 2000.

www.statcan.ca/Daily/English/000607/d000607b.htm
Industrial capacity utilization rates: first quarter 2000.

SETTING GOVERNMENT POLICIES

MYTH *"Wise economic policies can always control business cycles."*

Business cycles have always been the bane of capitalist economies. There was some hope in the 1960s that perhaps we had found the key to control and stabilize the ups and downs of the economy with wise fiscal and monetary policy. In time we've come to realize that controlling the business cycle is a naive hope. In light of less than perfect information about how the economy works, the question is whether a hands-on policy is better than a hands-off policy. It appears that the latter is the wiser and more prudent course.

If there's one thing the average person on the street doesn't need to hear from an economist, it is that times are tough when we're in a recession. It's obvious to the baker whose sales are down, or the steel worker just let go from his job, or the contract engineer when the city cancels the construction of a new subway line. The pain is apparent to anyone who has to endure the vagaries of the market; profits are down, inventories are high, and consumers' disposable incomes drop. In 1990, real GDP in Canada fell by $21 billion and unemployment rose from 7.5 percent to 11.5 percent by 1993. But just as there are bad times, good times eventually come around as businesses start investing and consumers start buying again. By early 2000, unemployment was just over 7 percent, the lowest in a generation. The ups and downs in the economy are another way to describe the boom and bust phases of the **business cycle**, phases characteristic of all modern and **mixed economies**. It can be argued that the major anxiety of Western economies is, when will the recession end? How long will the boom last? It can be said that permanence and stability aren't the hallmarks of modern industrial economies. Where does that leave government policy regarding the ups and downs of the economy? From what we know, the answer may be to do less rather than more.

WHAT GOES UP MUST COME DOWN: CAUSES OF THE CYCLES

One would think that with all the intellectual firepower directed at understanding modern economies, we would have figured out how to keep the economy from occasionally going into the tank, or control an overheated economy that seems to compel people to behave as if the good times will never end. Actually, we thought we had the key to steady economic growth back in the 1960s when some economists thought governments could fine-tune the economy by manipulating **monetary** and **fiscal policy**. When the economy is sluggish with rising unemployment and an overall drop in **aggregate demand**, and consumers are reluctant to get things going, all governments had to do, according to advocates of fine-tuning, was reduce taxes or spend more money on capital projects such as building roads. That's the fiscal side of the story. If that wasn't enough, the federal government, through the Bank of Canada, could step in and increase the money supply and drive down interest rates, making it less expensive for people to buy houses, cars, or that sound system the kids always wanted.

Policymakers would keep pushing on the monetary and fiscal levers until the economy was at full employment, or until everyone who wanted a job could get one. Now economists know that too much of a good thing, or sustained aggregate demand, can lead to unpleasant side-effects such as **inflation**. When that happens, the government simply puts monetary and fiscal policy in reverse until prices are stabilized while keeping employment at a high level. Some economists were so optimistic at the prospects of governments smoothing out the busts and booms in the economy that the whole system could be on automatic pilot: monetary and fiscal policy would kick in as soon as unemployment and inflation numbers reached certain levels. We already have in place **automatic stabilizers**, such as employment insurance, that automatically keep aggregate demand high when the economy slows down. Many of these insights came from John Maynard Keynes, the famous British economist, who argued that if governments had kept aggregate demand high enough, we could have avoided most of the misery of the Great Depression in the 1930s, which saw over 25 percent of the labour force without jobs in Canada.

What made economists optimistic about controlling the economy is that they observed when inflation was high, unemployment was low, and vice versa. This relationship is known as the **Phillips curve**, named after its discoverer, A.W. Phillips. In simple terms, what we have here is a trade-off between unemployment and inflation. If we want lower unemployment, we have to tolerate higher inflation; if we want lower price increases, we'll have to settle for fewer jobs. Those who hate inflation will advocate higher unemployment, while those who want more jobs will live with higher prices. Whatever side you choose, the elements for taming the business cycle are now in place: a steady and reliable trade-off between jobs and inflation, and to a great extent, government policy to control both. In either case, however, we can't have it all. Capitalist economies have to trade off lower prices with more unemployment and vice versa. That, in a nut shell, is the reason for the hope that we could finally control the business cycle. Optimism ran so high in the late 1960s and early '70s about the power of economics that the profession's esteem rose dramatically; economics was the *in* subject to study.[1]

ALL HELL BREAKS LOOSE

Just when everyone thought that the mystery of the gyrations in the economy was finally solved, along came the oil price increases in the mid-1970s to show how little we actually know about macroeconomics. Economists discovered what every student of economics knows: the subject is tough. The first thing to fall apart was the steady relationship between unemployment and inflation. Instead of one going up while the other fell, they both went up together creating the worst of both worlds—high prices and high unemployment. Existing mainstream theory told us that couldn't possibly happen. We now had a condition called **stagflation**: a stagnating economy with high prices. That had the effect of frustrating monetary and fiscal policy to the point where in the 1970s, the federal government resorted to imposing wage and price controls. Laws were used to do what economic policy couldn't. Then all hell broke loose. When controls were eventually removed, inflation went through the roof, hitting 11 percent by the late 1970s and early 1980s. To choke off the runaway inflation, the Bank of Canada pushed interest rates to over 20 percent, and in the process brought on one of the worst recessions since the 1930s.

Now economists were fighting in the halls of academe pointing fingers about who to blame. Those supporting Keynesianism were sent into retreat by the monetarists who argued that controlling the supply of money was a better way to direct the economy.[2] When the smoke cleared, we learned a few hard but important lessons.

First, economic growth and the creation of wealth in the long run are determined not by monetary and fiscal policy, but by the country's productive capacity, which means how much labour, capital, and technology a country has. One way to get more of these things is for governments to encourage higher savings and investments. Second, governments can nudge an economy to produce more goods and services in the short run by changing aggregate demand, if the policymakers know whether they are heading into a boom or into a recession. The message is that governments can still influence the economy in the short run, but we need a lot of good information about the economy. The key point is information, because without it we're flying blind. Third, in the long run there is no relationship between unemployment and inflation. In other words, there's no Phillips curve in the long run. That means that inflation can only be tamed by controlling the money supply. And finally, there may be a relationship between inflation and unemployment in the short run, which means that government policy can trade off a little inflation for more jobs. In other words, whatever employment benefits governments get from a policy of higher prices, they will be short lived if at all.[3] The lesson seems to be that Keynesianism is somewhat alive, in the short run, but not in the long run.

THE MYSTERY OF THE CYCLE CONTINUES: HANDS ON OR HANDS OFF?

Even though we know more about how business cycles work than we did twenty years ago, we still don't know very much. In fact, we're finding that the economy is much more difficult to manage than anyone imagined. So where does all this leave policymakers if they want to stabilize the economy? Even though policymakers might have some success in stabilizing the economy in the short run, the evidence seems to suggest a hands-off rather than a hands-on approach. And here's why:

1. The Role of Lags

One problem is that in order to react to a crisis in the economy, policymakers need information about what's happening, and that takes time. The economy is like piloting a big ocean liner: the ship only changes course long after the captain has given the order. And if you're not very good at the job, you'll compound one mistake after another, and drive the ship into disaster. Even if you know how to manage an economy, the information you need may be too long in coming. Economists differentiate between two kinds of lags in stabilization policy: *inside lags* and *outside lags.* The time between a shock to the economy and the time it is recognized and something is done about it is an inside lag, that could take months if not years. What makes it more complicated is that policymakers have to decide whether the crisis or shock, for example, an unexpected increase in unemployment, is self-correcting or needs government intervention.

Now assume the government decides to stimulate the economy with lower interest rates in reaction to higher unemployment. Changes in interest rates are especially slow because it takes time for them to wind themselves through the financial system before consumers and businesses get the message to start borrowing and buying: that's the outside lag. In both cases you need good information or you'll overshoot, or undershoot, your target and end up making things worse.[4] That's what many believe happened in the 1991–92 recession: the Bank of Canada, in its effort to fight inflation, overshot its inflation targets and drove interest rates to 5 and 6 points above rates in the United States. It managed to bring inflation under control, but drove unemployment to over 11 percent.[5] In many cases it takes years to study the data before coming to any conclusion about what happened and what to do about it. To this day economists still disagree about what caused the Great Depression, let alone what the best policy should have been.

2. *The Weakness of Forecasting*

In order to get better information about the economy, governments and businesses hire economists to forecast what's coming around the corner: Higher inflation? Lower aggregate demand? Lower interest rates? Lower unemployment? Useful as these forecasts are, they are far from infallible. Irving Fisher, one of the great economic minds of all time, predicted that the United States' economy would quickly recover after the stock market crash of 1929. His forecast was much too optimistic.[6] That was also the case in 1982, the worst recession since the Depression of the 1930s. No major forecaster, either in the private or public sector, predicted the depth or severity of that recession. In fact, most of them predicted what many thought would be a soft landing, a gradual decline in jobs over a long period of time, with plenty of time for policymakers to adjust. No one was prepared for the crash landing when it occurred. Economic models are great predictors when the economy is growing slowly and steadily, but are notoriously inaccurate when predicting disasters: they help most when they're needed least.[7]

This seems to confirm what Robert Lucas, the Nobel prize winner in economics, once said, "As an advice-giving profession we are in way over our heads." The reason is that people form expectations about such things as future inflation or the difficulty of finding a job. People also form expectations about how governments will react. If people anticipate that governments will fight high unemployment by stimulating the economy and causing inflation, they may frustrate government policy by building those expectations into their behaviour. Consumption may also be difficult to predict if people base their buying patterns on unexpected changes in income. It all sounds rather confusing, but Lucas makes the important point that we don't know enough about how people form expectations or how they affect government policy. And that makes forecasting all the more difficult.

3. *Economic Stability: A Statistical Illusion?*

Let's forget about the theoretical difficulties and see how successful governments have been in smoothing out the business cycle. After all, if government intervention has worked in the past, we don't have to worry how it works, only that it does. Some economists believe that since World War II, when governments became more active in the economy and took a more prominent role in maintaining full employment, economies in the West became more stable, with much less volatility in unemployment and real GDP; in short, we seem to be smoothing out the business cycle. If that's the case, who cares about what Lucas says about expectations, or the accuracy of economic forecasting? If government intervention works, just do it.

But is that what the data show? Are we in fact smoothing out the business cycle? Not according to Christina Romer, who makes the argument that the economy only seems more stable since 1945. And much of the illusion of a more stable business cycle has to do with better data since World War II. If we had better economic data before the war, the fluctuations in the business cycle would seem less extreme. Here's how she found out. Since she couldn't improve the quality of pre-war data, she constructed new 'bad' data for the post-war period. What she did, in fact, was build a post-war picture using only data series comparable with those available in the earlier period. She found that the economy is almost as unstable after 1945 as it was before then. This implies that stabilization policy is mainly a statistical illusion, which undermines the case that governments can do much good to control fluctuations in the economy.[8] Although her work remains controversial, most economists now believe that the economy is less stable than once thought.

THE NEW ECONOMY AND THE BUTTERFLY EFFECT

If policymakers and economists have discovered anything about business cycles, it's their fickleness and unpredictability. So unpredictable, in fact, that for many economists the economy is almost ungovernable. When you think of the economy as a metaphor for the extremely complex daily personal and commercial transactions of 26 million Canadians, you begin to grasp the enormous task of bringing such a system to heel. And the more complex a system, the less stable and predictable it becomes. Systems that are extremely complex can be influenced by the smallest impacts. That's why earthquakes and the weather are impossible to predict. In mathematics this is known whimsically as the **butterfly effect**: a theorem showing that a butterfly flapping its wings in the Amazon rain forest affects the weather patterns months later in Moose Jaw. In the short run, any external shock can have unknown and unpredictable effects, which explains why government policies don't often work. In systems as complex as that of developed economies, minor events, or statistically insignificant ones, can be very important without anyone knowing why or how.

Recent work by a number of respected economists shows that economics is much closer to an ever-changing biological system than to physics with set rules and principles. Learning economics is more than understanding how a machine works and then pulling the right levers to get it to full employment; the economy is an adaptive system, which makes it highly unpredictable. That is, consumers and businesses learn from past experiences and adapt to changing conditions. The **theory of rational expectations**, an influential branch of economics in the 1980s, held that because consumers and businesses are rational and take into account government policy, consumers and businesses can't be fooled. Rational expectation advocates held that the only way for government policies to work was for them to be random and unexpected. The irony is that such behaviour only made things more unstable! If that's the case, it becomes almost impossible to model the economy with any degree of accuracy, where raw chance plays a major role in what happens. This is referred to as the **Lucas critique** (named after the economist Robert E. Lucas), which states that estimating the effect of a policy change requires knowing how people respond to that policy change. That's the thinking of a number of prominent economists who are re-evaluating conventional economics in light of complexity theory.[9]

Where does this leave policymakers? For one thing, they have less control over the economy than they once thought, especially in the short run, and that means the average length of business cycles. If that's the situation, the less intervention in the economy the better. According to the famous management consultant Peter Drucker, it is better to follow the old maxim, 'when in doubt, do nothing,' especially in the short run. His message is to get the fundamentals right, keep inflation low, encourage savings and investment, promote competition and free trade, keep the debt and deficit under control, and ensure that you have a well-educated labour force. Does this imply, however, that governments should do nothing even in the face of severe economic crises? After all, advocates of economic intervention can argue that if the money supply had not been increased in Canada and the United States by the Bank of Canada and the Federal Reserve respectively after the stock market crash of 1987, we could have faced another depression. The point can still be made that the role of government should be reserved for such occasions, but trying to continually micro-manage the economy may only make things worse.

KEY TERMS

Business cycle	Inflation	Butterfly effect
Mixed economies	Automatic stabilizers	Rational expectations
Monetary policy	Stagflation	theory
Fiscal policy	Phillips curve	Lucas critique
Aggregate demand		

REVIEW QUESTIONS

1. a) Explain how, in theory, governments can fine-tune the economy by using monetary and fiscal policy.

   b) In each case, describe what kind of policies governments would have to pursue in a recession and boom.

   c) Explain how inside and outside lags make it difficult to fine-tune the economy.

2. Give two examples of automatic stabilizers and explain, in theory, how they work to smooth the business cycle.

3. What are three arguments in favour of less government intervention in controlling the business cycle?

DISCUSSION QUESTIONS

1. Does the fact that the economy is more complex than originally thought make all government action less useful?

2. "Many economists don't like to hear that economics is closer to biology than physics." Discuss.

NOTES

1. Again by early 2000, we seem to be in a perfect economy with low inflation, low unemployment, and a growing economy. Some say we are in a 'new paradigm' where the 'old rules' of economics no longer hold. Whether the rules have changed, only time will tell, but so far no one has shown that the laws of economics are now defunct.

2. This is a highly simplified view of the debate that actually took place. The monetarists, headed by Milton Friedman, argued that real GDP, growth after inflation, and money supply are closely linked; just make sure money supply doesn't grow faster than the ability of the economy to grow. The other schools that sprang up were the rational expectation school, the supply-siders, and the new classical economics. For a readable tour of these ideas see Alan S. Blinder, *Hard Heads, Soft Hearts* (Don Mills, ON: Addison-Wesley, 1987).

3. It should be said that not everyone agrees with these conclusions. New classical economists argue that even in the short run, monetary and fiscal policy won't work, but the four lessons outlined in the text are a good approximation of what many economists believe. N. Gregory Mankiw, *Macroeconomics* (New York: Worth Publishers, 1994).

4. Automatic stabilizers are fiscal policies that tend to reduce inside lags, but not outside ones.

5. Thomas Wilson, Peter Dungan, and Steve Murphy, "The Sources of the Recession in Canada: 1989–92," *Canadian Business Economics* (Winter, 1994).

6. One could argue that we have better models and techniques today. However, when comparing modern models today, we find they wouldn't have done any better predicting the Great Depression. Ibid., Mankiw, p. 325.

7. A consensus of 50 top economists in the United States predicted a continuation growth rate of 2.2 percent in GNP for 1982; the economy actually headed into a nose dive, falling 2.5 percent, a margin of error of 400 percent. Remember those are growth rates, and not percentage changes. The economist Robert Heilbroner wrote an interesting article about economic predictions for the *New Yorker* entitled "Reflections," 8 July 1901.

8. Christina D. Romer, "Is the Stabilization of the Postwar Economy a Figment of the Data?" *American Economic Review* (June 1986).

9. Two prominent economists at the forefront of complexity theory are the Nobel economist Kenneth Arrow and Brian Arthur at Stanford University. For an interesting discussion of economics and complexity see Charles R. Morris, "It's Not the Economy, Stupid," *The Atlantic Monthly* (July 1993).

WEBLINKS

www.fin.gc.ca/activty/ecfisce.html
Finance Canada: Economic and Fiscal Policy.

cepa.newschool.edu/het/essays/keynes/inflation.htm
Inflation and the Phillips curve.

deas.uqam.ca/ideas/data/Papers/nbrnberwo6230.html
Business Cycles Observed and Assessed: Why and How They Matter.

www.kva.se/eng/pg/prizes/economics/1995/ekeng.html
The Lucas critique.

HIGH UNEMPLOYMENT

 **"We can't do much about high unemployment."**

Many believe that high unemployment is an evil of modern society and that little can be done to reduce it. The natural rate of unemployment has stubbornly gone up over the last half century. Globalization has had some role to play in putting people out of work, but less than we think. Much of our unemployment is caused by home-grown factors. We know that unemployment is caused by tight monetary policy, poorly designed employment programs, payroll taxes, needless regulations, and the role of unions. The best policies are those that reduce the cost of hiring workers and remove impediments that restrict business from expanding.

Since the mid-1970s, Canada has been fighting a losing battle against unemployment. Even during the boom years of the late 1980s, unemployment never went below 7.5 percent, and promptly shot up over 11 percent when the recession hit in 1990–91. The United States, which went through the same recession, managed to keep its rate of unemployment 4 to 5 percentage points below Canada's. By the first quarter in 2000, unemployment was again below 7.5 percent, but the U.S. rate was an astonishing 3.8 percent. If the structures of our economies are roughly the same, and the United States buys 80 percent of our exports, why are our rates of unemployment double those in the United States?

We hear stories that unemployment is caused by everything from free trade to cheap foreign imports (not true) to globalization and technology (somewhat true). But much of our unemployment woes are home grown and have more to do with policy and institutional reasons that resemble Europe's more than the United States', such as our system of employment insurance. The reality, unfortunately, is that we can't bring unemployment to zero, but we can do a lot better. Before looking at the arguments supporting this claim, let's first examine how and why unemployment remains stubbornly high and why it's such a dilemma for policymakers.

THE RISING NATURAL RATE OF UNEMPLOYMENT

In 1999, over 8 percent of the labour force was out of work. Given a labour force of almost 14 million people, that's about 1.2 million people officially out of work. The good news is that we've been able to provide work for 12.5 million people, or around 92 percent of the labour force. Nevertheless, unemployment represents a tremendous waste of resources making us all worse off. Coupled with the added waste created by **underemployment**, where workers, talents, and skills are underutilized, we begin to realize the vast quantities of goods and services society is foregoing. But, Canada's rate of unemployment wasn't always this high.

In the 1950s, Canada's economy was close to full employment, with only 3 percent of the labour force unemployed. Today we consider it full employment when 8 percent of the labour force don't have jobs. Over the past 45 years, unemployment has fluctuated from below 3 percent to almost 12 percent, forcing the **natural rate of unemployment** to more than double from 4 percent to over 9 percent. What happened over those intervening years to change the face of unemployment so drastically? Part of the answer can be found in the role of the Bank of Canada, the employment insurance program, the role of organized labour, and demographic and labour-force changes.

Economists have long accepted that there's a given level of unemployment consistent with stable prices. Increasing employment above a "natural rate" comes at the expense of higher prices. In other words, there is what economists call a **nonaccelerating inflation rate of unemployment**, or **NAIRU**.[1] As NAIRU increases, so does the general level of unemployment. If a 10 percent rate of unemployment comes with a nonaccelerating 5 percent rate of inflation, and we want to reduce unemployment to 7 percent, we may have to accept a much higher rate of inflation. Some may argue that there's nothing wrong with more inflation if it comes with a drop in unemployment. They would be right if that were the end of the story, but it isn't.

Rising prices have a nasty habit of getting out of control. People learn quickly that lower levels of unemployment come with higher inflation rates and begin building higher prices and wage expectations into their behaviour. A 5 percent rate of inflation today becomes 10 percent tomorrow. We may even be able to live with that rate, but what about a 50 percent or 100 percent rate of inflation? What was once a reasonable rate of inflation quickly becomes intolerable. The natural rate of unemployment, or NAIRU, demands that we have to draw the line somewhere. Although the growth in the money supply determines inflation in the long run, it's in the short run that we live and have to determine policies to control inflation. We now turn to the Bank of Canada's role to control prices in the short run and the impact on employment.

ZERO INFLATION AND THE ROLE OF THE BANK OF CANADA

Policymakers face a dilemma, for while they want to reduce unemployment further, the Bank of Canada is committed to a policy of low inflation as a way of breaking the psychology of rising price expectations. Ever since inflation reached double digits in the early 1980s, the Bank of Canada has been steadfast in making sure it doesn't happen again. The Bank argues that we must eliminate inflation completely before embarking on any programs to stimulate the economy to full employment. So far it's succeeded in bringing inflation under control. However, the trade-off of lower inflation in the short run is higher **cyclical unemployment** levels. By early 1995, the annual rate of inflation was just over 2 percent as measured by the Consumer Price Index, but it came at the expense of a 10 percent rate of unemployment at a time when the economy had been out of recession for two years.[2]

Did we have to suffer such high rates of unemployment even though the federal government, through the Bank of Canada, was fighting inflation so vigorously? Although we can't avoid the basic reality of some level of unemployment if we want stable prices, the Bank of Canada may have gone too far in its fight against inflation.[3] Looking back, the Bank of Canada won its fight against inflation in a world that was deflating, making its own policies somewhat redundant. By mid-1995, there were signs that the economy was slowing down, but the difference between United States' and Canadian interest short-term rates were at historical highs. Some have argued that though the Bank may have fought inflation too strongly, it would be a shame to lose those inflation gains with a policy of lower interest rates. That may be true, but in hindsight it's clear that a zero-inflation rate policy came at the expense of slower growth and fewer jobs.

FRICTIONAL UNEMPLOYMENT AND THE ROLE OF EMPLOYMENT INSURANCE

Another factor driving up Canada's natural rate of unemployment is that the frictional or **transitional** level of **unemployment** has gone up. Frictional unemployment is the time it takes for many of us to go from one job to another. The labour market, like other markets, isn't perfect; it takes time and information to find work. If it didn't, we would instantaneously move from one job to another. Maybe in a world of perfect information, but not this one. You may have the perfect qualifications for a job in Moose Jaw, but by the time you and the job find each other, you've been counted as unemployed by Statistics Canada.

A key factor in increasing frictional unemployment is Canada's employment insurance (EI) program (formerly known as unemployment insurance [UI]). Although designed to ease the transition from one job to another, it invites abuse by providing unemployed workers the luxury of not taking the first job that comes along. Since 1971, when EI reforms were introduced, it's been estimated that EI alone has increased our rate of unemployment by 2 percentage points over unemployment rates in the United States.[4] By alleviating the hardships of unemployment, EI increases the amount of frictional unemployment, and raises the natural rate of unemployment.[5]

Although employment insurance isn't the only culprit for driving up the natural rate of unemployment, there's plenty of anecdotal and scientific evidence to suggest that EI is providing too many claimants with wrong incentives. Claimants only have to work 10 weeks to collect 40 weeks of benefits. It's not surprising that many people only work the required 10 weeks and take the rest of the year off and start the cycle all over again. And that's what the data tells us. One study found that 93 percent of workers on EI found work just before their benefits ran out, while almost 40 percent of EI claimants have used the system more than three times over a five-year period.[6]

Another problem with the EI system is that many cyclical industries have a greater tendency to lay off workers knowing that they are eligible to collect employment insurance benefits—in other words, forcing the taxpayer to subsidize their industries rather than keeping these workers on payroll until the economy recovers. The biggest users of EI, not surprisingly, are workers in seasonal industries such as agriculture, forestry, fishing, and construction. In forestry, for every dollar that industry and workers contribute in premiums, they take out about $9 in EI payments. In the construction industry, the ratio is $3 for every dollar contributed in premiums. The heaviest users of EI share two characteristics: their lay-off rates are higher than average, and their workers' weekly earnings are higher than average.[7] With such strong incentives, laid-off workers usually wait to be recalled without looking for more work. It is common knowledge that in fisheries, EI is used as an income supplement, and not an income bridge to a new job. There would be little need for reform if the program wasn't so expensive. Employment insurance, the centrepiece of Canada's social welfare system, has become one of the most expensive social programs in the country, costing around $18 billion each year. Americans, on the other hand, spend about $25 billion (Canadian) in total with a labour force 11 times that of our own. Canada spends four times more as a percent of GDP than does the United States on employment insurance.[8]

WAGES, TAXES, UNIONS, AND SELFISH WORKERS

It's been long known that sticky or rigid wages make it difficult for labour markets to clear, leading to higher levels of unemployment. If that's the case, workers aren't unemployed because they can't find work, but wages at the going rate are too high for firms to hire them. These workers are just waiting for jobs to become available. Why don't wages adjust to changing market conditions? As we've seen in Chapter 4, minimum wages provide a floor under which wages can't fall; and we know that those who suffer the most are the young with little job experience. If the law states that wages can't go below $6.85 an hour, as in Ontario, but some workers would take $5.00 an hour, that creates unemployment. Unions also have the power to keep wages above market levels. The wages of unions aren't determined by the supply and demand of workers, but by the negotiating ability of union leaders who often raise wages above their equilibrium levels. According to one study, an increase of 10 percentage points in the proportion of the labour force that is unionized raises the unemployment rate by 1.2 percentage points.[9]

The theory that explains how unions drive up unemployment is partly explained by the **insider–outsider** theory. This theory says that those on the inside with jobs care little about those on the outside without jobs. By driving up their own wages, those with jobs are depriving those on the outside of an opportunity to work if wages had been lower. It should be said that workers pushing to increase their wages do so without intending to deprive others of work, but their actions have the unintended consequences of keeping others outside the job market. With higher wage bills, firms react by hiring fewer workers and substituting capital for labour at faster rates. This theory belies the notion of worker solidarity.

Not surprisingly, countries that have a higher share of their work force belonging to unions have higher rates of unemployment. In the 1960s, both the United States and Canada had about 30 percent of their labour forces belonging to unions. Since then Canada's unionization rate increased marginally to 33 percent, while the share of unionization in the United States dropped to 16 percent. Part of the consequences of a higher rate of unionization in Canada is that during the 1980s real wages increased 30 percent relative to the real wage in the United States. One can understand why workers push for higher wages, but why would employers accommodate their demands? One explanation is the **efficiency wage theory**, which holds that some companies pay higher than normal wages, not because they are forced to by unions, but as a way to keep their best workers from leaving. Good workers are hard to find, and firms have an incentive to minimize worker turnover by paying higher than market wages to keep workers happy and productive.[10]

Although unions, minimum wages, and efficiency wages tend to drive up the cost of labour, cash-starved governments have also done their part to increase the cost of hiring workers by resorting to a variety of **payroll taxes** to increase revenues. From 1989 to 1993, wages and salaries grew by about 10 percent, yet payroll taxes, or supplementary labour income, grew by 40 percent. These payroll taxes now account for about 14 percent of total wages and salaries from around 6 percent in 1970. When the cost of hiring workers goes up, firms don't hire as many workers. And the evidence bears this out. One Bank of Canada study estimates that every time the payroll tax goes up 3 percent, there's a reduction in employment of 1 percent.[11] However, it should be noted that real wages stagnated over the 1990s and only recovered somewhat in 1999, driven partly by increasing labour productivity and a growing labour shortage.

WHAT ABOUT GLOBALIZATION, TECHNOLOGY, AND CHANGING DEMOGRAPHICS?

Important as the above factors are, the media's attention is drawn to more dramatic explanations of unemployment, such as the restructuring of our economy brought about by globalization, changing technologies, and shifting demographics. How important are these in explaining Canada's high unemployment?

Canada, along with the rest of the world, is in a transition from an economy where traditional skills are rapidly changing; we are moving from a goods-intensive economy to a knowledge-based economy. Although manufacturing isn't dead, there's no question that how we manufacture goods is changing, and that has implications for employment. In an economy based more on information and knowledge, most of us will be working in the production and transmission of information—an area that requires a whole new set of skills and talents. Together with a more global economy where capital, labour, and production are freer to move from one country to another, you can begin to appreciate the enormous changes taking place. This transition between sectors, called inter-sectoral shift, is matched by within-firm restructuring as firms become more competitive and cost-efficient, shedding expensive labour for relatively cheaper capital. That's why more Canadian firms, over the past decade, have been investing in automated systems and more efficient inventory controls.

Economists such as Richard Lipsey have dubbed this phenomenon a **paradigm shift**, a fancy term for a fundamental change in what we produce and how we produce it. In such a world, fewer of us are actually needed to produce anything tangible. Douglas North, an economic historian who won the Nobel prize in 1993, calculated that in the 1930s, 25 percent of the labour force was involved in the transmission of information; this includes teachers, lawyers, accountants, civil servants, designers, writers, consultants, and so on. Today, that number is over 50 percent. We're becoming a nation of information manipulators or, as some call it, **symbolic analysts.**[12] The less workers are engaged in goods production, the more complex society becomes, demanding new skills and technologies. Whole transitions to new ways of doing things bring with them changes in **structural unemployment** as people adapt to these profound economic transformations.

Given this structural shift in the economy, more workers are trapped between skills based on the old economy, versus those based on the new economy. Workers who will be affected the most are those working in regions and towns that rely on one industry. Even though jobs are being created in one sector and lost in another, some workers may never get the skills and education they need to go from a declining sector to a growing one. This phenomenon hasn't been helped by a shift in demographics. It was thought that in the mid-1970s, a growing labour force made up of young, inexperienced baby-boomers was pushing up the natural rate of unemployment, along with a steady increase in the female participation rate as more women entered the labour force.[13] Now an aging and growing population, as baby-boomers reach 50 in the late 1990s, can raise the NAIRU because older workers tend to have longer unemployment spells when laid off than younger workers.[14]

Along with these major demographic, technical, and global transitions, economists have added a new and novel explanation to a persistently high level of unemployment called **hysteresis**. This awkward term simply means that after a major outside shock to the economy, such as a dramatic oil price increase in the 1970s, the economy never quite settles down to employment levels before the adjustment. Shock after shock simply ratchets up the overall level of unemployment. Why does this happen? One explanation is that skills deteriorate after major changes to the economy, making it harder to re-employ older workers.

Interesting and important as many of these theories are, they aren't very useful in explaining Canada's persistently higher levels of unemployment compared to the United States. For example, try as they might, economists haven't found much evidence to explain how hysteresis plays much of a role in Canada's employment picture. As for the notion of paradigm shift and an aging work force, each has its place in explaining the difficulty of adjusting to a changing world and the transition for corporate restructuring. But these factors are a challenge to all industrial countries, not just Canada. What we're also seeing is that economies that rely more heavily on the state for economic growth and employment are finding the shift to a more global economy much more difficult.

Sweden is a case in point. Once a model for other social democratic societies, growth has dropped off to half the OECD rate since the 1970s. By 1994, unemployment reached 14 percent of the labour force, up from 3 percent two decades before. Today the public sector accounts for an astounding 70 percent of GDP, while a third of its work force works directly for the government. Sweden is facing the reality that its problems weren't created by external uncontrollable forces, but by internally designed policies that provided the wrong incentives for economic growth, making it more difficult for its labour force to adjust to change. In light of these high rates of structural unemployment, Sweden has taken drastic actions to cut back on the size of its public sector and stimulate private investment.

Canada, to a slightly lesser extent, is in the same boat. Countries that restrict trade and commerce with regulations are also prone to higher unemployment levels. That was a conclusion found in a study trying to explain why European unemployment rates were double those in the United States.[15] Canada's high unemployment rates are better explained by internal domestic policies rather than the attention-grabbing 'big picture' theories emphasized by the media.

WHERE DO WE GO FROM HERE?

The bad news about the unemployment rate is that it seems we'll never get it down to 3–4 percent of the work force. But that doesn't mean we're helpless in the face of changing demographics, technology changes, globalized markets, or even severe government budget constraints. The challenge for governments is not to get sidetracked with trendy policies that have small impacts, such as work sharing, which too often simply increase the cost of employment, and capital projects that use more machines than workers.[16] Even training programs have limited impacts on employment. The most effective programs are those that remove the incentives to stay unemployed, provide workers with better information about where jobs are, and reduce the cost to business of hiring more workers.

KEY TERMS

Underemployment	Transitional	Payroll taxes
Natural rate of	unemployment	Paradigm shift
unemployment	Cyclical unemployment	Symbolic analyst
Nonaccelerating inflation	Insider–outsider theory	Structural unemployment
rate of unemployment	Efficiency wage theory	Hysteresis
(NAIRU)		

REVIEW QUESTIONS

1. Define frictional unemployment and explain why economies will always experience some level of this sort of employment. Explain how Canada's employment insurance programs keep frictional unemployment high. Is frictional unemployment always a bad thing?

2. Critically evaluate the argument that labour unions drive up unemployment.

3. Define NAIRU and explain why Canada's natural rate of unemployment has been increasing over the years.

4. What are the differences between frictional, structural, and cyclical forms of unemployment?

DISCUSSION QUESTIONS

1. "The cruel irony is that government programs designed to help the unemployed often are a detriment to putting people to work." Comment.

2. Apart from reforming employment insurance, what would you do to reduce Canada's high natural rate of unemployment? *(Hint:* Think about the causes of unemployment, then outline policies that would reduce them.)

NOTES

1. The natural rate, discovered by Milton Friedman in the late 1960s, was later changed to the nonaccelerating inflation rate of unemployment because the original term implied there was something good, or natural, about unemployment. See: Paul Krugman, *The Age of Diminished Expectations* (Cambridge, Mass.: MIT Press, 1994).

2. The Bank of Canada isn't without its critics. WEFA, a forecasting and consulting firm, claims that the Bank's high interest rate policy drove the rate of unemployment from 8 percent to 10 percent in 1991. See: *Why Has Canada's Economy Performed So Poorly?* (Toronto: WEFA), March 1992.

3. Steven S. Poloz, *The Causes of Unemployment in Canada: A Review of the Evidence,* Institute for Policy Analysis, Policy Study 94–5 (University of Toronto, October 1994), p. 15.

4. This is an estimate by Professor Tom Courchene at Queen's University.

5. Rising frictional unemployment isn't always a bad thing if it means that people take more time finding the right job.

6. The Atlantic Institute for Market Studies 1995, and Department of Human Resources, 1994. The McKinley Global Institute found that regulations were a major cause of the EU's (European Union) high unemployment rates compared to those in the U.S. *Employment Performance* (Washington, D.C.: McKinley Global Institute, November 1994).

7. Not just the needy avail themselves of EI. The federal Department of Human Resources found 528 fishing families with average annual incomes of over $70,000 collecting EI. *The Globe and Mail,* 8 January 1995.

8. Michael Walker, "The Obvious Solution for Unemployment Insurance," *Fraser Forum,* December 1994.

9. Lawrence H. Summers, "Why Is the Unemployment Rate So Very High Near Full Employment?" *Brookings Papers on Economic Activity 2* (Washington, D.C.: Brookings Institute, 1986) pp. 339–383.

10. In 1914, Henry Ford began paying his workers $5 a day, twice the going wage, on the assumption that paying higher salaries was a way to get a more loyal and productive work force.

11. Ibid., Poloz, p. 12.

12. Term coined by United States Secretary of Labor Robert Reich under President Bill Clinton.

13. Female share of the labour force went from 34 percent in 1970 to about 45 percent in 1994, although there are signs the rate is now levelling off.

14. Ibid., Poloz.

15. On December 1, 1995, Human Resources Minister, Lloyd Axworthy, introduced changes to Canada's UI system that reduced the length of time people could access UI, especially for repeat users of the system.

16. Job sharing is often advanced as a cure for unemployment. But job sharing won't work for a number of reasons: First, shorter hours will create more jobs only if weekly pay is cut, otherwise cost per unit of output will go up. Second, not all labour costs vary with the number of hours worked. It usually costs more to hire two workers than one. See "One Lump or Two?" *The Economist,* 25 November 1995.

WEBLINKS

www.bankofcanada.ca/en/speeches/sp00-4.htm
The Canadian Economy: Finding the Right Balance

www.parl.gc.ca/english/senate/com-e/soci-e/08ap2-e.htm
Employment insurance reform.

www.clc-ctc.ca/policy/ui/research3.html
The Economic Impacts of Unemployment Insurance: The Case for the Defence.

www.fraserinstitute.ca/publications/books/unions/unions.html
Unionization and Economic Performance: Evidence on Productivity, Profits, Investment, and Growth.

Chapter

QUEBEC
AND
SOVEREIGNTY

24

 **MYTH** *"The cost of separation will be manage-able for Quebec and Canada."*

What will be the costs if Quebec separates and leaves Canada? Those in favour of separation believe the costs will be low if the federal government and Quebec bargain in good faith. However, there are those who believe if the negotiations are acrimonious the costs to Canada will be high. We know that the costs won't be trivial and could be extremely high in terms of lost investment and economic stability. In the end, the costs of separation, whatever they are, will fall mainly on Quebeckers themselves.

On October 30, 1995, Canada was on the verge of breaking up. In the end, Quebeckers voted to stay in Canada by the slimmest of margins: 50.6 percent voted no to independence compared to 49.4 who voted yes. Despite the second vote in a referendum where Quebeckers chose Canada over separation, the country may not be out of the woods yet. But what happens if Quebec eventually decides to separate?[1] What will be the economic costs to Quebec and the rest of the country? Quebec can clearly manage alone. Countries of similar size, such as Switzerland, have achieved one of the highest standards of living in the world. The real question is, what will be the cost of such a separation to Canada and Quebec? Many believe, particularly PQ supporters in Quebec, that separation need not be an economic burden and that the transition costs of separation would be manageable. They argue that our current federation wastes resources by duplicating government services at the federal and provincial level. It would be more efficient to eliminate one level of government. But those who believe the costs would be minimal are deluding themselves. The costs of breaking up the country would be high. How high would depend on the circumstances of separation. And since no one knows the circumstances under which separation will take place, no one can know the real costs.

THE ECONOMICS OF SEPARATION

Those who favour Quebec independence, or some form of economic partnership or **sovereignty association**, have a stake in minimizing the costs to both Quebec and Canada. A number of French-Canadian economists and members of the PQ assume that once Canadians confront the reality of separation, the Canadian government will bargain in good faith because it will be in its self-interest to do so. Separatists believe that negotiations will be tough, but calm, and the costs of adjustment to the breakup of the country will be low. Those who believe in a strong federal government make the opposite case: they feel that if Quebec decides to leave, "all bets are off" and forecast that the negotiations will be not only tough, but also acrimonious. As much was admitted by the federal Minister of Intergovernmental Affairs, Stéphane Dion. Under those circumstances, the costs in terms of lost income, less investment, and higher unemployment could drive the price of separation sky high for Canada, and especially for Quebec. This fundamental difference gives the overall impression that economists' opinions are widely scattered on the issue of the economic costs of Quebec separation. The projected costs vary from a high of 10 percent of GDP estimated by the Fraser Institute to a low of 1.4 percent of GDP estimated by the former Economic Council of Canada. It's important to note, however, that the differences of opinion are not based on disagreements about technical and purely economic questions, but rather on the political scenarios of separation. However, since the early 1990s, considerable work has been done on the economic impacts of Quebec independence. The three general observations about these studies are that, first, the costs of the breakup of the country will be greater the more decentralized the country becomes; second, the economic impact would be greater for Quebec than for the rest of Canada; and third, no one knows what the exact costs of separation will be because until it happens, no one knows the conditions under which the country will be divided.

The Low-Cost Scenario

The most optimistic forecasts of the impact of Quebec sovereignty came mainly from French-Canadian economists when they presented their briefs before the **Bélanger-Campeau Commission**, which dealt with Quebec's constitutional and political future under Premier Robert Bourassa in 1991. The studies that dealt with the economics of Quebec's independence arrived at two basic conclusions. The first conclusion was that the transitional costs involved in any separation would be minimal if the federal and Quebec governments negotiate rationally. The second conclusion was that the long-term costs would be low or negligible in terms of lost jobs and a change in standard of living. To reach these conclusions, the Bélanger-Campeau Commission made a number of crucial assumptions. The first assumption was that the trade relations with the rest of Canada and the United States would remain unchanged. This means that Canada would agree to a **common market** with Quebec in which they would behave much like the European Economic Community. They would also agree to reduce internal trade barriers between the regions of Canada as well as maintain common tariff and nontariff barriers with other countries. After separation, the United States, Mexico, and Canada would automatically allow Quebec to become a member of NAFTA with few variations to the existing agreement. At the same time, Quebec would quickly become a member of the WTO.

The second assumption deals with monetary policy. Here the commission assumed that Quebec would have a common monetary policy with the rest of Canada by adopting the Canadian dollar as its currency. Former Premier Jacques Parizeau has said often that an independent Quebec could take the Canadian dollar as its currency without Ottawa's permission or endorsement. A third assumption was that Quebec's budgetary position would change little after the formation of a new state. The secretariat to the Bélanger-Campeau Commission made the argument that Quebec should assume only 18.5 percent of the national debt rather than its share based on population, which would be around 25 percent.[2] On the issue of loss of federal equalization payments to Quebec, the sovereigntists argue that Quebec would lose little if anything after separation, given that Quebec's tax contributions to Canada (so say Quebec's nationalists) are the same as the transfers from Ottawa.

A study done by the Economic Council of Canada[3] estimated that under the conditions of separation, in which the federal government cut out all buying from Quebec and the province no longer collects equalization payments, the loss to Quebec would be a drop in welfare equal to only between 1.4 and 3.5 percent of its GDP.[4] Quebec nationalists were quick to use these numbers to show that the costs would be low for Quebec and practically nonexistent for the rest of Canada. But the council's findings only showed what would happen if the federal government removed taxes and transfers, and ignored the political consequences of splitting up the country. The picture changes considerably if international and national considerations are taken into account.[5] In the end, the PQ painted a rosy scenario in order to maximize their chances of gaining as much support as possible for separation. They even promised their fellow citizens that they would retain their Canadian passport even with an independent Quebec and have representatives on the Board of Governors of the Bank of Canada.

The High-Cost Scenario

If any one needed proof that political instability leads to economic instability, the Quebec referendum was a classic example of how international investors behave when their money is in jeopardy. During the month before the referendum when polls were showing surprising support for a "Yes" vote for independence, the Canadian dollar dropped from 75 U.S. cents to 72 U.S. cents, while prime rates jumped 1 percent just before the vote. Canadian stock markets also saw a sell-off of Canadian securities as investors took a wait-and-see attitude. The Canadian economy hadn't changed, but the political situation was highly uncertain, and that translates into jittery financial and equity markets. Immediately after the vote, the markets were so relieved that the No side won, that the dollar strengthened and interest rates dropped. How important are these changes? Although they are hard to measure, one study estimates that if international lenders charge 1 percent more to Canadian borrowers, the loss will slow growth in Canada's GDP equivalent to $8.6 billion (1986 dollars) over a 10-year period. Along with a higher borrowing rate facing governments, Canada could also expect less **direct investment**. Lower investment of $1 billion each year for 10 years means 1 percent less capital and machinery to work with a 0.5-percent drop in productivity and real wages. However, we may not have to wait for separation in order to be affected by higher interest rates and less investment. International investors know the political climate in Canada and are already charging Canadians a premium to hold government bonds.[6]

Most experts agree that Quebec will have little problem becoming a member of the WTO, but joining NAFTA is another matter. A "sovereign Quebec" will be negotiating with a "sovereign Canada," which means that Quebec will have to give up its industrial subsidies, forfeit protection of its financial institutions (i.e., the caisses populaires), open up its purchasing by government departments, stop Hydro-Quebec from subsidizing local industries, eliminate existing barriers against goods and services from other provinces, and repeal laws that discriminate against out-of-province construction workers from operating in Quebec. Those who remember how difficult it was to negotiate the free trade agreement with the United States should know that Quebec's negotiations with Canada and the United States will not be easy. Quebec was allowed to keep a number of its protective programs because of its sub-national status within Confederation—that won't be the case once it becomes a sovereign nation. As trade expert Gordon Ritchie said, "if it were easy to agree on free trade, it would not have taken us 50 years to get tariffs down to present levels."[7] Here Canada would be in a better bargaining position than an independent Quebec. Canada ships only 6.8 percent of all manufacturing output to Quebec, while Quebec in turn exports over 26 percent to the rest of Canada.[8]

The idea of a new **customs union** between an independent Quebec and Canada is unlikely because the rest of the country will not be willing to pay higher tariffs to protect the textile, clothing, and furniture industries in Quebec. Continuing to protect these sectors is important to Quebec because these "soft" industries are located mainly in Quebec and account for about 48.5 percent of total Canadian employment in those industries. Quebec has a considerable trade surplus in those industries that rely heavily on exports to the rest of Canada. Quebec exports 52 percent of its textile output to other provinces, 45 percent of its clothing, and 38 percent of its furniture and fixtures output.[9] After separation, Canadians would start buying these products from lower-cost producers around the world, such as those in the Far East and South America. The same principle applies to agricultural products. Quebec dairy producers supply almost 50 percent of Canada's industrial milk, cheese, and ice cream output at inflated prices protected by marketing boards. Direct and indirect federal subsidies to Quebec, including protection under supply-management schemes, amounted to over a billion dollars by the mid-1990s. If Quebec dairy farmers had to sell their products at world prices to the rest of Canada, they would stand to lose as much as $200 million annually. Some Quebec farm organizations have already advocated that existing supply management arrangements should remain, arguing that they have a right to continue exporting agricultural products to other provinces as part of their "historical market." Even though dairy quotas are slowly being eliminated because of international pressures, there is no chance that dairy producers in other provinces would ever accept this arrangement.[10]

Similarly, it would be naive to think that Canada would agree to some of the conditions put forth by Quebec nationalists regarding the national debt and the Canadian dollar. It's difficult to justify that Quebec assume only 18.5 percent of the national debt. This percentage is based on Quebec's share of total federal assets (buildings, Crown corporations, and the like). However since the debt was not incurred to purchase those assets, there is no reason to split the debt on that basis. In fact, the higher national debt was partly incurred to pay higher employment insurance and transfer payments to Quebec. The Bélanger-Campeau Commission estimated Quebec receives a net fiscal gain of $409 per capita, or $2.7 billion from the federal government. A closer estimate would be based on population share at 25.5 percent, or the amount of debt incurred by the federal government on behalf of each region in the country, which would bring Quebec's portion to 30.9 percent. This throws out any reasonable projections Quebec has about a manageable debt load, which would also increase the cost of borrowing internationally for an independent Quebec.[11] The PQ has always assumed that its main bargaining position in negotiations with Canada would be how much of the national debt it would assume in order to extract concessions from the rest of Canada. This would be a risky strategy given that Ottawa has control over pensions, employment insurance, and numerous transfer payments.

Finally, Quebec nationalists assume that Quebec will use the Canadian dollar as its official currency. According to separatists, the best option for both Quebec and Canada would be to continue with the status quo: a common currency with Quebec representatives sitting on the board of the Bank of Canada. It's believed that this option is preferable to Quebec issuing its own currency because it would minimize costs all around and reassure the international financial community of Quebec's economic viability.[12] But a common currency presents serious risks to the rest of Canada. What happens, for example, if a large Quebec financial institution goes bankrupt? If Quebec continues using the Canadian dollar as legal tender without permission, what does this mean for monetary policy in Canada? We got a glimpse of the problems in the last referendum when thousands of Quebeckers transferred their savings to banks outside the province. They were right to worry. In an independent Quebec there's no guarantee that their dollar deposits would be covered by the **Canadian Deposit Insurance Corporation (CIDC)**, which currently insures deposits up to $60,000.[13] Eliminating, or even the threat of removing CIDC protection, would cause a massive flight of capital out of Quebec.

It's ironic that Quebec would chose to adopt the Canadian dollar as its currency when, in effect, it will have no say over one of the most important levers of economic control—monetary policy. Quebec may end up having less economic independence than it has now if it allows the rest of Canada to unilaterally determine interest rates, money supply, and, ultimately, prices, output, and employment. Quebec may gain freedom, but without independence.[14]

THE LIMITS OF ANALYSIS

Trying to measure the costs of the breakup of Canada is virtually impossible. There are simply too many factors to take into consideration. One imponderable is land. Will Quebec be able to walk away with the area now under its jurisdiction? The Cree and the rest of Canada may lay claim to Northern Quebec and James Bay, which was ceded to Quebec in 1912 on the understanding that it would remain part of the country. That puts into dispute almost two-thirds of Quebec's approximately 1.5 million square kilometres of territory. Then there are the rights of Anglophone Quebeckers. Would they be entitled to remain in Canada and separate from Quebec? Stéphane Dion, the Minister of Intergovernmental Affairs, has often made the case if it is logical to split up Canada, then Quebec may also be split. It's impossible to know where the process would stop.

What is known is that any fragmentation of the Canadian economy erodes the gains from economic integration. These gains don't only include the benefits of producing for a larger market and reaping the benefits of "economies of scale," one of the more important reasons Canada signed a trade deal with the United States and Mexico.[15] Information and technology would not flow as smoothly between regions if Canada were to split up. People might not be able to work where they want to, nor would companies be able to go where they would earn the greatest profits. There's also the cost of uncertainty about Canada's future. Until that is resolved, Canadians will continue to pay higher interest rates from mortgages to business loans as foreign money lenders demand higher rates of return to offset the added risks of investing in a politically unsettled country. In the event that Quebec does leave, it's likely that Canadians will be resentful, making any negotiations long, acrimonious, and expensive.

Breaking up a country is never an easy and costless affair. Any impediment to the movement of money, people, and resources would, in the end, make us all poorer. But a perpetual constitutional crisis is also damaging.[16] We may not know the exact cost of separation, but we do know that if Quebec one day decides to leave Confederation, the transition costs won't be trivial, at least in the short run. Moreover, the biggest price will be borne by Quebeckers themselves.[17]

KEY TERMS

Sovereignty association	Common market	Canadian Deposit
Bélanger-Campeau	Direct investment	Insurance Corporation
Commission	Customs union	(CIDC)
		Clarity Bill

REVIEW QUESTIONS

1. Some have argued that the rest of Canada would be better off without Quebec given that Quebec gets more in transfer payments than it contributes to the rest of the country. What is the case against this line of reasoning?

2. It may be a relatively simple matter to determine net tax transfers from Ottawa to Quebec if separation occurs, but what are the economic costs that can't be measured in a more decentralized country?

3. What are some of the economic and political benefits Quebec now enjoys under Confederation that it would have to give up if it chose independence?

DISCUSSION QUESTIONS

1. Some have argued that Canada would be better off without Quebec. Do you agree with that statement from an economic point of view?

2. "The rest of Canada will negotiate rationally after separation because it will be in their best self-interest to do so." Discuss.

3. If Quebeckers are the big losers if they leave Confederation, why are so many willing to take that risk?

4. With the passing of the Clarity Bill, and low support for separation, do you believe the threat of separation is over?

NOTES

1. Lucien Bouchard, the leader of the PQ has indicated that there will be another referendum after the election of a new PQ government.

2. Based on that assumption, Quebec's overall debt would increase from 26.4 percent of its GDP to a high of 80 percent, making Quebec one of the most indebted nations in the world. This is equal to $144 billion, or $20,500 for each person in Quebec. See Robin Richardson, "L'addition s'il vous plait: Calculating and Paying Off Quebec's Separation Obligation to Canada," *Fraser Forum,* The Fraser Institute, May 1995. Also Patrick Grady, *The Economic Consequences of Québec Sovereignty* (Vancouver: The Fraser Institute, 1991) p. 43.

3. The Economic Council of Canada, A Joint Venture: *The Economics of Constitutional Options* (Ottawa: Supply and Services, 1991).

4. Small as a 3.5-percent decrease in GDP may seem, it translates into a drop in income of $1,800 per year for each family for an entire generation! See *The Financial Post,* 18 November 1991, p. 16.

5. The Canada Council study so angered the federal government, it was one of the reasons that the Council was disbanded by Prime Minister Mulroney in a wave of budget cutting measures in 1992.

6. Peter Dungan and Francois Vaillancourt, *Economic Impacts of Constitutional Reform: Modelling Some Pieces of the Puzzle,* Policy Study no. 91-8 (Toronto: University of Toronto Press, 1991).

7. Gordon Ritchie, "Putting Humpty Dumpty Together Again," in John McCallum, ed., *Broken Links: Trade Relations After a Quebec Secession* (Toronto: C.D. Howe Institute, October 1991), p. 18.

8. Grady, *The Economic Consequences of Quebec Sovereignty,* pp. 111-12.

9. Ibid., pp. 111–12.

10. W.H. Furtan and R.S. Gray, "Agriculture in an Independent Quebec," *Broken Links,* pp. 50-51.

11. Economic Council of Canada, *A Joint Venture,* p. 87.

12. David E.W. Laidler and William B.P. Robson, "Two Nations, One Money?" *Canada's Monetary System Following a Quebec Secession* (Toronto: C.D Howe Institute, September 1991). The second best option would be for Quebec to use the Canadian dollar without any influence over monetary policy. The worst option would be for Quebec to issue its own currency floating against the Canadian or U.S. currency. The option of a Quebec currency fixed to the Canadian or U.S. dollar didn't fare any better. The economist Bernard Fortin estimates that a separate currency could cost $40 billion.

13. Stephen Easton, "Separate Quebec Won't Use Dollar Long," *The Globe and Mail,* October 1995.

14. The losses for Quebec don't end here. Quebeckers would bear the costs of higher telephone rates and higher bilingualism costs, covering labelling and documentation now covered by the federal government. Who controls the shipping routes through the St. Lawrence would also be in question. Quebeckers would also risk losing about 25,000 federal jobs of those employed mainly in the Hull-Ottawa area. More Anglophones

and corporations would also move out of Quebec in the event of separation, taking even more needed talent with them. For more information, see Grady, *The Economic Consequences of Québec Sovereignty.*

15. A loss in the benefits of economies of scale could translate into lower capital and labour productivity. One study put this potential loss in total factory productivity at 2 percent in GDP over 10 years. See Dungan and Vaillancourt, *Economic Impacts of Constitutional Reform.*

16. Peter Brimelow writing in *Forbes,* (2 March 1992), argues that GDP per capita for the rest of Canada would actually rise if Quebec left Confederation because it is a drag, on the whole, through transfer payments. This ignores the dynamic, but immeasurable, gains Quebec and the rest of Canada enjoy as an integrated economy.

17. In the year 2000, much of this speculation about Quebec separation may be coming to an end. The polls indicate little appetite for separation in Quebec. The **Clarity Bill** would severely restrict Quebec's ability to leave Canada by insisting on a clear referendum question to be approved by Parliament. It seems remote that the majority of Quebeckers would vote to split the country. Nevertheless, this drama is far from over.

WEBLINKS

www.fraserinstitute.ca/publications/forum/1996/february/#fea
How to Balance the Federal Budget and Keep Canada Together.

www.fraserinstitute.ca/media/media_releases/unformatted/PR26.html
Canada/Quebec Divorce to Cost Quebec $143.9 Billion.

www.fin.gc.ca/newse95/oct17pre.html
Loss of NAFTA'S Protection and Use of the Canadian Dollar Doomed to Failure: The Dead-End for Quebec's Separation.

www.warrenmosler.com/docs/docs/essay2.htm
A Plan for Quebec Monetary Independence.

INCOME DISTRIBUTION

 **"The rich get richer and the poor get poorer."**

There is a strong perception that Canada is becoming a country with increasing income discrepancies between the rich and poor. Others argue that the proportion of the truly poor is greatly exaggerated and that today's poor are better off than at any time in our history. The answer is that both perceptions are correct. Poverty is both an absolute and a relative concept. The poor are better off today when compared to low-income Canadians in the past. The evidence also suggests that there is not a widening gap between income classes and that the middle class is not disappearing.

Many Canadians are becoming more distressed at the apparent growth in poverty in a country as rich as Canada. The media is full of stories about the desperate plight of the homeless sleeping on open grates throughout our big cities, or of overcrowded shelters now occupied by whole families. It seems one can't go down the streets of Canada's major cities without panhandlers begging for loose change or squeegee kids cleaning windshields for a handout. Food Banks, which were supposed to be a temporary stopgap to feed the poor, are a permanent fixture in many cities across the country. And every season brings with it a new food drive to help the destitute in our communities.

Stories such as these inevitably lead to the conclusion that something is profoundly wrong, especially when contrasted to the growing wealth enjoyed by others. Despite Canada's social welfare system, and a growing economy, many have come to the conclusion that a few rich are doing better, while poverty increases for many. How real are these perceptions? Is there a growing income gulf between the rich and poor, all the while squeezing out the middle class?

In order to think clearly about poverty, it's important to define what we mean by the term and how we measure it. To start, poverty is both a relative and absolute concept, but there is no hard and fast definition. You are poorer if you have less than your neighbour. The bottom 10 percent of income earners will always be, by definition, worse off than the other ninety percent. In that sense, the poor will always be with us. If your income rises 10 percent and that of your neighbour increases by 15 percent, you are better off but you are *relatively* worse off than your neighbour.[1] If we want to address the problem of poverty from the point of view of deprivation, or not having the income to provide for the bare necessities of life, then poverty becomes a concept where someone is *absolutely* worse off. Let's start with this idea of absolute poverty first.

POVERTY AS AN ABSOLUTE CONCEPT

Poverty today is a far cry from poverty years ago. It is hard for many born since 1960 to believe that poverty was once ubiquitous in Canada. Talk to anyone who lived through the Depression of the 1930s, or the aftermath of World War 2 in Canada, where most people had a hard time keeping bread on the table. Although hard to believe now, one in three Canadians was poor in 1951, poor in the sense that they could not afford the necessities of life. Fifty years ago, over 25 percent of Canadians had no indoor running water and malnutrition was common. One of the great accomplishments in Canadian history has been the almost complete elimination of extreme deprivation suffered by many Canadians. Real living standards have increased ten-fold over the past 100 years, and since 1950 economic growth has increased with real family incomes and consumption going up two and a half times. We live longer and are healthier and better educated than any generation before us. We have a standard of living that our grandparents could not have comprehended in their day. In only a half century, we've gone from a society where over a quarter of the population had no indoor plumbing, to one where virtually all households have at least one colour TV, 74 percent have cable, 84 percent a video player, and 40 percent have home computers. Even the poor have more. Today about 75 percent of poor households have cars compared with only 60 percent 20 years ago.[2] Simply put, the average Canadian today is better off in material terms than his or her grandparents.[3]

WHAT ABOUT THE HOMELESS?

Despite the strides Canada has made to eliminate absolute poverty, many would argue that we still have a serious poverty problem given the homeless living in the streets in Canada's major urban centres.[4] How can we say we've won the war against poverty when this evidence of poverty still exists?

An increase in the homeless population is a depressing manifestation in a country such as Canada that has a relatively high standard of living. But one of the main impediments to understanding the nature of homelessness is that we have no firm numbers of how many people are without homes. No clear survey has ever been done to accurately measure the number of people living on the streets, or whether the problem has become worse over the years. The matter of how many are living on the street has become a political issue, where poverty advocates have exaggerated the numbers to attract greater political attention in the hope of forcing politicians to allocate more resources to the problem. Too often the homeless are defined as simply lacking jobs and affordable housing. But the issue of homelessness is more complex than simply providing more jobs and housing.[5]

The roots of homelessness are often found in childhood where many grew up in poverty and were victims of physical and sexual abuse. And addressing the problem isn't always a simple matter of providing more money. In Toronto, for example, 86 percent of the homeless have had some form of mental illness or suffered from substance abuse. In the U.S., where billions of dollars have been spent trying to solve the problem, one study in New York City found that 50 percent of the homeless that were placed in permanent housing returned to the shelters.[6] By early 2000, despite the fact that the economy was producing impressive growth in jobs with historically low unemployment rates, the problem of homelessness goes unabated. How do we explain that persistent and almost intractable problem of the homeless? Part of the blame can be put at the door of government policy in the late 1970s, when the decision was made to deinstitutionalize the mentally ill and release them into the community without adequate support. This isn't to argue that all of the homeless suffer from alcohol or drug abuse or mental illness. Many are forced to the shelters through a series of adverse economic circumstances, but the issue of homelessness has to be treated not only as an economic problem but as a social and medical problem as well.[7]

POVERTY AND STATISTICS CANADA: THE PROBLEM OF MEASUREMENT

So, who are the poor in Canada? Given what's been said so far, it isn't an easy question to answer. According to Statistics Canada, any family that spends more than 54.7 percent of their income on the three necessities of life—food, shelter, and clothing—can be considered to be below the "poverty line," or poor according to that definition. For a family of four the poverty line, or **low-income cutoff (LICO)**, in 1998 was approximately $24,000 in rural areas and $32,000 in the larger cities. Anyone falling below those levels could be considered poor in Canada. Using that definition, 25 percent of Canadians live in poverty.

But the poverty line or LICO is a slippery concept. At best it's a crude measure of poverty because it also tends to capture many retirees whose income has dropped below the poverty line, but own their own homes and are now living off their investments. This measure also captures college and university students who are temporarily out of the labour market. Only the most literal of poverty advocates would include struggling actors, who make most of their income waiting tables, in the category of the working poor. Adding such individuals would be demeaning to the chronically poor who need the assistance of society to even make ends meet. Here we have to make the distinction between income disparities and distribution of wealth. Once the more obvious cases are removed, the numbers who are truly in need fall considerably. Some estimates put the real poverty rate as low as 2.5 percent of the Canadian population, which represents only a small fraction of Canadian families who can truly be defined as poor and lacking the basic necessities of life.[8] As already mentioned, one has to keep in mind that the 54.7 percent threshold used by Statistics Canada is essentially arbitrary. Even by this definition, that still leaves over 40 percent of their income for non-necessities. And who is to say that someone with that amount of discretionary income is poor?

In fairness to Statistics Canada, their analysts never intended LICO to be used as a poverty line. They knew the difficulties of setting a fixed number to a controversial political issue. To show the arbitrary nature of LICO, consider the following. In 1959 Statistics Canada, through the Family Expenditure Survey, found that the average family spent 50 percent of their income on the necessities of life. They then assumed that a family of four that spent 70 percent on such items should be considered poor. If one family spent 69 percent, they were automatically above the poverty line and no longer considered poor. However, Statistics Canada realized that as incomes rose, people would naturally spend a declining share of their earnings on food, shelter, and clothing, continually forcing the statisticians to revise their numbers. Today, the average family spends 34.7 percent on the necessities. Add 20 percent and we reach the new threshold. If we continued to use the old estimates, statistically there would be fewer families defined as poor. One begins to appreciate the changing nature of poverty as incomes rise over time. Statistics Canada is therefore caught in a dilemma when it comes to releasing poverty data. If the 70 percent income threshold is used to define poverty, only about 8 percent of all families fall below the poverty line. Using the 54.7 percent income cutoff, 23 percent of families are considered poor. Whichever definition is used, the concept of poverty is a moving target and a politically contentious issue.

To make matters more complicated, there are others who want to look at poverty from a completely different point of view. Some poverty analysts have made a strong case that poverty cannot be examined only from the perspective of consumption or even income levels, and that we need a more sophisticated and comprehensive measure of economic well-being that goes beyond a simple dollar cutoff point. Such an index, for both Canada and the United States, has been developed by two Canadian economists.[9] The index includes four key variables: consumption (per capita consumption and government spending), current wealth stocks, overall income inequality, and economic security. This last category is important because it tries to capture the anxiety of society and how people feel about the future; i.e., the chances of unemployment and the risks of illness, old age, and single parenthood. The index even measures the impact of pollution and the environment on individuals.

Although it is useful in measuring how we are doing as a society, this index is largely determined by the weight each variable receives, making it rather arbitrary. Nevertheless, it is an attempt, although an imperfect one, to get a broader sense of how we are doing as a country, rather than simply adding up how many people are rich and poor. What is implied by the construction of such an index is that economic well-being is drastically affected by the inequality of income distribution. Again we are back to thinking about poverty on a relative basis. Given these limitations, and based on this index, is Canada faring better or worse? The index shows that during the 1970s there was little change in the index, but it increased during the 1980s. But from 1991 to 1997, the index showed a clear decline in well-being for Canadians. However, because the data only goes to 1997 and the economy has improved dramatically since then in terms of increasing income and falling unemployment, there will inevitably be a positive effect on the index. And as the authors clearly admit, such a measure "inevitably requires a series of ethical and statistical judgements."

THE INCOME GAP: IS IT GROWING?

The data seem to be conclusive that there is no growing divergence in income between high- and low-income earners. This is surprising given all the anecdotal evidence to the contrary. If you break down income classes into five groups, called quintile shares, we see that there has been very little change in the distribution of wealth since 1950. For example, the top 20 percent of households, the richest group, earned about 43 percent of total income in 1950. The figure has remained pretty constant over the next 45 years. The fourth quintile group also held steady at about 25 percent, while the third quintile also didn't change much at 18 percent. If there was any change, it was in the second and in the lowest income household categories, which increased their share of total income marginally starting in the early 1980s and continuing into the 1990s. It appears that the rich are not getting richer at the expense of the poor.

Even if you look at the numbers a bit differently, we arrive at the same conclusions. The proportion of families making less than 25 percent of the **median income**[10] actually fell from 5.3 percent of the population to 3.9 percent from 1972 to 1992, and most likely improved still more throughout the rest of the decade. Over the same period, the proportion of families making more than 175 percent of the median income increased from 12.7 percent of the population to 15.3 percent.[11] Looked at from this perspective, both the high-income and low-income groups are doing better.

There has also been a lot of speculation that the **middle class** has been squeezed throughout the 1980s and the 1990s. The disappearing middle class is another version of the story that people are being pushed to the extremes of the income distribution scale. Again the evidence shows otherwise. As we've already seen, the share of total income of those at the bottom and top of the income scale has hardly changed. The size of the middle class, those earning 25 percent above the median income but less than 175 percent, has pretty much remained constant over the last three decades. To paraphrase Mark Twain, the rumours of the demise of the middle class are greatly exaggerated.

What we do know is that middle class incomes have stagnated mainly because of increasing taxes. The tax burden rose from 13.3 percent of median family income in 1971 to 17.6 percent by the early 1990s. In fact, the brunt of the tax burden fell on the upper middle class and the very rich.[12] It was the tax increases of higher income groups, and **income redistribution**, that allowed those at the bottom of the income scale to receive a greater share of government transfer payments, such as income assistance, employment insurance, workers' compensation, and so on. About 60 percent of those below the poverty line receive some form of transfer payments from government programs. Without these transfers, the rich would have been a lot richer, and the poor truly poorer. In the final analysis, the data suggests that there is no statistical evidence of income polarization between income classes in Canada, or that the middle class is disappearing anytime soon.

How we look at poverty has a great deal to do with how we view the problem. Those who see poverty as an absolute problem (that is, "do the poor have access to the necessities of life?"), would argue that the best government policy would be to provide people with employment opportunities rather than increase incomes through distribution from one class to another. This position usually comes with an emphasis on low taxes and controlled social spending. Those who see poverty as a relative concept through the concentration of wealth would make the case that the best way to resolve the problem is through aggressive income redistribution programs. And this usually means more generous social programs.

KEY TERMS

Low-income cutoff   Median income   Income redistribution
   (LICO)   Middle class

REVIEW QUESTIONS

1. If poverty is defined as a relative distribution of wealth, we will never completely eliminate it. Explain.

2. There was a drastic reduction in the number of families and individuals collecting social assistance in Ontario in the late 1990s even though welfare rates were reduced. Explain why these numbers fell. What was the lesson from that experience?

3. "The middle class has been squeezed over the years leading to a polarization of the rich and poor." Explain why this statement is generally believed and why it may not be true.

DISCUSSION QUESTIONS

1. Why does poverty exist in a country as rich as Canada? And what would be the best policies and programs to reduce it?

2. It has been argued that raising taxes to increase social programs and redistribute income may at times do more harm than good. Explain.

3. Discuss the complexities of the homeless problem in North America along with its main causes and possible cures. Is there a homeless problem in Europe? How do they approach the problem?

NOTES

1. In free markets there is no assurance that everyone's income will change at the same rate. Free markets reward some occupations more than others based on the needs of the economy. In many ways wage inequality is a good thing because it signals which occupations are most valued by society.

2. Despite the notion that the plight of the poor is worse in the United States, the average family living below the poverty line today is doing as well or better, in terms of material possessions, than middle-class families in 1971.

3. Another aspect of poverty is that someone poor today may not be poor tomorrow and vice versa. There is a great movement of people between the various classes of income earners. See *Myths of the Rich & Poor*, W. Michael Cox and Richard Alm (New York: Basic Books, 1999).

4. The homeless are not a new phenomenon in Canada. In the past they were commonly known as hobos looking for handouts and food while riding the rails across Canada.

5. Dr. Paula Goering, "Pathways to Homelessness," Clark Institute of Psychiatry, November 1997.

6. Heather MacDonald, "Real Roots of Homelessness," *Wall Street Journal*, 15 June 1993.

7. For a modern description of the plight of the homeless, see *The Globe and Mail* article written by John Stackhouse, December 18, 1999.

8. "Poverty in Canada" by Christopher Sarlo, The Fraser Institute, 1992.

9. Lars Osberg and Andrew Sharpe, "An Index of Economic Well-being for Canada and the United States," working paper presented to the American Economic Association, January 1999.

10. Median income is that value above which 50 percent of the observations lie.

11. Charles Beach and George Slotsve, "Are We Becoming Two Societies?" (Toronto: C.D. Howe Institute, 1996), pp. 2–3.

12. Ibid., pp. 11–12.

WEBLINKS

www.fraserinstitute.ca/publications/books/poverty/
Poverty in Canada.

www.lis.ceps.lu/canberra/canberrareport/sheridn2.htm
Statistics Canada's experience with low-income cutoffs.

www.ccsd.ca/pubs/2000/fbpov00/note.htm
The Canadian Fact Book on Poverty 2000.

www.statcan.ca/english/ads/13F0022XCB/highlight1.htm
Income trends in Canada.

GOVERNMENT
SIZE AND
PROPORTION

 **"We need big government to deliver the services Canadians want."**

Governments have grown enormously over the years. This has led to a proliferation of special interest groups, inefficiencies, and higher taxes. Many economists have come to realize that big government doesn't always mean better government, but too often big government brings bigger debts and deficits and ultimately a poorer economy. That's why Western economies are emphasizing more deregulation, privatization, and a greater role for free markets.

Here's a thought experiment; try to imagine life without government. Think of the roads, the hospitals, the schools, the national parks, the police. In fact, government services touch the lives of citizens every day. In today's world, the public sector dominates the economy. Governments at all levels account directly for 25 percent of Gross Domestic Product. But that percentage hardly captures the impact and prevalence of governments in the economy or our lives. When you take into account all the social welfare programs to individuals, subsidies to industry, and transfer payments from the federal government to the provinces, governments account for about 45 percent of GDP.

It wasn't always this way. In 1950, government spending was only half what it is today as a share of GDP. The biggest expenditure for governments then was **public goods**, such as national defence, police protection, transportation, and communications. Education, health care, and culture played a much smaller role in government spending, as did transfers to individuals. Today, the reverse is true. Expenditures on transfer payments, education, and health have grown enormously, while pure public goods have declined as a share of national income.

Why the drastic change? How did governments come to play such a prominent role in our lives and that of the economy? First, we'll examine some traditional reasons why governments have grown over the years, then we'll examine the growing disillusionment with big government, and finally we'll look at the myth that bigger is better and the trend to smaller governments and freer markets.

MARKET FAILURE AND THE ROLE OF GOVERNMENTS

Public goods

A traditional argument for the role of government is based on the notion of market failure. In a perfectly free economy without government intervention, markets would fail because they would not produce all the goods and services people need. The market might produce all the cars, ice cream, and rock CDs we want. There are profits to be made in the thousands of products we buy every day. But who'll build the roads, provide street lights, national defence, fight fires, and train the police to protect society? Traditionally, the strongest reason why we have governments is to provide these goods and services for everyone's benefit, paid for by everyone's taxes. But why should governments provide these goods and services? Can't the private sector produce them just as well?

One problem is that such goods are "collective consumption goods," that is, they are goods everyone can enjoy. When you buy a burger, you're the only one to enjoy it, but everyone benefits from safer neighbourhoods. And that's the problem: because everyone can enjoy a public good, there's no incentive for any individual to pay for it, and therefore no business is willing to provide it. This is what economists call the **free rider problem**; we permit governments to tax us in order to provide a service that otherwise wouldn't exist. Technically, one could exclude those not paying from using roads they didn't pay for, but the hassle would probably outweigh the benefits. If we charged everyone individually for national defence, you can be sure the armed forces would be much smaller. Now you have a strong case for government involvement. But is the free rider problem always a justification for governments to provide a good or service? Not always. We are beginning to realize that even traditional government services such as fire fighting can be contracted out to private companies. Inefficiencies and waste come from monopolies, whether in the public or private sector. Governments are beginning to realize that more competition is the key to lower prices and better service.

Externalities

Another example of market failure has to do with **externalities** or spillovers that may justify government intervention and regulations. Externalities are the unintended consequences on third parties of some economic activity. Take loud music as an example: if a person were to ride the bus to work each morning and someone with a loud radio makes it impossible to enjoy the trip, that's a case of a negative externality. Rules may be set in place to forbid anyone from playing radios on public transportation, but the problem is that, in an unregulated market, the price of the radio fails to take into consideration the discomfort others may suffer from its use. In the extreme case of pollution, the price of energy that comes from burning coal doesn't reflect the damage to the environment and the respiratory illness burning coal causes. The justification for government intervention in the economy is that markets, through the price system, simply don't capture the impacts of these sorts of external costs; that's why governments step in to tax and regulate the pollution of the environment.

But not all externalities are bad or negative. Some things people do benefit not only themselves, but also those around them. When your neighbour pays for her son's piano lessons and everyone can hear him playing Mozart, that's a positive externality. (That is if you like classical music.) Or if someone installs a catalytic converter in their car and reduces pollution for everyone, that's a positive externality. When someone gets more education, not only does the consumer of more education benefit, but so does all society because it now has a more informed and productive citizen. A strong argument for governments to get involved in the economy is to encourage and subsidize those things that provide positive externalities and tax or pass laws that cut back on those that give negative externalities. Externalities are everywhere: fluoride in the water, manicured lawns, drug rehabilitation centres, newly painted houses, day care, and well-behaved children. Can governments go overboard in subsidizing those things that give positive external costs to the community? The answer is yes—if the cost of getting more of the externality is higher than the benefits of the externality itself. Everything in the economy is subject to the law of diminishing returns. The first dollar spent by governments trying to get us to be better drivers is more effective than getting the last, worst driver to obey the law. To get the safest streets possible may not be worth the price, especially if we have to divert tax money from other activities. We live in a world of scarce resources where decisions have to be made about how best to allocate them.

ECONOMIES OF SCALE, OR BIGGER IS CHEAPER

Conventional wisdom has long held that small economies, such as Canada, could not afford to have many firms in certain industries, such as hydro, gas, rail, and telecommunications. In such cases, it is better to allow these industries to operate as **natural monopolies** and then regulate their behaviour. That way, society can still reap the benefits of longer production runs without suffering the side-effects associated with monopoly behaviour, such as higher prices and lower production levels.[1] For example, if Bell Canada wants to increase telephone rates, it has to justify such costs to the Canadian Radio-television and Telecommunications Commission (CRTC) before passing those costs onto consumers. Without tough regulations, it was thought, companies like Bell would overcharge its customers. We now know that's not the case, even where natural monopolies are concerned. When AT&T, the huge American phone company, was forced to break up its company in 1982, both local and long distance rates dropped. In Canada, the entry of long-distance carriers has also driven down the cost of long-distance calls. In countries that allow greater competition in telecommunications, prices have fallen more than in countries with heavy government regulation. The problem persists that remaining regulations compel telephone companies to charge more for long distance than local calls, which explains why so many companies are in the long-distance business.

The same goes for increases in hydro charges by such provincial monopolies as Ontario Hydro, whose rate increases are approved by the Ministry of Energy in Ontario. But even here, things are changing. Transmitting and distributing electrical power will likely remain a natural monopoly for a while, since it would be wasteful to have more than one set of wire systems, but the production of power is a different matter. Ontario Hydro, the biggest electrical utility in North America, realizes that its future depends on greater competition in the production of electricity. That's why it has deregulated hydro production. Ontario will now be buying power from a number of suppliers both inside and outside the province.

Governments are beginning to understand that, given the changing nature of the economy as new products and services are introduced, regulating monopolies isn't working as well as it did in the past. The answer in some cases is to deregulate monopoly restrictions and allow more competition as a natural antidote to monopolistic tendencies. Instead of controlling or owning monopolies, the Canadian government is selling off services once thought essential to Canada's nationhood. In the latter part of the 1980s, the federal government sold a dozen companies, including Air Canada. The government will also one day sell off CN rail. Many people are beginning to realize that there's no intrinsic reason for the government to own many of its Crown corporations. Critics of privatization argue that selling off Crown corporations saves taxpayers very little, but the evidence suggests the benefits are worth it. Encouraging more competition in the telephone business has meant lower prices and better services. Although Canada is just beginning to move in the direction of greater deregulation and privatization, other countries such as Britain are already reaping the benefits of less state intervention.[2]

OTHER CASES FOR GOVERNMENT INTERVENTION

There are other reasons why governments get involved in the economy. One compelling, if not overriding, reason is that even if markets are working well, we may not like the way in which they distribute incomes. We assign politicians not only with the task of making markets and the economy more efficient, but also with making them more equitable. Governments can and do intervene to alleviate poverty. The free market system may be the best way to achieve economic efficiency, but it does not guarantee an equitable distribution of income. Adam Smith, the great 18th century Scottish economist, was the first to recognize the genius of markets as a way of producing the maximum amount of goods for society. But even he realized that governments were needed to help the destitute by transferring income from the rich to the poor, not on economic, but moral, grounds.

Today, we have governments going beyond anything imagined by Adam Smith. Governments are heavily involved in helping the poor in a number of ways such as public housing, employment and training programs, welfare provisions, employment insurance, minimum wages, employment equity, farm support systems, along with an array of other income transfer programs. The question is, have these programs had an effect on alleviating poverty? There's no doubt that many of these programs help some of the poor. What many don't realize, is that most income distribution by government is not from the rich to the poor, but to citizens who are relatively well off. In other cases, the old have been helped, but at the expense of the young. The proportion of single persons aged 65 and over with incomes below the poverty line, as defined by Statistics Canada, has decreased from 70 percent in 1961 to 51 percent in 1991. For those under 25, it rose from 39 percent to 57 percent. Even though the proportion of families living below the poverty line has gone down, this decline is due to smaller average family size and the increased participation of women in the labour force.

One economist who believes governments do a bad job of helping the poor is Professor William Watson at McGill University. He claims that it would only take $13 billion to bring Canada's poor up to the poverty line. Yet Canada spends $300 billion annually on social transfer payments. In other words, it takes $9 to get $1 to where it is needed.[3] The rest of the money goes to middle income earners. Not only have we failed to properly design social policy to help the poor, but some policies also are making things worse.

When the Ontario Conservative government reduced welfare benefits in 1995, in an effort to reduce the deficit, there was considerable public outcry about hurting the weakest segment of society. The government wanted to reduce benefits to 110 percent of the national average for welfare recipients, still making it the most generous social assistance program in North America. These high rates had an interesting impact on economic behaviour. In 1981, 4 percent of Ontario's population was on some form of social assistance. By 1994, that rate had climbed to 12 percent. The increase cannot be explained by high unemployment rates alone. The welfare rates were climbing steadily throughout the 1980s even though unemployment was dropping. Many people saw the high social benefits as an alternative to working and withdrew from the labour market. What was intended as a program to help the poor, ended up encouraging high levels of welfare dependency.[4] This is a classic case of the law of unintended consequences. However, by 1999, the share of Ontario's population receiving social assistance dropped considerably to around 7 percent.

ARE GOVERNMENTS DOING BAD BY DOING TOO MUCH?

The main thrust of this book is that governments have, in many cases, gone too far and, in some cases, have hurt the very groups they want to help. We have seen how this is the case with rent control, pay equity, farm support systems, and minimum wages. But we haven't, as yet, explained why. Why do governments, with society's best interests at heart, end up doing more harm than good? In the past, that question eluded economists because their natural instinct was to look for failure in markets, not for failure in government. All that has changed. Economists in the last couple of decades have focused their attention on the behaviour of governments and bureaucracies and have come up with some interesting insights. One of them is that governments are poorer at delivering goods and services than private companies, even though government spending has never been higher.

For example, CN, the national railway, is less efficient than the private rail company, CP.[5] And when it comes to delivering the mail, companies such as United Parcel Service and FedEx do a better job than Canada Post. Even when it comes to picking up the garbage, governments are less efficient than private companies. In Ontario, it costs about $16 to collect a tonne of garbage when outside contractors do the job, compared to $27 when done by municipal workers who work directly for local governments.[6] Part of the reason for this difference is that the public sector tend to pay higher wages and provide more generous benefits than the private sector. The same is true in the United States; in cities with populations of over 50,000, garbage collection was over 30 percent cheaper when done by private companies. Government workers across the board tend to make higher wages and have higher pension and retirement benefits than do workers in the private sector. Government workers also enjoy better job security.[7][8]

PUBLIC CHOICE

Why is the public sector so generous? One explanation can be found in **public choice theory**. This theory attributes the same motives to politicians and bureaucrats as to business people; the latter are interested in maximizing profits, while the former want to maximize power and influence. To a politician, that means getting or holding on to power, while the objective of a bureaucrat is to have bigger budgets and departments. Saving taxpayer money is often of secondary consideration. As the famous economist Armen Alchian once said, "The one thing you can trust people to do is to put their interests above yours." That applies to both the public and private sector.

A group of investors who start a business have a strong interest in making sure it makes a profit or they risk bankruptcy. Now consider the same group of investors starting the same venture for the government and the venture fails. What happens? In most cases, nothing because there are no shareholders holding the investors accountable. Because no one likes to admit failure, bureaucrats are often rewarded with bigger budgets, bigger departments, and, unfortunately, bigger failure. That's one reason government union workers earn more than comparable workers in the private sector. Politicians buy labour peace with higher wages and benefits. Even when government programs fail on a massive scale, civil servants are seldom held accountable.[9] In the public sector it's not unusual for government departments to spend leftover budgets weeks or days before their fiscal year, whether they need to or not, just so they won't lose their funding for the next year.

SPECIAL INTEREST GROUPS

Another area that's received a lot of attention by economists is the role and proliferation of special interest groups and the demands these groups make on governments and the public purse. Traditionally, special interest groups were simply business organizations that persuaded governments to bestow privileges unavailable to others. Tariffs and import quotas have long protected farmers from competition the same way they protected the shoe and clothing industries.

Special interest groups now cover the whole spectrum of human experience. A sample of these interests are women's groups, such as the National Action Committee, gays, lesbians, artists, environmentalists, athletes, poverty groups, tenant associations, religious groups, multicultural interests, First Nations, anti-smoking groups, the elderly, and animal rights advocates. More and more people define themselves as members of groups in order to carry more political clout with politicians. And in doing so they can extract what economists call **economic rent** from their fellow taxpayers: privileges and money they could otherwise not have earned. These groups, or "**rent-seekers**," have been enormously successful in persuading governments of the justice of their causes. A compendium of federal subsidy programs runs to 950 pages listing the various benefits that companies and individuals can apply for. The Public Accounts of Canada, which lists grants of over $100,000 to various groups, runs to 110 pages of small print.[10]

In early 2000, the federal department of Human Resources Development Canada (HRDC) came under intense scrutiny because its budget was in many cases captured by special interest groups leading to hundreds of millions of dollars in questionable grants. Some economists, such as Gordon Tullock one of the original founders of public choice theory, believe that the enormous growth in government spending can be largely explained by the proliferation of rent-seekers.[11] Why does government give in? Part of the answer can be found in the idea of **rational ignorance**. Politicians are more likely to give support to a well-organized special interest group by passing on small costs to a less well-organized majority. The notion of dispersed costs and concentrated benefits explains a lot of what governments do. In politics the squeaky wheel does get the oil. And once special interest groups get their hands on the public purse strings, it is hard to cut them off without political consequences.[12]

Many of these groups are finding their support slipping away not because governments finally realized that these groups weren't worth funding, but because they simply couldn't afford them any more.[13] Ways had to be found to get the deficit under control, and when the public showed little support for many of these programs the government went ahead and slashed their budgets. In the end, special interest groups never had the wide public support many of them claimed. However, many of these groups aren't giving up without a fight; they are turning to the Charter of Rights and Freedoms to make their case in the courts and circumventing Parliament altogether.[14]

TREND TOWARD FREER MARKETS

All levels of governments in North America are undergoing a profound reassessing of the role of government in society. The popular catch phrase **reinventing government** is another term for how governments can redefine their role in society and concentrate on those things expected of them while letting the free market do the rest. Deregulation in the United States has lowered costs and improved services in a number of industries, including airlines, rail, and telecommunications, saving consumers billions.[15]

Countries such as the United Kingdom and New Zealand have revitalized their economies by privatizing and deregulating their industries. Even Sweden, the classic social democratic welfare state, is turning to markets to get out from under a mountain of public debt. In the United States, communities are finding ways for private businesses to operate their prisons and fire departments. Some public schools are turning over their management to private firms. The evidence suggests that countries with less regulated economies, where labour and goods and services have fewer restrictions, experience lower levels of unemployment and higher levels of economic growth.[16] It's estimated that regulations alone cost the Canadian economy $30 billion annually in added expenses.[17] Ottawa and the provinces are also looking to sell a number of Crown corporations such as VIA rail. Mike Harris, the Premier of Ontario, is even calling for the privatization of the CBC. The federal government is in the process of privatizing a number of activities, including air traffic control and the operations and management of airports. Even the bridge connecting Prince Edward Island to the mainland was constructed by money raised in the private sector. In Ontario, Highway 407 is a toll road that was built and managed by a private firm.

The role of government is changing rapidly. We're beginning to realize that more government spending doesn't mean more growth because higher taxes distort the incentives to save and invest, sending the economy into a spiral of higher costs and lower efficiency.[18] The pendulum of government intervention is swinging back from too much government to much less. Finding the right balance will be the challenge for the next decade or two.

KEY TERMS

Public goods	Natural monopolies	Rent-seekers
Free rider problem	Public choice theory	Rational ignorance
Externalities	Economic rent	Reinventing government

REVIEW QUESTIONS

1. Explain why free markets tend to produce all the rock and roll CDs consumers want, but don't supply enough national defence or police protection.

2. Distinguish between negative and positive externalities. Use examples to illustrate your answer. Explain why it makes sense for governments to intervene in a free market in the case of a) positive externalities b) negative externalities.

3. Explain the trend to greater deregulation of "natural monopolies." In your opinion, have such moves been effective?

4. Explain the role of special interest groups, and how they have come to play a major role in determining government behaviour.

5. a) What is the premise underlying "public choice theory"?

   b) Define "rational ignorance" and what impact it has on the economics of the public sector.

DISCUSSION QUESTIONS

1. "Governments are rethinking their roles not because they want to, but because they have to." Discuss.

2. Identify services now delivered by governments that could be handed over to the private sector. Give reasons for your selections.

3. In your opinion, what are the main forces driving the "reinvention of government"? Do you believe this trend will last?

NOTES

1. A natural monopoly is an industry in which average total cost is falling even when the entire market demand is satisfied. Because Canada has a relatively smaller market than the United States, there are more natural monopolies here than south of the border, and consequently more tolerance for monopolies. For a better understanding see the chapter on regulations and deregulations in Michael Parkin and Robin Bade, *Economics: Canada in the Global Environment,* 2nd ed. (Don Mills, ON: Addison-Wesley, 1994).

2. Eastern Europe and Latin American countries are rapidly selling off companies once owned by the state. In Britain, where more competition has been introduced into gas and electricity, gas prices have fallen 20 percent. See *The Economist,* 28 January 1995. Even for "merit goods" such as education and health, increased competition means more efficiency and lower costs. See "Public profit, public service," *The Economist,* 9 December 1995.

3. Wm. Watson, John Richards, and David M. Brown, *The Case for Change: Reinventing the Welfare State* (Toronto: C.D. Howe Institute, 1995).

4. Jack Carr, "High Rates Were Lure to Welfare Court Told," *The Globe and Mail,* 15 November 1995.

5. In one study comparing the private and public sector performance in rail transportation, the cost of running CN was 14 percent higher than CP, the private rail company. See Parkin, *Economics*, p. 551.

6. Don Dewees, Michael Trebilcock, Ian Freeman, and Brent Snell, *The Regulation of Solid Waste Management in Ontario,* April 1993 (University of Toronto paper).

7. Steven E. Rhoads, *The Economist's View of the World,* p. 70.

8. For an excellent review of the changing role of the state, see "The Future of the State," *The Economist*, 20 September 1997. It shows that small governments often mean better and more efficient government.

9. In the early 1980s, the Department of Finance lost billions of dollars to fraud and incompetence due to a badly designed program to encourage research and development. Marshall Cohen, the deputy minister and architect of the program, was later promoted and became president of Molson.

10. Some samples are $1.7 million to promote dialogue with South Africa; $470,000 to the Canadian Home Economics Association; $2,000 to the Yukon Prospector's Association; $16 million to First Nations bands for policy development and $138

million for administration; $101,000 to the Canadian Five-Pin Bowler's Association, etc. See Wm. Watson, *The Case for Change.*

11. Professor Tullock might be right. From 1981 to 1991, total government spending on social services went from 19.4 percent to 23.3 percent from a budget of $153.3 billion, while spending on resource conservation and industrial development dropped from 8.2 percent to 4.5 percent. In short, direct payment to individuals was the largest component of government spending. See *The National Finances,* The Canadian Tax Foundation, p. 43.

12. Analysts are more critical of so-called public interest groups who emphasize the "public" and altruistic nature of their cause. But as Professor William Standbury at the University of British Columbia states, groups don't have interests, but individuals heading up these groups do, and many times those interests are subjective and selfish. See "A sceptic's guide to the claims of so-called public interest groups," *Canadian Public Administration,* Vol. 36, No. 4 (Winter 1993).

13. When the federal Liberals brought down their budget in 1995, a number of special interests suffered major cuts, including women's groups, environmental and multicultural causes, and sports and cultural events. The only ones left unscathed were First Nations groups who received government grants.

14. In Ontario, poverty groups are arguing before the courts that any reduction in welfare benefits is a violation of their rights under the Charter of Rights and Freedom.

15. Clifford Winston, "Economic Deregulation: Days of Reckoning for Microeconomists," *Journal of Economic Literature* (September 1993).

16. Product market restrictions were identified as the culprit designed to protect existing interests, including existing jobs. The United States outperformed European countries in creating jobs of fewer market regulations. See *Employment Performance,* The McKinsey Global Institute, 1994.

17. John C. Strick, *The Economics of Government Regulation* (Toronto: Thompson Educational Publishing Inc., 1994), p. 115.

18. Professors Claude Montmarquette and Leonard Dudley have examined 50 countries where big government is an impediment to growth. They estimate that the most efficient size of government is half the size it is today. See *Policy Options,* The Institute for Public Policy Research, July–August 1995.

WEBLINKS

www.socialstudieshelp.com/Eco_Govts_Role.htm
The role of government in avoiding market failure.

www.msu.edu/course/prm/255/market_failure.htm
Market failure and externalities.

www.wlu.ca/~wwwpress/jrls/cjc/BackIssues/22.2/winseck.html
Canadian Telecommunications: Natural Monopolies.

www.independent.org/tii/BookExcerpts/TaxingChoiceCh5.html
Problems associated with rational ignorance.

THE NEW ECONOMY

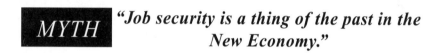

MYTH   *"Job security is a thing of the past in the New Economy."*

As Canada goes from an economy dominated by the goods and resource sectors to services, there is general concern that this trend will signify a more unstable labour market. Conventional wisdom also tells us this will only be made worse by globalization, freer trade, and the greater use of technology. This chapter argues that the trend to less job stability is not backed by the data, and that workers in the New Economy have more bargaining power than they think.

As we move into the era of the **New Economy**, we've all heard the good news about the benefits of faster economic growth and higher levels of productivity. The news may be good for how we produce and consume products, but **conventional wisdom** tells us that the news is bad for workers, especially younger ones, with the move to globalization, freer trade, and deregulation. Under this scenario we can now look forward to a highly volatile labour market where jobs are unstable, temporary, and constantly changing.[1] Labour will be in a state of flux and anxiety as workers move from one job to another as firms hire and fire workers to become more competitive. It appears that the message has gotten through. Students are now routinely told that they will go through many career changes over their working lives with no expectation of being at any one job for more than a few years. And with so many job changes, workers will be constantly training and retraining: "learning to learn," as some describe it. Loyalty will also be a dead concept in the New Economy as workers and employers look out for their own best interests. If that's the conventional thinking on how labour operates in the New Economy, how does it square with theory and the evidence? Not very well, it seems.

JOB SECURITY AND THE NEW ECONOMY

There is little question that we have moved to a new economy, one dominated by the service industries. From the mid-1970s to the late 1990s, the services industries have grown from 67 percent to 75 percent of total employment with most of this growth taking place in consumer and business services. One would expect that job stability and **job duration** would suffer as we move from jobs in the goods and re-source-producing sector to more service-oriented jobs. But that hasn't happened. According to Statistics Canada, the average duration of jobs in the early 1980s was around 45 months; about 15 years later it rose to around 50 months. And the proportion of jobs that lasted between 5 and 20 years stayed the same over the 1980s and 1990s. The data also shows that the probability that a job that lasted 6 months would last 5 years or more actually increased from the early 1980s to the mid-1990s.[2] And lifelong jobs are also not a thing of the past. About 7 percent of all jobs lasted more than 20 years, a proportion that hasn't changed since the early 1980s.

But not all sectors of the economy are created equal. The highest level of job security and duration can be found, not surprisingly, in the public service where the average job lasted 67 months. This was followed by distributive services at 56 months, business services at 51 months, and manufacturing at 50 months. Consumer service jobs lasted on average only about 32 months, while the construction sector (a sector most susceptible to cyclical swings in the economy) was at 21.6 months.[3] When people think of high job turnover rates, they usually think of consumer services alone. What we find is that job duration in the service sector varies less than that in the goods-producing sector of the economy during the ups and downs of the business cycle.

If conventional wisdom tells us that jobs aren't as secure as they once were, why has there been such little change in the duration of jobs in general? And will this trend last? A number of factors explain job stability in the Canadian labour market. First, more women are entering the labour market. As the female participation rates increase, especially among educated women, there is a tendency for job duration to increase. Women occupy jobs that last on average slightly longer than males' jobs. The reason is that women tend to stay at their jobs longer then men. A second factor is that job stability increases as education increases. Workers with 11 years or more of education have average job durations almost twice as long as those with less education. Men with low levels of education are particularly vulnerable to short employment duration rates.[4]

A third factor is demographics and Canada's ageing baby boom cohort. The age of the work force has changed since the early 1980s: it has shifted toward older more educated workers. And we know that older workers tend to stay at their jobs longer, mainly because they have usually found a good match and their desire for security increases as they see retirement looming over the horizon.[5] However, one segment of the work force that was affected by changing labour markets and corporate restructuring during the recession of the early 1990s were older workers over 50 with high seniority. For workers between 50–59 years of age with 15 years of tenure, the probability that that job would last another 5 years declined by 32 percent. Unfortunately, the data isn't clear about what caused this decline in jobs for this age group. No doubt much of the job losses were caused by corporate restructuring during the severe recession in the early 1990s; but many workers took early retirement, not because they had to, but because they could afford to.[6]

If job security and job duration haven't changed over the years, why is there so much worry among the general public that there's more instability than there actually is? One possible answer is that workers aren't responding to an actual drop in job stability, but to the cost of losing one's job. That means, if someone loses a job it takes a long time to find another one. The longer it takes to find a job, the more costly it is to the worker. The evidence seems to bear this out by looking at the 1981–82 and 1990–91 recessions in Canada. If someone lost her job during the 1981–82 recession, she would be able to find another one rather quickly when the economy began to pick up, which means the **hiring rate** was strong. During the recession in the early 1990s, hiring rates were down considerably, which meant that unemployed workers found it harder to find work and this pushed up the cost of being unemployed. And when it gets harder to find jobs, the quit rate among workers drops. That's what happened during the recession of the early '90s. The memory of that recession gave the impression that job stability and security were things of the past, and that concern was reflected in less job security.[7]

WORKERS IN THE DRIVER'S SEAT

One overlooked factor for job stability and longer job tenure rates has to do with the changing behaviour of corporations and employers toward their workers. Contrary to all the hype, the notion that companies pick up and relocate if they can find cheaper workers elsewhere is more illusion than reality. Training and re-training workers is expensive and businesses would rather keep their good workers than find others. Today virtually all companies offer their best workers some form of deferred compensation in hopes of buying their loyalty. But because most companies offer their better workers more benefits, sometimes through generous **stock options**, higher pay in itself is becoming less of a reason to stay. Workers have to feel that companies can respond to their needs and lifestyles. That includes everything from working flexible hours from home to providing day care. As the population ages and more experienced baby-boom workers start to reach retirement age by 2010, there is considerable worry that there could be a significant short-term labour short-age. This will force companies to do even more to keep their workers, especially older ones, happy.

In the late 1990s when the economy showed strong growth, there is no doubt that the majority of jobs created were in the category of self-employment rather than in traditional full-time paid jobs. Over the 1990s, full-time jobs accounted for only 18 percent of net job creation, compared to 47 percent a decade earlier. The pro-liferation of self-employment was much greater in Canada than in the United States over that same period of time. Does this mean that there is a fundamental change in Canada's labour market? Probably not. By the late 1990s and early 2000, full-time jobs were outpacing part-time ones as businesses felt more confident about sus-tained economic growth. There seems to be little correlation between short-term economic conditions and self-employment over the business cycle according to studies by Statistics Canada. The move to more self-employment could become a stronger trend if unemployment persists for longer periods of time.

But that doesn't seem to be the case. In the United States, where competitive pressures have been more intense than in Canada, there is no general movement to more self-employment.[8] But in the New Economy, workers, especially well-edu-cated workers, are in the driver's seat when it comes to determining their terms of em-ployment. And the main reason has to do with the structure of the New Economy. In the old economy a company's capital was measured by machinery and fixed assets. In the New Economy there's a general acknowledgement that knowledge is the core resource; the raw material of the new industrial revolution. And when skilled work-ers walk out the door, they take with them more than their wage or salary. Smart com-panies know this and will do what they can to keep valuable workers and remain competitive.[9]

KEY TERMS

New Economy	Job duration	Stock options
Conventional wisdom	Hiring rate	

REVIEW QUESTIONS

1. The evidence is clear that job stability has actually increased since the early 1980s. What are the reasons for this stability? Explain why you believe this trend may or may not hold, paying particular attention to demographic changes.

2. Even though overall employment has increased after the recession of the early 1990s, the level of self-employment has also increased. Do you think this was caused by structural changes in the economy or was it driven by the needs of workers rather than the labour market?

DISCUSSION QUESTIONS

1. Do you believe that the labour market of the future will be dictated by the changing nature of the economy or the needs of employees? That is, will workers adjust to what the labour market needs, or will industry adjust to accommodate the demands of the work force?

2. "Job security is a function of swings in the business cycle and education, and not a function of the New Economy." Please discuss.

NOTES

1. See Jeremy Rifkin, "The End of Work" (New York: Putnam & Sons, 1995). Rifkin paints a bleak picture of work in the future where workers will be at the mercy of ever-changing corporate needs.

2. Andrew Heisz, "Changes in Job Duration in Canada," in the *Canadian Economic Observer*, Statistics Canada, Vol. 54, No. 2, 1999.

3. Ibid., p. 3.4.

4. D.A. Green, and W.C. Riddell, "Job Duration in Canada: Is Long-Term Employment Declining?" in *Transition and Structural Change in the North American Labour Market,* edited by Morley Gunderson (University of Toronto, 1998).

5. Changes to Canada's Employment Insurance Act may also have contributed to higher job stability rates. If workers who quit their jobs have more difficulty collecting employment insurance, they tend to stay at their jobs longer.

6. However, in the late 1990s and early part of 2000, older experienced workers were back in demand as the supply of labour tightened to meet the needs of a growing economy. Many workers who had taken early retirement were now back in the labour force as consultants with the firms they once worked for.

7. Now job stability isn't always a good thing. Job retention rates tend to be cyclical, that is high during recessions when job alternatives are poor and low when the economy is growing. Short job tenure for younger workers can also be a positive sign as they experiment with different jobs until they match their talents with the right occupations.

8. G. Picot and A. Heisz, "The Labour Market in the 1990s," *Canadian Economic Observer*, January 2000.

9. For an excellent analysis of how companies are keeping their best workers, see Peter Cappelli, "A Market-Driven Approach to Retaining Talent," *Harvard Business Review*, January–February 2000.

WEBLINKS

www.newecon.org/
New Economy Information Service.

www.statcan.ca/english/IPS/Data/11F0019MIE96095.htm
Changes in job tenure and job stability in Canada.

www.statcan.ca/Daily/English/000120/d000120c.htm
The labour market in the 1990s.

Chapter 28

THE
BRAIN
DRAIN

 **MYTH** *"Canada is (or is not) suffering a brain drain."*

The controversy about how many highly skilled people are leaving Canada has become a serious problem for public policy. There are those who argue that the problem is nothing new and that emigration has been worse in the past. There are others who argue this time it's different and that Canada is losing its best and brightest to the United States because of lower taxes and better job opportunities there. There are strong arguments to suggest that this latter interpretation has some credibility, but until we have better data, the total cost of the brain drain may remain a mystery.

Canadians aren't strangers to the brain drain. It's hard to imagine the American entertainment industry without stars such as Jim Carrey, Dan Ayckroyd, Neve Campbell, or Shania Twain; all Canadians. But that's not the sort of **brain drain** that has occupied the country since the early 1990s. The problem now is the loss of highly skilled Canadians going south of the border. On an anecdotal basis, it seems many of us know of someone who has moved to the U.S. or is thinking of it because of the job opportunities or lower taxes. But does this anecdotal evidence add up to much? How serious is the brain drain for the Canadian economy? Some don't see it as an issue at all, while others are convinced that the problem is serious and getting worse.

Even the government is split on the issue. Prime Minister Jean Chrétien dismisses the problem as a myth generated by opposition members and journalists. Yet his Minister of Industry, John Manley, admits that Canada is indeed losing skilled workers, who are attracted by lower taxes and higher income in the U.S., and this poses a serious threat to Canada's standard of living.[1]

Even economists can't agree on how serious the problem is. While some argue that although **emigration** from Canada is nothing new, the number of Canadian-born citizens leaving for the U.S. since 1990 isn't that significant compared to other periods in Canada's history. Others argue that the numbers may be small in relation to the overall work force, but we should be concerned with the quality of the workers we're losing. Which side is right in the brain drain controversy? The intention of this chapter is to briefly present both sides of the argument and then come to some conclusions about how to think about the issue.

What does traditional or classical economic theory say about the economics of migration? It is usually argued that emigrants do not lower the standard of living of those they leave behind, because they take with them not only their "hands," used in production, but their "mouths" to consume. That is, when people move, we may lose their ability to produce, but society saves in no longer providing social services for them. There is little problem if the level of emigration is small compared to the overall population where those emigrating produce roughly the same amount as they consume. This is certainly the case for low-skilled migrants who came to Canada after the Second World War. These emigrants, many from southern Europe, left countries that had a surplus of low-skilled workers, so their departure was a benefit to these countries. Coming to Canada, they were more valued because of the shortage of labour in this country.[2] Classical theory tells us that emigration of this sort benefits both countries by increasing the wages of those left behind, increasing the wages of those coming to Canada, and increasing overall economic output.

CASE 1: THERE IS NO BRAIN DRAIN PROBLEM

One of the economists who argues that the brain drain is not a problem for Canada is Professor John Helliwell at the University of British Columbia. He makes the case that the brain drain isn't that much of a problem because the levels of emigration today from Canada to the United States are relatively small compared to levels in the past. Between 1966 and 1976, it is estimated that over 900,000 Canadians left Canada. From 1991 to 1996, the number of Canadians leaving the country was about 178,000. The number of Canadian-born residents in the United States has declined steadily throughout the 1980s and 1990s.[3][4] However, it was expected that about 52,000 would return to Canada. So the number of Canadians permanently leaving the country was around 126,000. Even since the signing of NAFTA in 1989, which has encouraged the freer movement of goods, services, and labour, Helliwell estimates that only about 10,000 native-born Canadians are, on average, leaving the country annually. Of these, only about half hold university degrees. And given the fact that for every Canadian that leaves, about four new immigrants arrive, one can begin to understand why some don't see the brain drain as a problem; especially because many of the new immigrants coming to Canada are young and well educated. For example, recent immigrants were close to twice as likely to have university degrees compared to native-born Canadians.[5]

Professor Helliwell gives a number of reasons for the small numbers of emigrants. First, many highly skilled Canadians, who are more apt to move, are now getting their graduate education in Canada rather than in the U.S., making it more likely that they will remain here. In the past, with more Canadians earning their degrees in the United States, they tended to work there as well. Second, the income gap between Canada and the U.S. has narrowed in the 1990s compared to the 1970s. In 1960, per capita GDP in Canada was 40 percent below that in the United States, while in 1990 that gap was less than one-third as great. Professor Helliwell also expects the number of emigrants to decrease as unemployment drops in Canada and incomes rise. His third argument is that immigration still makes up a small percentage of the population of any country and therefore is a relatively rare event. Consequently, it has a small overall macroeconomic impact. And that is certainly the case, given that emigration makes up only about 0.2 percent of the population; a number that hasn't changed since the early 1930s.

He concludes by arguing that the pool of skilled and willing immigrants coming to Canada are filling job vacancies and therefore lessening the inflationary bottlenecks that would have occurred without them. One example is the growing number of immigrant doctors located in northern Canadian locations—jobs that Canadian-born doctors don't want. Putting all these arguments together, it makes a compelling case that Canada isn't suffering from a brain drain. But that isn't the end of the story.

CASE 2: THERE IS A GROWING BRAIN DRAIN PROBLEM

Is Professor Helliwell correct in his conclusions that the brain drain is not a serious problem and that policies to correct it, such as lowering taxes, are counterproductive? There are those who disagree based on a different reading of the evidence. Some scholars, such as Professor Don DeVoretz at Simon Fraser University, say that although Canada was a traditional importer of human capital, these trends are declining. If one takes into account such factors as skill comparability, DeVoretz concludes that from 1989–1996 Canada had a minor net inflow (1,971), after accounting for Canadian emigration to the United States. However, this net inflow was negative given the productivity costs to the Canadian economy. In other words, it didn't matter that more arrived than left, Canada was still a net loser because the replacement costs of those who left are estimated to be over $13 billion. The skilled immigrant could not compensate for the value of the lost Canadian-trained emigrant to the United States. DeVoretz further makes the case that many professionally trained Canadians were in effect getting a highly subsidized education in Canada, and moving to the U.S. for higher paying jobs. Canadian students pay tuition fees that have historically covered less than one-fifth of the cost of a university education. The amount that taxpayers invested in these emigrants was around $5.2 billion in education.

That's the main point made by those who believe the brain drain is a serious public policy problem for Canada. We're not just losing workers, but highly trained ones with high levels of human capital. Although the numbers of people leaving the country is not large in absolute terms, the quality of these leaving is affecting Canada's standard of living. These losses are concentrated in the knowledge-intensive sectors of the economy. From 1982 to 1996, 54,000 highly educated Canadians largely from business, medicine, and science left the country. In 1982 Canada had a net outflow of only 330 professionals and managers. That number steadily increased to about 5,000 by 1997.[6]

Although we hear much about the loss to the U.S. of doctors and nurses (who make up the largest emigrating groups among the professions), there is also a net outflow of engineers, managers, and post-secondary teachers. In 1997 Canada lost about 4 percent of its 1995 graduating class of engineers (12,300), and 1 percent of its natural scientists (18,900). During the last decade, faculty leaving for U.S. universities outnumbered those coming to Canada by a margin of 2 to 1. The loss of these high achievers provides another argument for why the cost of education should be borne mainly by the student through higher tuition fees for programs such as business studies, computer science, and medicine.[7]

Now there is the question of the actual numbers leaving Canada. Professor Helliwell estimates that approximately 10,000 Canadian-born workers per year are migrating to the United States. These workers are usually the ones who have applied for permanent immigration. However, under NAFTA, Canadian workers, in qualifying occupations, can readily gain entry into the U.S. only by showing proof of their qualifications and a job offer from a U.S. employer. While this permit is valid for only one year, the maximum number of renewals is unlimited. In other words, more people may be remaining in the United States for extended periods of time without converting to permanent resident status. These numbers are captured by Canadian tax filing data. According to this data, the number of taxfilers who left Canada, whether permanently or temporarily, has increased steadily over the years from around 15,000 in 1991 to about 29,000 in 1997. If we add the dependants to this data, Statistics Canada estimates that the annual average emigration to the United States in the 1990s was in the range of 22,000 to 35,000. Taxfiler data indicates a steadily rising number of emigrants, although it is still small as a share of the Canadian population. And those leaving the country are also high-income earners with above average levels of education.[8]

Many analysts and commentators have argued that concerns about the few thousand highly skilled workers leaving Canada annually for the U.S. are overblown. After all, well-educated immigrants are replacing Canada's loss by a ratio of 2 to 1. But there are important counterarguments to refute this claim. To begin with, although Canada has traditionally relied on the inflow of immigrants, these flows have been erratic over time. Although the immigration of skilled workers has been high over the last decade, we can't assume that will continue. Another factor has to do with the innate quality of immigrant workers. The knowledge-based economy requires a special kind of teamwork between leaders and research teams. It appears that Canada is having difficulty in attracting individuals who are team leaders at the most productive phases of their careers. In short, although the number of skilled immigrants is sizeable, they aren't replacing the quality of workers Canada is losing to the U.S.[9]

THE BRAIN DRAIN AND ECONOMIC GROWTH THEORY

There is another strong case regarding the cost of the brain drain that's provided by the **new growth theory** in economics. Assume that brain drainers tend to work in professions that create new knowledge, products, and services. These are considered to be valuable to society because they create **positive externalities**, or benefits for others. That means that they create benefits in research and insights that can be used by others in society. For example, Canadian research in cancer is a benefit not only to the researcher involved, but to many suffering from the disease. Traditional or classical economic theory would argue that where the discovery is made is not important because we will all eventually have access to the benefits. In short, whether the invention is made in Canada or elsewhere, the difference is the same for Canadians. However, new thinking on the subject brings a different conclusion. Michael Porter, at the Harvard Business School, argues that firms and companies tend to cluster around certain regions of the world. For example, the world high-tech sector is concentrated south of San Francisco in Silicon Valley. A smaller high-tech region has also emerged in Kanata, a city outside Ottawa. The world's largest **agglomeration** of pharmaceutical companies can be found near Basel, Switzerland.

Why does this matter? Firms that are located in the same region encourage competition and innovation, thereby encouraging economic growth. But more important, they create externalities that are a benefit to the larger community and society of which they are part, and that can't be captured solely by the inventors and owners of capital. The clusters are characterized by a strong synergism among all firms, universities, and applied research institutes. They also rely heavily on purchases and skilled labour from the surrounding communities. The benefits and externalities do not go to the world at large, as traditional theory would predict, but mostly to the many firms within such clusters. The reason is that the process of innovation involves frequent and informal contacts between the employees, entrepreneurs, and financial agents in the cluster. Very little of the spill-over effects reach other regions and countries. When Canada loses skilled workers to these clusters, new growth theory suggests the contributions of these workers go to the clusters and regions where they work, and not to Canadians. For example, when a software engineer graduating from the University of Waterloo (a school with an international reputation in mathematics and computer science) moves to California, it leads to a reduction of economic wealth for Canadians left behind.[10]

Because those leaving Canada are among the most highly educated and talented workers, one can further argue that their contribution to society far outweighs the amounts paid in taxes by this group of individuals. The best and brightest are by definition different from the highly skilled. And when we lose them, for whatever reason, it creates quite a burden for the country. It is recognized that only a small group of professionals in their respective fields become truly productive. In the field of economics, it is determined that 10 percent of the scholars produce 74 percent of all cited works in their field, while the bottom 50 percent produce only 0.2 percent. This means that when Canada loses a top-notch economist, medical researcher, or entrepreneur, it loses much more than the taxes paid by these individuals. This is especially the case with entrepreneurs who potentially create considerable amounts of wealth. When the best and brightest leave Canada, employers fail to recoup the investment they have made in the training of these individuals.

John Helliwell alluded to the fact that the brain drain isn't as bad as it was in the 1970s because Canada was narrowing the income gap with the U.S. But the opposite may be happening. There is growing evidence that the income gap may be widening and not closing. Comparatively higher Canadian taxes and more job opportunities south of the border can only make the situation worse and not better.[11] [12]

FINAL OBSERVATIONS

Where does all this leave us? It would appear that even though the numbers of emigrants don't appear to be large, the problem isn't getting better and is probably getting worse. The issue isn't so much how many people are moving, but who is moving. If they are our best and brightest, the problem is a serious one and politicians need to implement good public policy to address it. New growth theory also suggests that the brain drain isn't as innocuous as classical theory would suggest and that taxpayers are unwittingly contributing to the problem by subsidizing the tuition costs of those leaving the country. And although skilled immigrants are coming into the country, they are not replacing the crucial leadership skills of those leaving. But one must keep in mind that we need better data to truly assess the costs of the brain drain. Until we get a handle on the data, we may never know the dimensions of the problem.

KEY TERMS

Brain drain	New growth theory	Agglomeration
Emigration	Positive externalities	

REVIEW QUESTIONS

1. Would you argue that the brain drain is more a theoretical problem than a quantitative problem?

2. Even without the proper emigration data, could one make the argument that it is a greater problem today than it was in the 1970s?

3. In light of the fact that a disproportionate number of highly skilled workers go to the United States, and given that Canadian taxpayers pay the bulk of education costs in Canada, does this imply that those acquiring professional degrees should pay a greater share of their tuition?

DISCUSSION QUESTIONS

1. If you believe there is a brain drain problem, what policies would you recommend to the government to reverse the situation?

2. On a personal level, would you consider moving to the United States after graduation? What conditions would motivate such a move? How much does patriotism count?

NOTES

1. *National Post*, 16 February 2000.

2. The assumption that workers are paid an amount equal to what they contribute to output is fundamental to some of the most central propositions in the theory of wages and of income distribution.

3. John F. Helliwell, "Checking the Brain Drain: Evidence and Implications," PEAP Policy Study 99-3, June 1999, University of Toronto.

4. John Zhao, Doug Drew, and T. Scott Murray, "Knowledge Workers on the Move," *Perspectives on Labour and Income*, Summer 2000.

5. Canada has traditionally received more skilled workers than it lost. From 1967 to 1987, Canada received almost $43 billion worth of post-secondary trained workers from immigrant flow.

6. "The Brain Drain: Causes, Consequences, and Policy Response," The Fraser Institute Conference, November 13, 1998.

7. "Knowledge Workers on the Move," *Perspective on Labour and Income*, Statistics Canada, Summer 2000.

8. Ibid., p. 34.

9. Daniel Schwanen, "Putting the Brain Drain in Context," *Commentary* (Toronto: C.D. Howe Institute, April 2000).

10. Herb Grubel, "The Effects of the Brain Drain on the Welfare of Canadians," Fraser Institute conference papers on the brain drain, November 13, 1998.

11. A Canadian reaches the top tax bracket of 53 percent with an income of around $50,000. To reach the 50 percent tax level, a U.S. worker would have to earn $250,000. Although falling, Canada's unemployment rate is still higher than that in the U.S.: 7 percent in Canada in January 2000, compared to 4 percent in the U.S.

12. John McCallum, "Will Canada Matter in 2020?" *National Post*, 19 February 2000. Another economist, Elhanan Helpman of Harvard, estimated that Canada's current standard of living equalled that in the United States in 1979! (*Source*: Lecture to the Canadian Institute for Advanced Research, Banff, Alberta, June 1999.)

WEBLINKS

www.statcan.ca/Daily/English/000524/d000524a.htm
Brain Drain and Brain Gain: The Migration of Knowledge Workers into and out of Canada.

www.nsf.gov/sbe/srs/issuebrf/sib98316.htm
Brain Drain or Brain Circulation?

www.well.com/user/bgm/ngt2.html
New growth theory.

www.essential.org/antitrust/ms/cfa/four.html
Positive externalities.

Glossary

Agglomeration (p. 244) The clustering of firms within a defined geographical area.

Aggregate demand (pp. 94, 189) The total spending of all consumers, businesses, governments, and foreigners on a country's final goods and services.

Allocative efficiency (p. 141) The efficient combination of inputs that produces maximum output at the lowest opportunity cost.

Allocative inefficiencies (p. 20) The nonoptimum use of a nation's scarce resources that does not maximize the number of goods and services produced.

Arbitrage (p. 77) The business of buying low and selling high to make a profit on the margin between two prices. Although the activity can be profitable, the arbitrageur risks losses if prices change during the transaction.

Automatic stabilizers (p. 189) Policies that reduce the fluctuations in the economy without deliberate actions by government. For example, automatic increases in aggregate demand through employment insurance when the economy slows down.

Balance of trade (p. 76) The value of all exports minus the value of all imports.

Beggar-my-neighbour policiese (p. 84) A course of action in which a country tries to export its unemployment and protect its domestic industries by raising trade barriers.

Bélanger-Campeau Commission (p. 208) Committee established by the Quebec government to assess the financial and economic implications of separation.

Black markets (p. 14) An illegal trading arrangement in which buyers and sellers do business at a price higher than the law allows.

Blue Box program (p. 153) Municipal program to encourage households to separate bottles, cans, and newspaper for special pick-up and recycling.

Braindrain (p.240) a net loss of talent, or educated work force, mainly to the U.S., over a specified period of time.

Brundtland Report (p. 166) Study by the United Nation's Commission, entitled *Our Common Future,* chaired by Gro Harlem Brundtland (former Prime Minister of Norway) to study the relationship between economics and the ecology.

Budget deficit (or **budget surplus**) (p. 128) The difference between government revenues, or taxes, and government spending over the year. If revenues exceed spending, government has a budget surplus. If spending is greater than revenues, government has a budget deficit.

Business cycle (p. 189) Economy-wide fluctuations in output, incomes, and employment.

Butterfly effect (p. 193) The notion that a small inconsequential change can have massive, unpredictable results on systems such as the weather and the overall economy. (Term taken from chaos theory in mathematics that a butterfly flapping its wings in Brazil can affect the weather in Toronto.)

Buy Canadian (p. 84) Government programs that encourage people to buy products made in Canada with the purpose of keeping jobs at home.

Canadian Deposit Insurance Corporation (CIDC) (p. 212) Federal insurance program that protects the investments of depositors in Canadian financial institutions to a maximum of $60,000.

Canadian Wheat Marketing Board (p. 29) Federal agency with the mandate to sell Canadian wheat abroad.

Capacity utilization (p. 183) The ratio of actual to potential output. This can relate to firms as well as whole economies and gives a measure of the proportion of the total capacity that is being used.

Capital intensive (p. 69) The ratio of capital to labour in the process of production. The more capital employed, keeping other factors constant, the higher the level of capital intensity.

Cartel (p. 148) Producers who come together to restrict output in order to raise prices and profits.

Clarity Bill (p. 215) Federal legislation that would permit Quebec, or other provinces, to hold a referendum on separation with the proviso that the question is clear and approved by Parliament and that a "clear" majority is attained.

Club of Rome (p. 146) International group of businesspeople, statespeople, and scientists that commissioned a study in 1972 entitled *The Limits of Growth* to determine the relationship between population growth and the global economy.

Command and control (p. 137) A central planning authority that determines *what* and *how* goods and services are produced. It is the predominant form of planning in Communist countries.

Common Agricultural Policy (CAP) (p. 29) A program of agricultural price supports and grants used by the European Economic Community to help increase incomes in agriculture.

Common market (p. 209) A group of countries that reduce trade barriers among themselves but maintain common external trade barriers to non-member countries.

Comparative advantage (p. 61) A country is said to have a comparative advantage if it can produce a good or service at a lower opportunity cost (or more efficiently) than any other country.

Competition policies (p. 84) Policies that deal with promoting effective competition between suppliers by regulating practices that may restrict or distort competition in the market place.

Consumer Price Index (CPI) (p. 179) The most popular index number that measures the average level of prices of a basket of goods and services consumed by an urban Canadian family.

Consumer sovereignty (p. 163) Consumer preferences that determine what goods and how much will be produced.

Conventional wisdom (p. 235) Prevailing knowledge or belief among the general public.

Countervailing duties (p. 86) Tariffs that are imposed on imports to enable domestic producers to compete with subsidized foreign producers.

Crowding out effect (p. 128) An increase in government spending on goods and services that has the effect of reducing the level of private sector spending.

Currency appreciation (p. 76) The increase in the value of one currency in relation to another currency.

Currency depreciation (p. 76) The fall in the value of one currency in relation to another currency.

Customs union (p. 210) A group of countries that eliminate trade restrictions among themselves but retain external trade barriers against other countries.

Cyclical unemployment (p. 199) The unemployment that occurs when the economy slows down or goes into a recession.

Dead-weight loss (p. 110) A misallocation of resources and loss of production to the economy, caused by restricting output below its efficient level.

Deficit (p. 126) A situation in which ongoing spending exceeds income or revenues at a specific point in time.

Deindustrialization (pp. 69, 86) A sustained fall in the share of national income accounted for by the industrial and manufacturing sector.

Direct investment (p. 210) Any expenditure on physical assets, such as plant, machinery, and inventory.

Dispute settlement mechanism (p. 63) Arrangement in which a binational panel under the Canada–U.S. free trade agreement is the final arbiter of trade disputes between the two countries.

Dumping (p. 86) Selling goods in a foreign market at prices lower than those charged in the domestic market.

Economic rent (p. 231) The amount earned by labour, or any factor of production, beyond what could normally be earned given a worker's level of skills or training.

Economies of scale (p. 61) The savings a firm or industry realizes through increases in quantities produced.

Economies of scope (p. 174) The decrease in average total cost made possible by increasing the number of total goods produced. For example, McDonald's can produce hamburgers and fries at a lower cost than if they were produced by two different firms due to the sharing of specialized food storage and preparation facilities.

Efficiency principle (p. 109) An objective of tax policy that tries to maintain an efficient economy by distorting purchasing patterns as little as possible.

Efficiency wage theory (p. 201) Theory that states that firms can increase productivity and profits by keeping real wages above equilibrium levels.

Efficient level of pollution (p. 139) The theoretical point where the marginal benefits of reducing pollution to the environment and the public are equal to marginal costs associated with pollution abatement equipment.

Elasticity of supply (p. 148) A measure of how responsive supply is given a change in price. It is calculated by dividing the percentage change in the quantity supplied by the percentage change in price.

Emigration (p. 241) An exodus of people from one country to another.

Emission credits (p. 141) Unused portion of pollution permits that firms can sell or exchange on the open market.

Entropy (p. 153) A term borrowed from physics that, when applied to economics, means that physical limitations prevent all materials in the production process from being recycled.

Equal pay for equal work (p. 18) The principle of paying women the same wages as men for doing identical jobs.

Equal pay for work of equal value (pay equity) (p. 19) The principle of paying equal wages to jobs judged to be of comparable worth.

Equity (or equity base) (p. 30) An owner's financial or capital stake in a business.

Equity principle (pp. 36, 109) An objective of tax policy that attempts to shift the burden of taxation from the poor to the rich (*see* **Progressive (income) tax rate**).

Excess supply of labour (p. 36) More labour than is needed to perform a certain task measured by the level of unemployment.

Externalities (pp. 137, 226) Costs or benefits that result from an economic activity that fall on a third party for which there is no corresponding compensation or payment by those generating the externality (e.g., air pollution is a *negative* externality).

Fallacy of composition (p. 101) The false notion that what applies to the individual also applies to the group or the whole (e.g., if individual households must live within their means so must governments).

Fertility rates (p. 103) The average number of births per woman.

Fiscal policy (p. 189) Government action using spending and taxation in order to influence the economy.

Fixed capital formation (or fixed investment) (p. 131) Current level of investment in plant, machinery, equipment, or other durable capital good.

Flat tax (p. 121) Another term for proportional tax where all income earners pay the same percentage of their income in taxes.

Flexible exchange rate (or floating exchange rate) (p. 76) Exchange rates between countries determined by market forces in the absence of central bank intervention; whereas a fixed exchange fixes one country's currency value, or exchange rate, in relation to another country's currency and is maintained as a matter of policy by the central bank.

Floor price (pp. 28, 36) Legal minimum price that may be charged, usually above what the market would normally set under conditions of supply and demand (e.g., minimum wages).

Free rider problem (p. 225) A problem intrinsic to public goods. Because people can enjoy the benefits of public goods without being excluded, everyone is disinclined to pay for them. An example is public radio that relies on donations from listeners.

Free Trade Agreement (FTA) (p. 60) Comprehensive trade agreement signed in 1988 by the United States and Canada creating a free trade area between the two countries.

G7 (p. 127) Group of seven nations making up the leading economies in the world—United States, Germany, France, the United Kingdom, Japan, Italy, and Canada.

General Agreement on Tariffs and Trade (GATT) (p. 34) A multinational institution set up in 1947 to promote the expansion of international trade by restricting governments from imposing artificial impediments to trade such as tariff and nontariff barriers.

Generation X (p. 42) The post-baby boom generation born approximately between 1960 and 1975.

Globalization (p. 56) The trend to greater trade, financial, and economic integration among countries around the world.

Goods and Services Tax (GST) (p. 108) A value-added tax introduced by the federal government in 1991 that taxes consumption rather than production.

Gross Domestic Product (GDP) (p. 180) Value of all final goods and services produced within Canada whether by residents or nonresidents.

Guaranteed annual income (pp. 40, 120) A minimum level of income provided by the government for those falling below the poverty line with the objective of eliminating poverty without destroying the incentive to work (also known as a negative income tax).

Hiring rate (p. 237) The pace at which firms bring on new workers.

Human capital (pp. 43, 92) A form of intangible capital that includes the skills and knowledge that workers acquire through education, training, and experience.

Hysteresis (p. 203) The long-lasting influence of history, such as on the natural rate of unemployment.

Income-contingent loan (p. 49) A loan's payment that is based on income earned.

Income effect (p. 118) The change in the amount consumed of a commodity given a change in income.

Income redistribution (p. 221) The distribution of income between classes of income earners.

Industrial strategy (p. 171) Government policy that attempts to encourage industrial development by picking and helping promising sectors in the economy and discouraging the losers.

Inflation (p. 189) A persistent increase in the average price level sustained over time.

Information highway (p. 174) The common expression used to describe a wide range of communication services available to providers and users on the Internet.

Insider–outsider theory (p. 201) The theory that workers with jobs have an influence on wage bargaining while those on the outside looking for work have no influence.

Intergenerational conflict (p. 101) An expression to describe the friction between the younger and older generation when it comes to competing for jobs and resources. This term is usually used to highlight the tension between the older baby boomers and the younger "Generation X."

International Monetary Fund (IMF) (p. 130) Founded in 1945, the IMF is an agency of the United Nations whose purpose is to encourage international monetary cooperation along with promoting trade and exchange rate stability. One of its main functions is to lend money to countries experiencing severe balance of payments problems.

Interprovincial trade barriers (p. 84) Provincial trade obstacles preventing the free movement of goods, services, and labour between provinces.

Job duration (p. 236) The average length of time workers remain employed with one employer.

Key money (p. 14) Extra payment demanded by landlords or vacating tenants in lieu of rent increases. Usually illegal and prevalent when governments impose rent controls.

Labour force (p. 102) The number of people working plus all those who are unemployed.

Laffer curve (p. 118) A graph made prominent by economist Arthur Laffer that relates tax revenues to the tax rate.

Law of diminishing marginal returns (pp. 44, 92) The tendency for marginal output to diminish as more labour is employed, while other factors of production (e.g., capital, land) are held constant.

Life-cycle hypothesis (p. 129) The theory that households make lifetime consumption decisions based on their expectations of lifetime income.

Long run (p. 15) A period of time in which a firm can vary all factors of production.

Low-income cutoff (LICO) (p. 219) Level of income determined by Statistics Canada that defines the current poverty line in Canada.

Lucas critique (p. 194) The argument that traditional policy analysis does not account for how people form their expectations of the future. Without knowing how people form these expectations, government runs the risk of failed policies.

Luddites (p. 69) Members of English artisan bands who destroyed machinery in the late 18th and early 19th century. Often refers to anyone who obstructs progress.

Manufacturers' Sales Tax (MST) (or federal sales tax) (p. 109) Tax replaced by the GST that formally imposed a 13.5 percent tax on manufactured goods.

Marginal cost (pp. 44, 137, 154) The increase in total cost resulting from an increase in total output by an extra unit.

Marginal Revenue Product (MRP) (p. 19) Extra revenue earned as a result of increased sales by using an additional unit of labour or capital.

Marginal revenue (p. 154) The increase in total revenue resulting from an increase in sales associated with an extra unit of output.

Marketing boards (p. 29) Quasi-government bodies that have the right to restrict agricultural output using quotas to keep farm incomes up.

Median income (p. 221) The median income where 50 percent of all observations lie.

Mercantilism (p. 85) Seventeenth-century economic doctrine that maintained exports were preferable to imports. The objective of commerce and government policy was to increase exports in order to amass gold and increase wealth.

Middle class (p. 221) General term to describe the population that earns more than 25 percent but less than 175 percent of the median income.

Mincome (Manitoba Basic Annual Income Experiment) (p. 120) Federal experiment and study to determine if a negative income tax, or guaranteed annual income, would alleviate poverty without destroying the incentive to work. Mincome was a multi-million-dollar study started in 1975 and completed in 1991.

Mixed economies (p. 189) Economies that have a blend of both capitalism and state ownership. All advanced modern economies exhibit a combination of both to varying degrees.

Monetary policy (p. 189) The tools that the Bank of Canada uses, such as open-market operations, to influence the money supply, which in turn affects interest rates, which in turn affects the goods market and output.

Moral hazard (p. 51) A term used to express that businesses (or individuals) will take increasing risks if the costs of those risks are partly paid by a third party.

NAFTA (p. 60) Acronym for the North American Free Trade Agreement signed by the United States, Canada, and Mexico.

National debt (p. 125) The federal government's accumulated indebtedness resulting from previous deficits.

National treatment (p. 63) The condition under the free trade agreement that government policy cannot discriminate against American companies in Canada and Canadian companies operating in the United States.

Natural monopoly (p. 227) Usually, a utility company, such as a supplier of energy or cable TV, that is the sole provider of a good or service. With deregulation of markets, natural monopolies are becoming less prevalent.

Natural rate of unemployment (p. 198) Although difficult to define it usually refers to the sum of *frictional* and *structural* unemployment.

Negative income tax (p. 120) (*see* **Guaranteed annual income**).

New Economy (p. 235) An economy dominated by the service sector and heavily dependent on technology.

New growth theory (p. 244) A theory of economic growth based on the idea that technological change results from choices people make in the pursuit of profit.

Nominal interest rate (p. 78) Interest rate not adjusted for inflation.

Nonaccelerating inflation rate of unemployment (NAIRU) (p. 198) The level of unemployment that does not contribute to excess demand and hence an increase in inflation.

Nonrenewable resources (p. 146) Natural resources that are fixed in nature and not self-generating, such as oil, gas, and minerals.

Not-in-my-backyard syndrome (NIMBY) (p. 157) A term to describe objections by citizens who do not allow activities near their neighbourhoods that would cause their property values to fall. Such activities are landfills, polluting industries, halfway houses for prisoners, and drug rehabilitation centres.

Open economy (pp. 63, 79) An economy that relies on exports and imports as a major share of its GDP.

Open market operations (p. 8) The purchase and sale by the Bank of Canada of government securities in the open

market. It is a tool to expand or contract the amount of reserves in the system and hence the money supply.

Opportunity cost (pp. 44, 54, 61) A fundamental concept in economics. The opportunity cost of an action is the value of the forgone alternative that is not chosen.

Organization for Economic Co-operation and Development (OECD) (p. 32) An intergovernmental organization of twenty-four nations including Canada, established in 1961 to promote economic development around the world.

Organization of Petroleum Exporting Countries (OPEC) (p. 147) A cartel of major oil-producing countries composed mainly of Middle Eastern countries and also including Venezuela. It was established to control the supply of oil and its price on international markets.

Paradigm shift (p. 202) A term used to describe a major economic transformation, such as the change from an economy based on agricultural production to one based on manufactured goods.

Participation rates (p. 94) Percentage of men or women of working age in the labour force.

Payroll taxes (p. 202) Taxes based on wages and salaries that are partially or fully paid by the employer and reduced at source, such as employment insurance and the Canada Pension Plan.

Phillips curve (p. 190) A relationship that holds that for lower levels of unemployment, higher levels of inflation must be tolerated. The inverse also holds that low rates of inflation can only be attained with higher unemployment levels.

Physiocrats (p. 69) Those who follow the economic ideas of eighteenth-century French economists who believed land was the sole source of income and wealth in society.

Positive externalities (p. 244) Benefits that accrue to society above that captured by the consumers of the product.

Predator pricing (p. 87) The practice of selling into a market at prices below cost of production in order to weaken or eliminate competition.

Price ceiling (p. 11) Legal maximum price that may be charged, usually below what the market would normally set under conditions of supply and demand (e.g., rent controls).

Price support programs (p. 28) A way of supporting prices above those set in the market in order to increase or stabilize incomes. Usually applied by governments to support farm incomes.

Price system (p. 146) A character of an economy where *what* to produce, *how* to produce it, and *for whom* it is produced is determined by the free interactions of buyers and sellers.

Producer Subsidy Equivalent (PSE) (p. 27) The income value of tariffs and quota protection if these were to be converted to direct subsidies for farmers.

Productivity (p. 183) The amount of output produced by a unit of input. Usually measured in terms of output per person-hour.

Progressive (income) tax rate (p. 36) The principle that the average tax rate paid by a taxpayer increases as income rises.

Proportional (income) tax rate (p. 121) The principle that the average tax rate remains the same as income rises. Another term for flat tax.

Public choice theory (p. 230) An approach to economic theory that assumes elected and nonelected public officials act in their own self-interest, just as those in the private sector behave.

Public goods (p. 225) Goods or services provided by governments that do not exclude anyone from their use.

Quotas (p. 29) A nontariff barrier that limits the level of imports or a restriction on the quantity of a good a firm is allowed to sell.

Rational expectations (p. 194) Theory that assumes that people optimally use all available sources of information, including current and prospective government policies, to make decisions about the future.

Rational ignorance (p. 231) The decision not to acquire information because the cost of doing so would outweigh the benefits of having it.

Reaganomics (p. 117) Term named after President Ronald Reagan that usually describes a policy of lower taxes designed to stimulate more investment leading to higher economic growth and hence higher government revenues.

Regressive tax (p. 110) The principle that the average tax rate decreases as income rises.

Reinventing government (p. 231) The expression to describe how governments are rethinking the services they now provide and how they can work more efficiently to deliver the services they now provide.

Renewable resources (p. 146) Resources not fixed by nature that can be managed and restored (e.g., lumber and agricultural produce).

Rent-seekers (p. 231) Groups or individuals who attempt to receive special favours from government, such as financial benefits or changes to legislation, rather than protect their interests.

Retirement Savings Plan (RSP) (p. 103) Government incentive program to encourage savings by deferring taxes to the future.

Return on investment (pp. 46, 52) Commonly defined as the ratio of profits to capital employed, or as earnings from the investment of capital.

Ricardian Equivalence (p. 133) First developed by the eighteenth-century English economist David Ricardo, it is the idea that financing public deficits by issuing debt (borrowing and paying interest) or raising taxes are equivalent and have the same effect on the economy. (The reason is that people take full account of the future tax if debt is used to cover a deficit and will act rationally to accumulate wealth to meet future tax liabilities.)

Right to pollute (p. 137) A restriction on pollution in which a firm can pollute only if it purchases the right to do so.

Set-aside programs (p. 175) Government procurement policies that reserve a share of all government purchases to small or minority-designated businesses.

Short run (p. 12) A period of time in which a firm can vary only one factor of production, usually labour, but not all factors of production.

Social returns to education (p. 46) The excess return on education above any earnings obtained from being educated.

Sovereignty association (p. 208) The position of the Parti Québécois that advocates political independence but economic integration with the rest of Canada after separation.

Specialization (p. 62) The process in which a country devotes its resources to the production of a few goods.

Stagflation (p. 190) The simultaneous presence of inflation and economic stagnation.

Stock options (p. 237) Equity or company shares available to employees as long as they remain with the company for a fixed period of time.

Structural unemployment (p. 203) Long-run unemployment caused as a result of rapid changes in the economy.

Substitution effect (pp. 117, 179) The substitution of one product for another given a change in their relative prices.

Supply management (p. 31) Another term for describing the activity of agricultural marketing boards where prices are determined by controlling the amount of produce or good that is supplied on the market.

Supply side economics (p. 116) The branch of economics concerned with the productive side of the economy. Supply side theorists advocate stimulating the economy with lower taxes and fewer restrictions on production.

Sustainable development (p. 166) The concept that economic growth is achievable without the destruction of the earth's ecology.

Symbolic analyst (p. 203) A professional manager of "information" in the New Economy.

Tax base (p. 100) The total pool of income that authorities can tax.

Tragedy of the commons (p. 142) The consequences of overexploiting a common resource when there is no clear ownership of that resource. The disappearance of the cod off the coast of Newfoundland is a clear example of "tragedy of the commons."

Transitional unemployment (p. 200) A type of unemployment that tends to disappear when the economy begins to grow or recover from recession.

Underemployment (pp. 182, 198) Factors of production, such as labour or capital, not used to their maximum potential or efficiency.

Unemployment rate (p. 182) The percentage share of the workforce looking for work.

Value-added tax (VAT) (p. 112) A tax based on taxing the value added at each level of the production process in a country. It does not discriminate against any activity as do specific taxes such as excise taxes. The GST is considered a form of value-added tax.

Venture capital (p. 173) Investment funds that are available solely to take advantage of high-growth income opportunities such as start-ups. These funds are usually associated with high risk ventures.

Voucher system (p. 15) Vouchers issued by governments that can only be redeemed or spent on certain goods and services.

World Trade Organization (WTO) (p. 33) The new name for the international trade organization known formally as the General Agreement on Tariffs and Trade or GATT.

Zero sum game (p. 36) A situation in game theory in which players compete for a fixed payoff, so that one player can only win at the expense of the other.